WOMEN, STATE, AND IDEOLOGY

1,3,4

Women, State, and Ideology

Studies from Africa and Asia

Haleh Afshar, Editor

STATE UNIVERSITY OF NEW YORK PRESS

First published
in USA by
STATE UNIVERSITY OF NEW YORK PRESS
Albany

For information, address State University of New York
Press, State University Plaza, Albany, NY 12246

Printed in Hong Kong

Library of Congress Cataloging-in-Publication Data
Women, state, and ideology.

Includes index.
Contents: Women and the state in Nigeria/Carolyne
Dennis—Women in Zimbabwe/Susie Jacobs and Tracey
Howard—The state and the regulation of marriage/
Penelope R. Roberts—[etc.]
1. Women—Developing countries—Social conditions.
2. Women—Developing countries—Economic conditions.
3. Developing countries—Social policy. I. Afshar,
Haleh, 1944–
HQ1870.9.W656   1987   305.4′2′091724   86–14432
ISBN 0–88706–393–4
ISBN 0–88706–394–2 (pbk.)

Contents

Acknowledgements

I would like to thank the Development Studies Association for funding and supporting the Women and Development Study Group. Thanks are similarly due to Steve Curry, who organised the Development Studies Conference at the University of Bradford, where many of the chapters of this book were presented. My thanks also to each of the contributors for participating in our numerous and heated discussion sessions and for making this book possible.

I would also like to thank Maurice Dodson, without whose constant help, support and encouragement this book would never have been completed. And Marlene Ellison for typing and circulating the reports of the group's meetings as well as the numerous drafts of some of the chapters, and for remaining patient, cheerful and unperturbed and for working beyond the call of duty to see this book through.

HALEH AFSHAR

Notes on the Editor and Contributors

Haleh Afshar is a Lecturer in Economics at the University of Bradford, currently on secondment at the Centre for Health Economics, University of York. From 1972 to 1974 she worked both as a civil servant and a journalist in Iran. She is a founder member of the Development Studies Association's Women and Development Study group and edited the group's first book *Women and Work in the Third World*. She is the editor of *Iran: A Revolution in Turmoil*, also published by SUNY Press.

Delia Davin is a lecturer in Social and Economic History at the University of York. She taught in Beijing from 1963 to 1965, and worked as a translator there from 1975 to 1976. She has written extensively on women and the family in China, and her publications include: *Woman's Work: Women and the Party in Revolutionary China.*

Carolyne Dennis taught and did research for seventeen years in Cameroon and Nigeria in West Africa on rural industrialisation, the labour market for women, the provision of health and plantation systems. She is now a Lecturer at the Project Planning Centre at the Univesity of Bradford and is doing research on the labour market for women in West Yorkshire and a study of the institutional context within which Third World planners take decisions.

Tracey Howard is a pen-name.

Susan Jacobs is a Senior Lecturer in Sociology at St Mary's College, University of Surrey. She did her most recent fieldwork in Zimbabwe during 1983–4 when she was a Research Associate at the Ministry of Community Development and Women's Affairs.

Patricia Margaret Jeffery, after one year reading medicine, took a degree in Social Anthropology from Newnam College, University of Cambridge. She first visited South Asia while doing postgraduate research at Briston University on Pakistani migrants (*Migrants and*

Refugees, Cambridge University Press, 1976), and carried out further research among Muslims in Delhi in 1975–6 (*Frogs in a Well: Indian Women in Purdah*, 1979), returning to India in 1982 to carry out the research reported here. She is currently Lecturer in Sociology (part-time) University of Edinburgh.

Roger Jeffery read Economics at Churchill College, University of Cambridge, and did postgraduate research in the Sociology Department, University of Bristol with fieldwork in Lahore, Pakistan. He carried out further research in Delhi 1975–6 on the medical profession and medical policy-making (*Health and State in India*) and has acted as a consultant to maternal and child health programmes in India since 1979. He returned to India in 1982 to carry out research reported here. Currently Lecturer (part-time) in Sociology, University of Edinburgh.

Jocelyn Kynch is a research assistant to Amartya Sen on the Leverhulme Trust funded project on forms and content of sex bias in living standards. She is an associate member of the Institute of Economics and Statistics, University of Oxford. She has visited India twice, conducting a nutritional survey of a village in Uttar Pradesh (supported by the ODA). Previous publications were in the areas of epidemiology, agricultural economics and criminology.

Andrew Lyon read Economics and Sociology at Edinburgh University and had an ESRC award for postgraduate research linked to the project reported here from 1981 to 1984. He is currently writing a PhD thesis for the Sociology Department, University of Edinburgh.

Christine Pelzer White is a Research Fellow at the Institute of Development Studies, University of Sussex, with research interests in the socialist transformation of agriculture and women in socialist societies. During the academic year 1985–6 she is a visiting Associate Professor at the Graduate School of International Studies, University of Denver. She is co-editor of *Revolutionary Socialist Development in the Third World* (1983).

Penelope A. Roberts teaches at the University of Liverpool. She is an anthropologist and has carried out research in Ghana and Nigeria. She has co-edited a book on rural development in Africa and written several papers on women, rural development, and agrarian economies of Africa.

Maila Stivens was born in Australia and studied Anthropology at Sydney University and the London School of Economics. She has carried out research in Sydney on kinship in a middle-class suburb and in Negeri Sembilan , Malaysia on gender and underdevelopment. A founding editor of *Critique of Anthropology*, she lives in London with her spouse and child and teaches at the University College, University of London.

Ann Weston is a development economist, currently working for the Commonwealth Secretariat, concentrating on international trade issues. She wrote this paper while employed as a research officer at the Overseas Development Institute.

Carol Wolkowitz is employed at the University of Bradford, where she is involved in a research project on women and home working, and has a one-year-old son. She has been active in the Conference of Social Economists.

Nira Yuval-Davis has been involved in anti-sexist and anti-racist struggles in both Israel and Britain, where she is a Senior Lecturer in Sociology at Thames Polytechnic, London, and where she is currently involved in a project on ethnic and gender divisions in south-east London. Her writings include topics such as the Israeli–Arab conflict, the interrelations of socialism and nationalism in radical Jewish movements and the theorisation of gender versus class ethnic and national divisions.

Glossary

abusua dihyie royal matrilineage

adat matrilinear practices

adidi sika chop money

aliya wave of immigration

asetena bo marriage ceremony

a-sudh naturally impure, also called na-pak

awowa a pawn

ayefere adultery fee

Ayurvedic an indigenous system of sophisticated 'high culture' medicine derived from the Sambrit vedas (Hindu religious work) and associated with Hindu culture

babaso gonorrhoea

bhangan female member of the Hindu Bhangi caste whose traditional work is to sweep away the night soil, an occupation which makes her a member of the untouchable caste

chamar a Hindu intouchable caste, traditionally leather workers

chen charm the women's corp of isarael army

chikan embroidery

co giao Miss Teacher

dai traditional village midwife with no training

desi local, with undertones of inferiority; of superiority when compared with some non-local items

di amoen drink the gods

diyat blood money

eddeh a two- or three-month waiting period observed by Muslim women on divorce, before re-marriage

egya full marriage

esiase to put her behind (divorce payment)

ganda filthy, dirty with undertones of natural impurity, e.g. 'ganda-kam' means dirty work

goan village or settlement

goan ki dai the village traditional birth attendant

harijans 'Children of God', Gandhi's term for the 'untouchable'. According to the ideology of caste, their very touch is polluting.

hejab the Islamic veil

hoshiyar intelligent, knowledgeable, clever

issar extreme generosity

kaam work, job

Kanouneh Vokala the Law Association

kari-to-ye a debt on the wife to be thrown away

kɔkɔ knocking-fee

majbour neccessary

majbouri main of neccessity (literally in neccesity)

Majlis the Iranian Parliament

mpata pacification money

Mojtahed Shiia religious leader; entitled to interpret the Quranic dictum for his followers

Mojtahedin plural of Mojtahed

naal a tube or pipe, in the context of birth and new-born baby the umbilical cord

naal khatney-wali the woman who cuts the cord, the cord-cutter

na-pak naturally impure, the same as a-sudh

oman state

omanhene head of state

parda literally 'curtain', but used to describe the system of seclusion for women

parda-nashin a woman who keeps purdah; also 'respectable women who are debarred by national custom from appearing in public' (Indian Famine Code)

qanouneh Taazirat secular code relating to legal matters not specifically stated in the Quran

qassas the Iranian law of retribution

safohenes head of subordinate royal lineage

seh palat altering the pattern of a woman's birth order by prescribing treatment to ensure the sex of a foetus is male (or female).

sharm shame or embarrassment

sharm ki baat embarrassing matters

soma gya a marriage established by the payment of kɔkɔ

Thanh Tam agony aunt

ti nza head rum, a form of marriage payment

ti sika head money

tutu prostitute

Unani or Greek (medicine) a system of sophisticated 'high culture' medicine brought to India by Mogul invaders from the Middle East and associated with Muslim culture

yishuv the pre-state Jewish settlement in Palestine

zabandar behaving in a speaking manner

zahal Israel defence army

Introduction
Haleh Afshar

The formal recognition of the vital contribution of women to the process of development has been long in coming, and despite the recent international 'Decade of Women' there has not been much improvement in the lives of women in the Third World. This book is the result of two years work by the Women and Development Study Group of the Development Studies Association and its 1984 Conference at Bradford. The authors examine the position of women in African and Asian countries and evaluate government policies directed at women and the underlying ideologies that often have a contradictory impact.

The state and its bureaucracy are increasingly important in the people's daily lives in the Third World. In particular, policies concerning population, the family and household are centred more and more on women, their sexuality and fertility. The part played by wives and mothers, both in terms of the survival of the nation and as unpaid or cheap sources of home-bound labour is invaluable, but not recognised. Since many governments endorse the domesticity of women and the unwaged services they provide for the family, it is never easy to suggest and initiate measures that would provide alternative and more lucrative opportunities for them. As a result, much of the legislation concerning women has been directed at controlling them, their sexuality and fertility, and endorsing their subordination.

THE STATE

The states in the underdeveloped world have complex and different formations, and it is not the intention of this book to make universal generalisations about their nature. Different historical, economic and ideological frameworks have produced different bureaucracies with differing stated and implicit aims. As the case studies in this book show, these may lead to diametrically opposite policies in nations which share a degree of similarities; the Chinese Government is finding it necessary to advocate one-child families for the Hans, whereas the Malaysian government is encouraging ever larger families

1

for the Malay population. Nevertheless, without making any claims to universality, it is true to say that the part played by the State in these countries is becoming more and more extensive and the implications of policy decisions spread beyond economic planning at the national level and influence the private and personal lives of individuals.

The nature of these policies and their direction varies historically, and may, at times, appear inconsistent and contradictory. This may be explained in terms of the character of ruling classes and the role played by the state in the underdeveloped world. Given the history of imperialism experienced by most of the countries examined, we observe, in greater or lesser degrees, the emergence of an uneasy power struggle at the level of decision-making. The State includes, and must accommodate, the landed classes who are no longer feudal but may also be owners of capitalist landed property, the bourgeoisie who aspire to and depend on Western interests and the local industrialists who have a more ambivalent relationship with foreign capital, being at one and the same time threatened by it and collaborating with it.[1] Ultimately there is an uneasy alliance among these groups: none is seeking the overthrow of the existing social order. But, in the short term, they pursue conflicting interests aimed at gaining ever larger shares of the country's wealth at the expense of one another. In this context, the educated middle classes who fill the positions of power in the state apparatus structure find themselves mediating the rival interests and gaining considerable power and authority over the dominant classes. As a result, the state often becomes increasingly powerful and centralised, and some of its actions may even threaten the interests of the bourgeoisie. But, as the cases of Iran and Nigeria demonstrate, these measures, which are often initiated against the background of populist rhetoric, may hinder capitalist development, but do not usually undermine its institutional and structural base.[2]

Within state structures, the bureaucracy in turn may have an ambivalent part to play, and is likely and able to undermine measures which threaten it or the classes it represents. Thus we note a wide range of differences between the formulation of policies at the national level and their implementation through agents who have greater or lesser degrees of autonomy and commitment and are unlikely to implement those which they see as directly threatening to their own survival.

There is, however, a commonalty shared by the states which we have examined in terms of their ideological definition of gender and the part ascribed to women. Even where, as in the case of Vietnam, this ascription is intentionally opposed and policies initiated to alter it, a combination of social forces and economic needs for a cheap or unwaged source of domestic labour has, in practice, undermined some of the best-intentioned measures.

WOMEN

Although all state policies have gender implications and affect the social status of women as well as their control over their livelihood, in the context of this book we have discussed specific policies concerned with sexuality, fertility, health, and paid employment in the public and private sectors, where the intentions of the State in relation to women may be more clearly demonstrated.

Although women are not a single sociological category, gender remains more than a physiological category, and is an important means of social differentiation everywhere. There is a general identification of women with the sphere of domesticity, even though the roles and obligations of women within this sphere and the definition of domesticity itself are culturally and economically specific. There are, of course, shared experiences between those men and women who bear the brunt of poverty, or those who bask in the comforts of wealth. Nevertheless, it is women – rather than men – who are responsible for nurturing the family. The degree to which women depend on their kin and family to provide gender ascribed services, and the extent to which the provision of care, welfare and education are located within the family or kin network, varies between societies and among classes within societies. Given the absence of centralised and national or commercialised provisions in most of the countries studied in this volume, we find that women have the responsibility of raising the family without necessarily having the economic means for fulfilling such duties.

Third World states in general, and even particular countries, however, do not have coherent policies about women, nor do they usually have structural facilities for co-ordinating their decisions. Given the tensions within bureaucracies and the almost total absence of discussion between the separate branches of the executive, it is not surprising to find the introduction of policies which have radically opposed implications for the lives of women and make at one and the same time contradictory demands of them. Thus, for example, we find that the Chinese on the one hand initiate a one-child planning policy, and on the other embark on rural reforms which make familial labour an essential asset for farmers.

Modernisation policies which, to different degrees and in different guises' have been adopted by most of the nations studied in this book, do not necessarily aim specifically at affecting gender relations, but they have invidious and complex implications for women. In rural areas for example, capitalisation of agriculture has been experienced, in the first instance, in terms of male migration and the distressful plights of women and children who have been left without any formal titles to the land nor any visible means of survival. In the case of Malaysia, where there are close kin ties, the remuneration paid by women migrants to their relatives in return for child-care, generates viable and economically rewarded child-care facilities. But more often the male migration is followed by that of females who do not gain access to the formal labour market and who are condemned to eke out a living on the margins of starvation.

IDEOLOGIES

Many states, moreover, have a strong ideological fear of women who are not clearly confined to the sphere of domesticity. Under the banner of fundamentalist ideologies, such countries embark on oppressive measures directed against those women who, of necessity, have flooded the labour market and threaten the survival of more traditional familial relations. In these societies, modernisation policies frequently meet with a barrier of middle-class ideologies which hark back to a golden age and decry the disintegration of the family and domestic bliss. It is in this context that we find repeated references to working women as symbols of corruption and agents of moral disintegration. It is not only the religiously minded who have such deep fears of women; even the educated middle classes, who may live the lifestyle of the Western cultures, may still carry both the ideas and the familial convictions of their culture. They often endorse views that advocate control of women and their sexuality and equate such control with social morality and harmony. Similarly, the ruling classes may need to appeal to the idioms and ideologies of traditionalism to obtain or maintain their legitimacy. Without such ideological force it would be difficult to justify the survival of the state.

There are, of course, occasions where the state intentionally intervenes in an effort to alter aspects of the ideological structure. On coming to power, modernists and traditionalists alike seek to make such interventions using the educational system and, more importantly, the media. In the context of countries where literacy remains low, broadcasting – both audio and visual – becomes a major propaganda tool, as does the cinema. These campaigns are usually backed by severe censorship and any material that is in any way contradictory to the official views is strictly banned.

Where, as in the case of China, the state already enjoys a considerable degree of legitimacy in the eyes of its people, even draconian measures such as the one-child policy, with its serious threat to the traditional religious and cultural beliefs, may be implemented with a degree of success. Where women are concerned, however, such propaganda campaigns have not always been successful. Where the State does not have such support, as is the case of Iran before the revolution, measures which may be viewed as positive and liberating to women meet with only temporary success and may even contribute to a fundamentalist backlash.

WOMEN AND THE STATE

Although all policies affect women, for the purpose of this book we have selected those issues where the state specifically articulates its ideologies on women. The first part discusses the tensions and contradictions arising from State intervention at the level of household and analyses its implications for women.

The fundamentalist view of women as sources of evil has led governments as diverse as those in Zimbabwe, Nigeria, Ghana and Iran to formulate policies that have similar results in marginalising women.

Carolyne Dennis's article on Nigeria demonstrates that the present military government's policies concerning women, appear to be based on the assumption that those who are economically independent may not only be perceived as a threat to men, but the State could construe them to be potentially subversive and a threat to the stability of the nation. Women had benefited to some extent from the expansion of the Nigerian economy and the post-colonial policies, but the recent recession and political crisis has revealed the deep-rooted fears of the disruptive potentials of independent women.

The perception of women as agents of 'corruption' plays a part in the recent 'clean-up' policies of the government in Zimbabwe. Susie Jacobs and Tracey Howard's chapter places the measures aimed at rounding-up vagrants and prostitutes in the context of an ideology that attaches the stigma of immorality to women migrants. The 'clean-ups' are excluding the poorer women from the towns without offering them viable alternatives in the countryside. In rural areas, women's rights to land remain mediated by men, who are dependent on this unpaid familial labour and unlikely to welcome policies that would provide alternative waged employment for them.

Prostitution and moral panic is studied in the context of the matrilinear Sefwi Wiawso society in Ghana by Penelope Roberts. In this chapter, Roberts looks at the 1930s political crisis which was caused in part by the impotence of the newly enthroned ruler. Female witchcraft was blamed and there followed an attempt to curtail prostitution and promiscuity, and impose male control on female sexuality. Roberts considers the general implications of this case for understanding attempts by patriarchal authority to control female sexuality in the context of a matrilineal society.

The conception of women as 'seditious' agents is central to the oppressive attitude of the Iranian theocracy. Haleh Afshar's chapter shows that Iranian politicians seek to hide their paranoid fear of women's sexuality under the guise of protecting their 'honour' and 'dignity'. By making them the single most important symbol of family honour, the Iranian State justifies the virtual imprisonment of women within the household. Outside the home, the mere sight of any part of a women is thought by the regime to be 'seditious' and to under-mine the very sanity of men.

The second part of the book is concerned with specific State policies on health, welfare and the control of fertility. The first chapters in this section compare two contrasting policies in this respect. In China, the Government is seeking to enforce a one-child family planning regulation for the Hans, while in Malaysia, the Government has abandoned family planning programmes for Malay women and is encouraging them to have numerous children.

Maila Stivens' chapter places the pro-natalist policies of the Malay-sian State in the context of kinship relations, and the position of women within them. Stivens sees the family as both an instrument and an object of social policy, and discusses the co-option of kinship morality by the state in lieu of provision of welfare facilities. Despite large-scale migration to towns, women maintain close kinship ties with rural areas and continue their reciprocal services by providing subsistence for kin and care of grandchildren.

By contrast, in China there is little migration and the state policies on one-child families are backed by clear material benefits. But, as Delia Davin's chapter on this subject demonstrates, welfare benefits are inadequate compensation for such draconian intrusion on the lives of women. Davin argues that although the policy is directed at both parents, in practice it is women who are the main target of formal and informal pressures. Not least among the serious implications for women is the rising tide of female infanticide, as well as denigration of mothers who give birth to daughters, and the encouragement of late abortions for women who already have one child. In the battle between the State and the family for the control over women's bodies and fertility, it is women who emerge as the losers.

Population control in China is seen as a means of preventing the re-emergence of famine. Jocelyn Kynch's case study of Indian policies of famine relief and medical facilities provided during epidemics, shows that women on the whole received less care and less provision than men. Kynch argues that this was in part because in times of crisis scarce resources are allocated to the most 'efficient' recipients and that men were assumed to be more productive than women. But, as this chapter demonstrates, evidence does not support this assumption, which seems to be rooted in ideology rather than reality.

By contrast, where it is important to operate in the context of traditional views, the State does not always seem to share or endorse the prevalent ideology. The chapter by Patricia and Roger Jeffery and Andrew Lyon shows that Indian programmes for improvement of the standard of health care during labour and childbirth have had little success, since they were formulated without accommodating the notions of pollution at the time of birth and the low status of birth attendants who are soiled by the very act of cutting the foetal cord. In India, these programmes also suffer from the loss of credibility of a government whose legitimacy was seriously undermined by the sterilisation programme.

The third part of this book analyses the impact of stated and implied ideologies in constraining the participation of women in the labour market and the public sphere. As these chapters show, where domesticity is seen as the natural role for women, then employment is envisaged as little more than a sideline and therefore accorded low payment and low status. But even in Israel, India and Vietnam, where there is a stated intention to include women in the public sphere, traditional views persist and pose limitations on such activities.

Ann Weston's chapter on women and handicraft production in India, discusses the problems that have bedevilled the promotion of home-based production; an industry which was compatible with the perceived domestic role of women. But, as this study shows, if women succeed in this sector, as they did in the case of lace-making, then there follows an increased division of labour, in which men take over the better paid entrepreneurial functions and the artisan's earnings fall. Women are prevented from marketing their own products by social conventions and blacklisting. Weston argues that the fragmented nature of domestic production has not only curtailed the access of women to the export market, but also that the expansion of this market may result in their exclusion altogether. As the handicraft sector becomes more lucrative, production moves out of the homes, outside which traditions bar women from working. It is ideology and not ability or skill that excludes women from the labour market.

Even in the context of an advanced capitalist country such as Israel, with a clear policy of including women in all spheres of life, it has not been easy to eradicate their subordinate economic and social position. The chapter by Nira Yuval-Davis looks at the military, where the inclusion of women has changed rather than ended their subordination. Yuval Davis shows that in the extremely hierarchical and bureaucratic modern army, gender differentations are far more formal and extreme than in the civil labour market. Yuval Davis argues that the division of labour within the military labour market must be analysed in terms of the national strategies. In Israel, these strategies envisage motherhood as the primary function of women, and participation in the military labour market as a temporary task for young women before childbearing. However, the military establishment never treats Israeli women as a unitary category; even during their national service their roles are defined by class, ethnic origin and ideological and religious locations as well as their gender.

In considering the impact of ideology on women's activities in the public sphere, attention has to be given to women's participation in public office as well as their relation to the labour market. The article by Carole Wolkowitz is concerned with the ideological construction of women politicians, and with the role of such constructions in accommodating women's presence in public office. She looks at the example of women legislators in Andhra Pradesh, India, where many women politicians are seen as the dependents of their male kin, thereby confirming rather than challenging the more general definition of women as primarily wives. This is one way in which the state, through the actions of the ruling party and its leaders, curtails potentially disruptive influences on notions of women's social identity.

However, as Christine Pelzer White's analysis of state attempts to revolutionise the cultural context of Vietnamese society shows, even fundamental changes in the systems of production (co-operatives) and reproduction (the family) are not sufficient to cause a complete transformation of gender relations. Pelzer White argues that this is in part because a State is itself the product of that which it governs and is deeply influenced by the 'traditional' attitudes that it is attempting to transform. This, in part, explains the apparent failure of national and even international efforts such as the Decade of Women to have an immediate impact on the lives of those women who are in greatest need of help. Nevertheless, what is clear is that once women's invaluable contribution to society have been recognised, particularly when such recognition includes payment for womens work, then it becomes easier to begin the long process of ideological change and the gradual erosion of the oppression of women.

Acknowledgement

I am most grateful to all the contributors for participating in our study group meeting and helping to write this introduction and produce the book. I should also like to thank Bina Agarwal who provided many of the ideas discussed here, and Patricia Jeffery for all her help and her meticulous comments on an earlier draft of this chapter.

Note

1. H. Alavi, 'State and Class Under Peripheral Capitalism', in H. Alavi and T. Shanin (eds), *Introduction to the Sociology of 'Developing Societies'* (Monthly Review Press, 1982) p. 298.
2. Ibid., p. 295.

Part I
Women and the State

1 Women and the State in Nigeria: the Case of the Federal Military Government 1984–85

Carolyne Dennis

The present Federal Military Government in Nigeria came to power on 31 December 1983.[1] The circumstances surrounding the *coup* were an immediate political crisis largely caused by the impotence of the Shagari Government in the face of an economic crisis which it had not created but had certainly exacerbated. Confronted by such a cruel dashing of Nigerian hopes for a better future, the Federal Military Government (FMG) sought to explain the causes of the crisis and thus provide an agenda for resolving it. The explanation offered which, of course, also provided the rationale for the *coup* itself, operated on many levels. However, the dominant theme of the internal causes of the crisis which were diagnosed, centred around the notion of 'indiscipline'. 'Indiscipline' ranged from those smuggling large quantities of petroleum and currency out of the country to market traders who profited from scarcity, to unconscientious salaried workers. Among the other groups guilty of anti-social behaviour of this kind, three categories of women were identified as contributing to the breakdown of social discipline: wives and mothers who failed to devote their time to the upbringing of their children; single women who provided a source of temptation to men; and petty traders who hoarded essential goods and created congested urban centres. This chapter examines the background of the relationship between women and the State in Nigeria in order to explain why, confronted with the worst economic crisis in the history of Nigeria since Independence, the Federal Military Government should offer an explanation of the crisis which laid considerable stress on the alleged results of women neglecting their 'traditional' roles and responsibilities.

The position of women in pre-colonial Nigeria differed from one society to another. There were variations in kinship structure and the

13

division of labour which determined the role of women within the economic structure. The history of State formation, development of religious ideologies and religious conversion also differed and thus so did the position of women within the public as opposed to the domestic sphere.[2] The majority of women within all societies spent their lives within the household, but such households depended on a range of economic activities with variations in the sexual division of labour and also in the division of labour within those economic activities reserved to women.

Nigerian societies had predominantly patrilineal and patriarchal kinship structures in which women married into a Yoruba or Igbo patrilineage or a Hausa *gandu*[3] were expected to produce sons to ensure the future of the kinship group. The position of the young wife as the newest members of a lineage, required to earn approval from its older members, improved as she grew older, bore children and gained the right to assistance from younger wives, leaving her free to engage in activities outside the household. In many societies like Igboland, women played an important role in agriculture. In Hausa society, the prevalent interpretation of Islam confined women to the household, except for the wives of men who were too poor to obtain other sources of labour.[4] The opportunities for women to participate in other economic activities such as manufacturing and trade varied from one society to another. They were probably greatest in Yoruba society in which the responsibility of a woman to provide for her family was interpreted as meaning providing the material resources for such care,[5] and the pattern of settlement in large towns created a division of labour with the possibility for the development of special-ised occupations. Under particular conditions of economic and social change and uncertainty, a minority of Yoruba women were able to achieve spectacular positions of economic and political power.[6] Under more stable conditions women, born into or married into ruling families often exercised considerable political influence indi-rectly, but it was rare for such influence to be exercised in public except by the leaders of the women market traders.[7] The religions of many Nigerian societies recognised the social importance of women by emphasising the place of female gods of fertility and social peace, but women were also associated with witchcraft which appeared to symbolise the potential social danger of women exercising power uncontrolled by men.[8] A 'purified' Islam increasingly confined Hausa women to the household. In societies with other forms of political economy and ideology, the role of women in agriculture, manufacturing and trade could be very important and women possessed an important, if restricted, religious role. However, systems of religious belief also provided an important space for explanations of the dangerous results of women acting outside their appropriate social role, unconfined by men.

Even before the imposition of colonial rule, Nigeria had been incorporated into the international economy as a supplier of raw materials. The colonial administrators and missionaries brought with them patriarchal conceptions of the appropriate social role for women. The cultivation of cash crops for the international market became a male preserve confining women to the growing of food crops for which returns were lower. This process was intensified by bureaucratic efforts to improve agriculture which were focused on men, cash crop farmers. The import of cheap manufactured goods from Europe and later Japan, led to the decline of craft industry, except for a limited range of luxury goods which in some regions affected the significant proportion of women engaged in such manufacture. The creation of the colonial economy thus tended to marginalise the position of the majority of women.

The establishment of a colonial bureaucracy and a network of European trading companies created opportunities for those Nigerians who managed to obtain the stipulated educational qualifications for salaried employment. The provision of educational facilities always lagged behind the insufficient facilities for men so this affected a very small number of women.[9] The fact that a limited number of women were able to accumulate considerable economic resources or obtain salaried employment in Southern Nigeria enhanced their social position as they were able to meet their domestic responsibilities more successfully. But these changes reinforced the reservations surrounding a woman with financial independence who might not give to her husband and his family the respect to which they felt they were entitled. The legal system established by the colonial administration institutionalised a new form of marriage by 'Statute' and codified 'customary' marriage. Statute marriage reflected the patriarchal assumptions of British society and does not appear to have worked in Nigeria as intended. A woman's family rather than the law could intervene to secure her position within her husband's family.

The colonial state in Nigeria reinforced the process of the economic marginalisation of women. The colonial administrators and Christian missionaries introduced the assumptions of European patriarchy into a situation in which considerable potential for tension existed between women's domestic responsibilities and the ideological explanation of their appropriate social role. Throughout the colonial period there was a series of protests by Nigerian women, first against particular colonial policies and later against colonialism itself. These actions often originated in opposition to the obstacles placed in the way of women performing their duties towards their families by the colonial State.[10]

Since Independence there has been a continual problem, which has varied in intensity, of ensuring the viability of the Nigerian State. The 'instability' has primarily been the result of competition for the resources of the State by different sectors of the Nigerian bourgeoisie. All post-Independence Nigerian Governments have pursued a policy of 'development', to be achieved by economic growth, particularly the expansion of the industrial base.[11] The growth of the oil extraction sector altered the structure of the economy by releasing the Federal Government from its dependence on revenue from the cash crop sector, thus ensuring the decline of cash crops in addition to food crops. It also altered the relative resources of Federal and State Governments as the revenues from oil accrued to the Federal Government.[12] But it intensified existing trends in economic policy rather than altering its direction, by making it appear that Nigeria could become the 'Brazil' of Africa by virtue of its demographic and natural resources and indigenous capitalist experience. The successive military *coups* in Nigeria have occurred at times when the senior officers of the Nigerian Army have perceived that the activities of the political class were such as to threaten this objective.

The competition within this class and the activities of any other group which does not appear to be contributing to the prescribed path of 'development' is often perceived as a problem of 'indiscipline'. Campaigns against manifestations of 'indiscipline' have punctuated Nigerian public life and the present Federal Military Government has articulated very clearly the view that Nigeria's problems are due to 'indiscipline' in its War Against Indiscipline.[13] In such a situation, the question of which social groups are identified as being the cause of indiscipline and therefore of sabotaging national development becomes very important. In order to answer it adequately, it is necessary to analyse briefly the context within which such campaigns take place, especially as women have been a very important target of accusations of 'indiscipline'. This discussion will begin with an analysis of major trends in the Nigerian political economy since Independence, followed by a discussion of the manner in which the War Against Indiscipline has affected Nigerian women.

Successive Nigerian governments have pursued a remarkably similar agricultural policy to that of the colonial administration. Food farming and marketing have been consistently neglected and productivity has dropped as the incomes of farmers have fallen dramatically in relation to returns to other sectors of the economy.[14] This decline has included the large number of women working in agriculture and the processing and marketing of local food. The production of food has declined to the point at which Nigeria is now a net importer of food.[15] Under the colonial regime and until the early 1970's, the cash crop sector was the most important source of Nigerian Government revenue through the pricing policies of the marketing boards. The returns to farmers have declined as a proportion of the world price, and this gap has been allowed to increase as the exploitation of oil has provided the Federal Government with an alternative source of revenue to the excise duties on cash crops. Thus, the production of cash crops is now also declining.[16] The agricultural policies of the Nigerian Government have always stressed the importance of supporting the larger 'more efficient' farmers and have made very little contribution to improving the position of the small peasant farmers, the agricultural sector which includes the majority of women engaged in agricultural production, processing and marketing.[17]

Educational facilities have expanded very rapidly in Nigeria since Independence. Educational expenditure is the largest item of public expenditure at both the Federal and the State level.[18] The historical experience of Nigeria has created a great disparity in the educational provision which is available in the different regions, notably between the North and South. The provision of primary education has expanded dramatically since Universal Primary Education was introduced in 1975, although major discrepancies in facilities still exist. More recently there has also been rapid expansion in secondary and tertiary education but very major differences exist between regions and also in the facilities available in schools, teacher training colleges and universities established recently by comparison with those which have been in existence for longer. At all levels the system is characterised by the discrepancy between the numbers of girls and boys being educated. At the primary level this has ceased to be very

significant in the South but is still very important in the North, both
for religious reasons and due to the importance of children's labour in
the home and for agriculture. At the secondary level, the disparity
between the sexes is even more significant and at the tertiary level,
very striking indeed.[19] In the Muslim North the factors militating
against education for girls are relatively clear and a significant change
in the numbers receiving more than a primary education probably
depends on radical measures such as reducing the cost of education to
parents and raising the minimum age of marriage. The first has been
adversely affected by the present economic crisis and the second is
unlikely to be introduced or enforced. In the South the situation is
more complex and the tradition that women have financial responsibilities to their own and their parents' household has meant that girls
have been eager to take up the educational opportunities available.
But 'women's occupations' like nursing and primary school teaching
have developed while far fewer women train for the professions; and
in universities, 'women's subjects' have emerged, the majority of
female students being concentrated in the humanities with relatively
few in medicine and engineering.[20] It is possible that in spite of the
indigenous assumption that a woman should have an income-creating
occupation, the stereotypes of the appropriate education and occupations for women found in British education have been imported along
with the educational system itself.[21] The lack of educational provision
for women in many parts of the country has left large numbers of
women with no means of legally earning a living within the cash
economy but with considerable domestic responsibilities, which is
relevant to how they are perceived by the present Government.

Post-Independence Nigerian Governments at both the Federal and
State level have energetically pursued a policy of industrialisation.
There are a number of small factories usually run by Indian, Leban-
ese or Chinese management, in association with Nigerian partners
since the passing of the Indigenisation Decree in 1978.[22] Larger
industrial enterprises have usually been established by an agreement
between the Federal or a State Government and foreign technical
partners.[23] Their control of oil revenues has also made it possible for
the Federal Government to embark on a series of large construction
projects: road networks, dams, irrigation projects and administrative
buildings. The construction sector has developed into the most profit-
able and fast growing sector of the Nigerian economy,[24] in which the
most lucrative contracts and probably the highest rates of corruption
obtain. The present world recession and the resulting surplus of oil

has had a particularly severe effect upon Nigeria, which was identified by the industrialised countries as the 'weak link' in OPEC and therefore most likely to reduce the price of oil under pressure.[25] The severe economic crisis which is now taking place in Nigeria has revealed the relative lack of return on the very high levels of public expenditure during the years of 'oil boom' and has led to a search for those responsible.

The parameters within which both political and intellectual discourse take place in Nigeria appear to exclude any discussion of class, except by a small group of Marxists. There has thus been a consistent tendency to identify the cause of Nigeria's problems as being 'indiscipline' – the failure of particular social groups to perform adequately their prescribed social role, preventing society from functioning as it should. This type of explanation has a particular attraction for military governments and is the fundamental basis of their claims to legitimacy. In a situation in which minor administrative procedures have become extremely problematic, in which the commitment of medical personnel to provide minimum levels of medical care is often limited and observance of driving regulations often appears to be non-existent, the predictability of everyday life appears fragile and the emphasis on a lack of discipline as the cause of the economic and social crisis is understandable. However, the members of the present Federal Military Government perceive themselves as being engaged in a 'fundamental' reform of Nigerian public life by the 'War Against Indiscipline'.

I wish to argue that different groups of women have been especially singled out as being the cause of 'indiscipline', either because of their own failure to perform adequately their allotted social role or because of the manner in which they encourage indiscipline in men. In the attention focused on the manner in which the awarding of contracts was abused, the wives of army officers and civil servants have been especially singled out as being responsible for corruption. The latter part of this chapter will analyse the significance of the identification of three groups of women who have been singled out as being responsible for 'indiscipline': petty traders, single women, and working women with children. These categories would appear between them to encompass most Nigerian women.

Outside large shops in a few urban centres, retail trade in Nigeria is largely in the hands of traders selling small quantities of food, cloth and other consumer goods in open markets. These traders, many of whom are women, stand at the end of a long list of wholesalers and middlemen or women. The economic crisis in Nigeria has led to a very high rate of inflation in the prices of consumer goods, and in many regions to an absolute scarcity of household necessities such as detergent, soap and matches, for example. In 1983, before the *coup* which brought the present Military Government into power, there were serious shortages of staple foods and an astronomical rate of price increases in food supplies.[26] The consumers' understandable reaction to this intolerable situation has been to blame the retailers they see – the petty traders – for hoarding goods and creating a scarcity of essential commodities. It is not so easy to explain the reaction of the Federal Military Government. Apart from the spectacular opening of a number of warehouses owned by wholesalers, full of hoarded foodstuffs, the concentration upon the idea that it is petty traders who are responsible for scarcity and price increases has been encouraged by the Military Government. The most extreme manifestation of this has been the large number of occasions in early 1984 when soldiers entered markets, beat the women traders and forced them to sell their goods at lower prices. This has benefited a few consumers. However, in a society in which considerable resources are devoted to creating monopolies in imported goods and inequitable distribution systems for local foodstuffs, the concentration upon the activities of the least powerful members of the retail distribution chain lacks credibility.[27] It also avoids addressing the issue of how the large number of women who attempt to meet their domestic responsibilities through petty trade are to do this if the retail system breaks down.[28]

This concentration upon the informal trading sector and especially on women traders within it as being responsible for the crisis, has been manifested in other ways. The formation of military officers in underdeveloped societies appears to create a particular conception of 'modernisation' and the characteristics of a 'modern' society.[29] This extends to particular conceptions of the characteristics of cities and the purpose of urban planning, reinforced by a limited knowledge of cities in industrialised societies. Petty traders who work on the highways, blocking the pavements and in unofficial markets contradict this notion and are taken to be a reflection on the 'modern' character of cities such as Lagos. The State Military Government in Lagos has carried out a constant campaign to remove traders from the streets and replace them with trees by tree planting campaigns.[30] These activities demonstrate a concentration upon the superficial consequences of the structural characteristics of Nigerian society and

show a lack of appreciation of the relationship between the petty
trade sector and low wage earners in the formal sector who depend
upon it for their food and commodity supplies.

This articulation of women's economic activities as undisciplined
and a bad reflection on the modern character of Nigerian society is a
particularly clear example of the policies pursued by the colonial
administration and subsequent Nigerian Governments. As outlined
above, this involved a concentration upon the cash crop sector during
the colonial period and an emphasis on large-scale farming and
particularly industrialisation since Independence. By implication and
sometimes overtly, this has also meant the characterisation of other
activities, particularly peasant farming, as backward sectors awaiting
modernisation or as anomalies in large industrial cities which will
either become extinct or – if a real problem for planners – must be
abolished, like petty trade. It arises out of a division of economic and
social sectors into 'traditional' and 'modern' which leads to particular
policies of economic growth and development.[31] The assumption
underlying this approach is that the existing industrialised societies
are modern and that modernisation and development means evolving
an economic and social structure like theirs.[32] One of these assumptions concerns the 'proper' economic and social place of women. The
patriarchal assumptions derived from European experience made it
impossible to understand the economic role played by women in
indigenous Nigerian societies and, therefore, to grasp the reality of
those societies. These assumptions have been inherited in a particularly strong form by the present Federal Military Government with its
modernising and disciplining mission. The significance of the attacks
on women petty traders is that, in a situation of deep economic crisis
caused largely by structural contradictions in Nigerian society and its
external relationships, the most vulnerable and marginal sector in
which women attempt to meeet their domestic responsibilities has
been singled out as the cause of the inability of Nigerian families to
obtain food and essential commodities without paying exorbitant
prices and investing much of their time.

Other policies of the Federal Military Government towards women
are more directly the result of a particular ideological orientation. In
the cities of Northern Nigeria, especially Kano, there has been a
campaign against single women in cities and an attempt to push this
further towards the forcible marriage of women who remain single
and in a city. The assumption is that single women are by definition
prostitutes, that by tempting men, they are responsible for immor-

ality, and by demanding money from men cause armed robbery, bribery and all other manifestations of 'indiscipline' which the Government wishes to eradicate. This group of urban migrants are also an affront to 'modern' urban planning as they do not contribute to the desired characteristics of urban centres.[33] The reasons behind prostitution and women moving to cities without an adequate regular source of income have been outlined above: the marginalisation of women within the economy and regional and gender disparities in the provision of education. This marginalisation has been intensified by the employment and trading difficulties caused by the present crisis. But the idea that single women outside marriage and therefore not controlled by a man are a potential threat to the social order is widespread in Europe, Asia and Africa. Perhaps in African societies it is intensified by a fear of women who have the potential power of witchcraft. However, in Northern Nigeria it is an assertive militant Islam which drives the campaign against single women and identifies them as prostitutes. The Kano State Government has been eager to appropriate this perception and its corollary of forced marriages as part of its own campaign against 'indiscipline'. It is a particular example of the phenomenon discussed below, in which the necessity of women assuming their 'traditional' role is stressed in societies undergoing rapid and unpredictable social change.

In many situations in which 'indiscipline' is diagnosed as being the cause of social problems, the lack of discipline is traced to the inadequate socialisation of the individual.[34] In Nigeria this lack of discipline is identified as being caused by the inadequate socialisation of the individual resulting from the failure of wives and mothers to perform their domestic duties properly.[35] The argument rests on the implicit and sometimes explicit assumption that a woman's place is in the home, that the rearing of children is an entirely female responsibility and that if young people are delinquent or indisciplined, it is the fault of their mothers for not training them. It also implies that the young are the most serious examples of 'indiscipline', which is not self-evidently true in Nigeria.

It is certainly true that in the polygynous structure of Nigerian society, a mother does carry the primary responsibility for her own children and may see herself as competing with the claims of other wives and their children for the attention and resources of her husband, but that duty has always been perceived in material as well as nurturing terms. In many households this has required the wife to search for a source of income which will complement that of her husband. It has also meant that if she is pursuing a personal 'career' which includes trading, she needs to build up a network of contacts through social rituals. This also provides her with the necessary potential social support in the problems confronted by women in a polygynous society. The attack by the members of the Federal Military Government on women who spend their time working and attending social functions appears to derive from a particular conception of the characteristics of a 'modern' society and its family relationships. It resembles the patriarchal European assumption that the place of women is in the home, engaged particularly in child rearing which is an exclusively female responsibility. In indigenous Nigerian societies bringing up children has never been the exclusive responsibility of the mother; the assistance of older and younger female relatives has meant that women have been able to carry domestic responsibilities other than housework and child care. It is possible that, faced with the rapid decline in the accessibility of the extended family and the availability of domestic servants which made it feasible for their wives to work outside the home and manage it without their assistance, Nigerian bourgeois men have chosen to redefine domestic management and child-care as being the sole responsibility of their wives, to which they have to find a solution by themselves within the context of the immensely difficult everyday conditions of the economic crisis.

The persecution of the informal sector reflects an assumption about the proper operation of a disciplined economy which bears particularly heavily on those excluded from formal employment – who are disproportionately women. The explanation of social problems as being caused by personal indiscipline, projects structural processes on to the individual and the home, the home being assumed to be the responsibility of women. This tends to be an accurate reading of the division of responsibility within the home, but the emphasis on women's responsibility for child-care ignores the fact that women also carry the financial responsibility for feeding their families, which for many of them means working within the informal sector. For those lucky enough to have wage-earning employment, arranging for child-care, which is regarded as their sole responsibility, raises serious problems.

These ideas have been current in Nigerian society for a long time but appear to be articulated in a particularly emphatic manner in the present crisis. In a situation of great uncertainty, women are perceived as the guardians of tradition and dire consequences are pre-

Full reported
to be Traditional

dicted for a society if they deviate from their 'traditional' role and
responsibilities. In this situation, and one suspects, many others, the
'tradition' which acts as the reference point is largely mythical. It is
significant that while 'modernisation' is being stressed as the goal for
Nigerian society, an increasing emphasis should be placed on women
conforming to 'traditional' expectations.

It is also significant that it is the present Federal Military Government which has articulated this unease in its clearest official form
since Independence. In part this reflects the fact that they have been
confronted with a more severe economic crisis than any previous
Nigerian government. But it also derives in part from the particular
formation of senior army officers in a bureaucracy which is regarded
as 'modern' and is certainly masculine, hierarchical and has an
emphasis on high technology. In other words, they live within an
organisation, the members of which tend to be regarded as the
vanguard of 'modernisation' and which is furthest removed from the
concerns of petty traders, peasant farmers and women. It is understandable that they should blame petty traders and working mothers
for being the cause of Nigeria's failure to become a 'disciplined'
modern State. In the North of Nigeria, this scapegoating of women
has been reinforced by a militant Islam, paradoxically a reaction to
the particular form 'development and modernisation' have taken in
Northern Nigeria. This same reaction can be observed in a more
diffuse form in other parts of the country.

before domestication - more
marginalised

The obligations which Nigerian women possessed within indigenous Nigerian societies contradicted the assumptions of a 'purified'
Islam, evangelical Christianity and the colonial State. The changes
which have occurred in Nigeria during the colonial period and since
Independence have tended to marginalise the majority of women
into food production and petty commodity production and trade,
although a minority have been able to take advantage of growing
public sector employment and lucrative contracts for public works. A
major economic crisis like that now occurring in Nigeria demonstrates very clearly how such an economy works and the character of
the contradictions within it. One of these contradictions results from
women trying to meet culturally prescribed obligations in a situation
in which they are marginalised and in which powerful imported
ideologies assert that they should have a purely domestic role. The
present Federal Military Government has interpreted this contradiction as a cause rather than a symptom of Nigeria's present predica-
ment.

Notes and References

1. This chapter was written before the *coup* in Nigeria on 27 August 1985. The *coup* appears to have been caused by the economic austerity without the prospect of growth and the abuses of 'human rights', especially the imprisonment of editors and journalists.
2. See Yusufu Bala Usman, *The Transformation of Katsina 1400–1883* (Ahmadu Bello University Press, Kaduna, 1981); G. I. Jones, *The Trading States of the Oil Rivers: a Study of Political Development in Eastern Nigeria* (Oxford University Press, 1963); and R. Henderson, *The King in Every Man: Evolutionary Trends in Onitsha Ibo Society and Culture* (New Haven: Yale University Press, 1972).
3. See Polly Hill, *Rural Hausa* (Cambridge University Press, 1972).
4. Polly Hill, *Rural Hausa;* I. A. Ogunbiyi, 'The Position of Muslim Women as Stated by Uthman B. Fudi', *Odu: A Journal of West African Studies*, n.s., 5, no. 2 (October 1969) pp. 43–60; Mary Smith, *Baba of Karo: a woman of the Muslim Hausa* (London: Faber, 1954).
5. Simi Afonja, 'Changing Modes of Production and the Sexual Division of Labour Among the Yoruba', *Signs* vol. 7, no. 2 (Winter 1981) pp. 299–313.
6. See two Yoruba plays by Akin Isola, *Madam Tinubu* and *Efunsetan*.
7. Ibid.
8. In relation to Yoruba religion, see P. Morton-Williams, 'An Outline of the Cosmology and Cult Organisation of the Oyo Yoruba', *Africa*, vol. 34 no. 3 (1964); K. Barber, 'How Man Makes God in West Africa: Yoruba Attitudes Towards the Orisa', *Africa*, vol. 51 no. 3 (1981) pp. 724–45; Francis Speed and Peggy Harper, *Gelede: A Yoruba Masquerade* (Institute of African Studies film, University of Ibadan, 1968).
9. A. B. Fafunwa, *History of Education in Nigeria* (London: Allen & Unwin, 1974); Bolanle Awe, 'Formal Education and the Status of Nigerian Women', in A. Ogunsheye, K. Awosika, Carolyne Dennis and C. M. Di Domenico (eds), *Nigerian Women and Development* (Ibadan, 1982) pp. 404–24.
10. Nina Mba, *Nigerian Women Mobilised: Women's Political Activity in Southern Nigeria 1900–1965* (Institute of International Studies, University of California, 1984).
11. See *Third National Development Plan 1975–1980*, vol. I (Central Planning Office, Federal Ministry of Economic Development, Lagos, 1975) p. 147: 'The Nigerian economy is now faced with the challenge and opportunity of creating an industrial base that can guarantee self-sustaining growth in the future.'
12. Gavin Williams (ed.), *Nigeria Economy and Society* (London: Rex Collings, 1976); T. Turner, 'Multinational Corporations and the Instability of the Nigerian State', *Review of African Political Economy*, 5 (1976).
13. See *West Africa*, no. 3477 (9 April 1984) p. 796, for the launching of the present War Against Indiscipline' by the Federal Military Government.
14. See Frances Stewart, *Planning for Basic Needs* (London: Macmillan, 1985) section on the Nigerian economy.

15. The composition of imports into Nigeria has shifted in the past twenty years. Food and beverages were 9.2 per cent of imports in 1965 and 17.1 per cent in 1980, which in the context of a rising total of imports is a considerable foreign exchange bill for food imports, World Tables (Baltimore: Johns Hopkins University Press for the World Bank) p. 526.

16. The food and beverage component of Nigerian exports has fallen from 64.5 per cent of the total in 1962 to 3.6 per cent of the total in 1980, which has left the economy almost entirely dependent on oil exports. See World Tables, p. 518.

17. 'The land tenure system is mainly responsible for the fragmentation of holdings and the difficulties in mechanisation and modernisation of agricultural production', Third National Development Plan 1975–1980 vol. I (Central Planning Office, Federal Ministry of Economic Development, Lagos, 1975) p. 63. 'The required transformation from peasant production to modernised production calls for a new breed of entrepreneurs with sufficient training and expertise', ibid, p. 64.

18. The 1984/5 Budget after the coup saw a shift of expenditure towards Agriculture with N826 836m, 21 per cent of the capital budget. The Army received N569 244m in recurrent expenditure and N359m of the capital budget. Education, Science and Technology which at the Federal level is tertiary education, received N272m of the capital budget, with each State Government devoting a considerable proportion of its Budget to primary and secondary education. See West Africa, no. 3483 (21 May 1984) p. 1093.

19. For the figures of the relative enrolment of men and women at the different levels of the educational system, see A. Ogunsheye, 'Formal Education and the Status of Women in Nigeria', in A. Ogunsheye, K. Awosika, Carolyne Dennis and C. M. Di Domenico (eds), Nigerian Women and Development (Ibadan, 1982) pp. 425–50.

20. See Bolanle Awe, 'Formal Education and the Status of Nigerian Women: an Historial perspective' and Olajumoke Peters, 'Female Students in Residence: An Analysis of the Problems, Attitudes and Aspirations of undergraduates in Queen Elizabeth Hall', in A.Ogunsheye et al. Nigerian Women and Development, pp. 404–24 and 510–17.

21. Eileen Byrne, Women and Education (London: Tavistock, 1978).

22. Paul Collins 'The Political Economy of Indigenisation', African Review, no. 4, 1975; E. O. Akeredolu-Ale, 'Private Foreign Investment and the Underdevelopment of Indigenous Entrepreneurship in Nigeria', in Gavin Williams (ed.), Nigeria Economy and Society (London: Rex Collings, 1976) pp. 106–22.

23. See S. A. Afonja, Carolyne Dennis and C. P. M. van Rest, 'Rural Industrialisation: the example of the Westexinco factory at Ado-Ekiti', Proceedings of the Annual Conference of the Nigerian Anthropological and Sociological Association, ed. W. Ogionwo, 1973; S. A. Afonja and Carolyne Dennis, 'Social Aspects of Rural industrialisation: the Ado-Ekiti example', Proceedings of the Conference on Social Research and National Development in Nigeria (Ibadan, 1976) pp. 756–89; Carolyne Dennis, 'Capitalist Development and Women's Work: a Nigerian case study', Review of African Political Economy, no. 27/28, pp. 109–19.

24. Frances Stewart, *Planning for Basic Needs* (London: Macmillan, 1985) section on the Nigerian economy.
25. See *West Africa*, no. 3420 (28 February 1983) p. 527.
26. It is almost impossible to estimate inflation levels in an economy such as that of Nigeria but in the period before the *coup*, it must have been running at 100–200 per cent and does not appear to have been significantly reduced since then. See *West Africa* no. 3465 (16 January 1984) p. 126. It is provided as one of the justifications for the *coup*.
27. *West Africa*, no. 3465 (16 January 1984) p. 126. General Buhari's first economic policy speech focused among other issues, on the need to 'check the activities of hoarders, smugglers and all other social and economic saboteurs'. This was interpreted by soldiers as permission to try to force prices down in markets by beating traders which resulted in the closing of shops and stalls.
28. Gloria Marshall, 'Some Patterns of Trade Among Women in Western Nigeria', *NISER Conference Proceedings*, 1962; Niara Sudarkasa, *Where Women Work: A Study of Yoruba Women in the Market Place and in the Home* (Ann Arbor Museum of Anthropology, University of Michigan, 1973).
29. J. M. Lee, *African Armies and Civil Order* (London: Chatto & Windus, 1967); Billy Dudley, *The Social Characteristics of the Nigerian Military* (Ibadan, 1973).
30. See *West Africa*, no. 3476 (2 April 1984) p. 748 'Lagos State Government has issued an edict prohibiting street trading in Lagos. . . . Since January efforts have been made to clear traders from the streets and 'illegal' markets that characterise Lagos. The markets have been burnt down by the soldiers and police and council workers have been arresting the street hawkers!
31. *Third National Development Plan 1975–1980* (Lagos: Central Planning Office, Federal Ministry of Economic Development, 1975).
32. Henry Bernstein, 'Modernisation Theory and the Sociological Study of Development', *Journal of Development Studies*, vol. 7, no. 2 (1971).
33. See 'Women in Nigeria Press Release', *Review of African Political Economy*, no. 31 (December 1984) pp. 104–6. See also the chapter on Zimbabwe in this volume for a similar phenomenon in a different political and ideological context and *West Africa*, no. 3478 (16 April 1984) p. 848, for the drive against criminals and prostitutes in Nigerian cities.
34. Talcott Parsons and R. M. Bales, *Family, Socialisation and Interaction* (London: Routledge & Kegan Paul, 1956) for the paradigm of this approach.
35. See 'Women in Nigeria Press Release', *Review of African Political Economy*, no. 31 (December 1984) pp. 104–6. The denigration of working women is demonstrated by Governor Popoola of Oyo State warning that 'Public officers, especially women, who were fond of travelling overseas to buy goods for sale in their offices would be dismissed if caught', *West Africa*, no. 3480 (30 April 1984) p. 951. An equivalent campaign is 'Operation Keep Oyo State Free of Destitutes', *West Africa*, no. 3501 (22 October 1984) p. 2145.

2 Women in Zimbabwe: Stated Policy and State Action

Susie M. Jacobs and Tracey Howard

INTRODUCTION

This chapter will examine aspects of state policy towards black women in independent Zimbabwe. Although the woman question in state policy making is intertwined with more general social, economic and political questions, there are nevertheless areas of State policy which are specifically gender-based and which bear separate examination. These areas include laws affecting women' female participation in production, fertility and the recent 'clean-up' campaigns.

While the colonial state in Rhodesia did enact some policies specifically oriented towards African women, most existed on a *de facto* basis; for example, black women did not have equal citizenship rights and were considered legal minors, under the protection of male guardians. African women, then, had no *direct* relationship to the colonial State. Most affairs considered relevant to them were administered under African customary law. One of the more important changes that has come with Independence is in this relationship, so that for the first time African women enjoy (at least formally) full citizenship rights, and can make demands directly, on their own behalves. It is from this changing relationship that many contradictions also arise.

We begin with an analysis of state policies concerning women. ZANU is not the only party in Zimbabwe, but it does form the present government and thus largely directs State policy. The main institutions which articulate policy towards women are the ZANU Women's League, and the Ministry of Community Development (CD) and Women's Affairs (WA). The former is an arm of Party organisation; the latter, while having a measure of autonomy, is one of the weaker ministries.[1] So the policies of the above two institutions can be seen as largely, although not wholly, subsumed under stated government policy.

Moreover, any analysis of state actions must take account of struggles against the state, both inside and outside its apparatuses. Such struggles continue to prevent absolute determination of policy by the ZANU leadership. However, these conflicts may not be readily visible due to the increasing amount of control the leadership is able to exert over most aspects of the state machinery and the increasing repression used to maintain this. Thus many policies which may have been the objects of struggles can only be considered in their outcomes and not in the process of construction.

B. N. Ong[2] has identified common strands between the Zimbabwean, Angolan and Mozambiquan ruling parties' conceptions of the subordination of women and the ways in which this should be tackled in a newly 'socialist' society. Like the revolutionary movements in Mozambique and Angola, which faced similar difficulties and resources, ZANU (PF) and (PF) ZAPU in Zimbabwe adopted policy positions on women broadly similar to those of states in Eastern Europe and the USSR.[3] Official Soviet policy is based on Engels' and Lenin's belief that the key to female emancipation lay in incorporation into productive work outside the home. However, little attention was (or is) paid to women's subordinate role within the home and the family.[4]

Penelope Roberts quotes President Machel of Mozambique to exemplify this position: 'Women's liberation is to be achieved by the abolition of private property and women's entry into social production, both of which are inseparable from socialist strategy itself and therefore requiring no separate struggle.'[5] She comments that Machel has defined the limits of 'permissible feminism' indicating that feminism is a secondary issue which confuses women, especially as it suggests that men might be in part responsible for the maintenance of gender divisions.

The official political rhetoric relating to women in these southern African societies may be rooted in a model derived from Engels, via the Soviet Union, but the actual situation they face today bears little resemblance to that of the USSR. In Zimbabwe particularly, policymakers are caught between several ideological and material contradictions, which are especially pertinent to women-oriented policies. The dominant ideology has been shaped by two belief-systems, opposed in their conceptions of women. Marxism vies with a model deriving from the pre-colonial society, in which women's capacity to reproduce the lineage, socially, economically and biologically, was crucial and in which lineage males controlled women's labour-power.

Arising from this, there have developed conflicts between the political rhetoric which pledges ZANU to the total emancipation of women, on the one hand, and the enactment of State policies which entrench women's dependence on men, on the other. Thus statements about the need to bring women into 'social production' co-exist with the State's reinforcement of men's control over women.

There is however a degree of conflict between rural and urban women. Historically, most black urban dwellers in Zimbabwe have been male. Women living in towns are relatively privileged to live there, since they have access to more services than do rural women. But this difference is often misconstrued as being one of simple socio-economic stratification, so that all urban women are seen as (relatively) well-off materially and all rural women as poor. This division, we would argue, should be seen rather in class terms, and in the context of the migrant labour system characteristic of southern Africa. In towns, there is a small stratum of petty-bourgeois women as well as a stratum of very impoverished and unemployed women. In rural areas most women are engaged in subsistence farming or in cash-cropping, but the (largely female) peasantry is also differentiated by class factors. It should be noted as well that many people of both sexes are not exclusively settled in either townships or Communal Lands, but have bases in both. In conclusion, aspects of State policy in Zimbabwe do affect all black women, though this does not mean that they should be construed as a unified group or that policies affect all women evenly.

We now turn to a closer examination of ZANU's stated position, which aims to mobilise women to become 'effective participants in the development process'.

Consistent with our socialist philosophy of equality of man and woman and our desire to enhance the status and image of the woman, the ZANU Women's League will play a crucial role in mobilising and conscientising women so that they become effective participants in the development process:
To this end we will:
(a) encourage women to participate in income generation activities and engage in co-operative economic enterprises;
(b) train our women to develop marketing strategies for goods they will have produced;
(c) encourage women to take full advantage of adult literacy and other beneficial programmes;

(d) ensure that outdated or restrictive legislations pertaining to the status or well-being of women are amended.[6]

Point (a) reiterates the common, but completely mistaken, assumption that women are not *already* engaged in productive work. In fact it remains part of the colonial legacy that women perform the bulk of agricultural tasks, especially in subsistence production.[7]

Point (b) indicates the success of the ZANU Women's League and the Ministry of CD and WA in some areas in setting up small cooperatives for activities such as sewing and bakery. Whilst these may increase the amount of cash available to the household, women are expected to take up any such opportunities *in addition* to their other work in the fields or at home. But the income from such products may be appropriated by men: that is, it is not controlled by women.

The third aspect of stated policy (c) implies that women need to be *encouraged* to take part and that it is their 'backwardness' which prevents them from attending. Again, preliminary research[8] shows that for most women, the unrelieved burden of work leaves no time or energy to attend classes for most of the year. The opposition of husbands and the relative lack of facilities may also prevent women from attending.

The last section mentioned in the extract from the ZANU document relates to the legal sphere. This is often seen as crucial in maintaining and/or altering women's position in society. It is both an arena of social control in a direct, coercive sense, and, at the same time, a major vehicle of State ideology. In Zimbabwe, one of the main ways in which women's issues have been taken up is in terms of their own status before the law. This is reflected both in the heated debates which have taken place about legal changes[9] and in the complexities of the set of laws facing women in Zimbabwe.

RECENT LEGISLATION

The major piece of legislation passed since Independence which was directly aimed at women is the *Legal Age of Majority Act 1982* (LAMA). The effects of LAMA which have received most attention in Zimbabwe are the conditions of marriage and divorce for black women. It must be noted that the LAMA generated strong reaction

within the country. For instance, Bishop Muzorewa published a
criticism of it in the UANC election manifesto,[10] in which he alleged
that the LAMA 'allows children to disobey their parents on attaining
the age of eighteen'. The reply of N. Shamuyarira, Minister of
Information, Posts and Telecommunications, was instructive, 'the
LAMA was intended to give the right to vote, not to disobey parents
– legal misunderstandings are soon to be clarified'.[11] A few days later,
Mugabe himself supported this view when he declared, at a meeting
with chiefs, that the Act had been passed in order to enable women
to vote and that the interpretations of the courts had not been
foreseen, adding that the Government is 'reviewing the law to see if it
can be amended'.[12]

In spite of the LAMA, two separate systems of law remain in
Zimbabwe: Civil/General Law which applied originally to whites,
and Customary Law for blacks. Since 1981, Zimbabweans have been
able to elect for one or the other. However, as with many aspects of
law relating to women, the scope and practice of it is severely limited
by lack of knowledge of its provisions, so that the situation has not
changed significantly. Most rural cases are still tried under Customary Law and most cases under Civil/General Law are urban. However, black men, especially urban men, are still able to refer to the
type of law which they find beneficial. For instance, men married
under Civil Law sometimes marry second wives under Customary
Law, although technically such second marriages are bigamous.

Prior to the LAMA, black women had to have their guardians'
permission to marry under either the Marriage Act of 1964 (which
comes under Civil/General Law, and is therefore monogamous) or
the African Marriages Act of 1951, which requires an 'enabling
certificate'. LAMA, however, has retained the clause requiring consent, for Customary Law marriages. N. Makamure suggests that this
is an indication of the absence of any state intention to use the
LAMA as an instrument to bring about full legal emancipation of
women.[13]

Despite the Government's lack of commitment to challenge what
has come to be seen as 'tradition',[14] it is still necessary to consider
why women themselves choose to marry under Customary Law.
Rural women remain largely ignorant of the ways in which the
changes in law might potentially affect them, despite some attempts
at education by the Ministry of CD and WA.[15] Hence they are likely
to choose the Customary form. Also women frequently place a high

priority on satisfying their own families' wishes, which are often for a Customary marriage.[16]

As to divorce in Zimbabwe, the issues which most concern women are the custody of children and the provision of property and/or maintenance. In giving women full legal status, LAMA entitled unmarried mothers and wives to become sole guardians of children upon divorce. But the situation is unchanged in some rural areas,[17] since to win guardianship, a woman must have detailed knowledge of the law, and needs to initiate the proceedings. Rural women are much less likely than urban women to have such knowledge.

In any case, many women married under Civil/General Law are divorced illegally under Customary Law: and outside the courts. In this situation, the families concerned usually decide the matter according to the husband's wishes. The woman is unable to get fair treatment since she lacks the resources to secure a court hearing. Once again, women are unable to obtain justice, because of their own ignorance of the laws and a lack of commitment by the authorities to implement them.

One final aspect concerning women's legal status should be noted here: that of 'damages'. Under Customary Law if a wife or unmarried daughter was found to have had sex with a man other than her spouse, her guardian was able to sue the 'seducer' for damages. Since LAMA there has been considerable confusion about this, particularly when the woman in question has been leading an urban lifestyle and so is likely to come under Civil/General Law. This was highlighted in a case recently,[18] in which a man, ordered to pay damages to a woman's father by a primary court, took the case to the Supreme Court. The Supreme Court ruled that the father was unable to claim damages for the daughter as she was a legal major, and that a woman who came under General Law could conceivably claim damages in her own right!

This shows the extent of legal confusion about the implications of LAMA. However, the Act remains at present largely irrelevant for most black women. There are vociferous calls from within[19] and from outside the Ministry of CD and WA for stronger and more specific laws protecting women's rights in marriage, divorce and widowhood. Ministers, including Mugabe, who are keen to ensure the support of a large proportion of the urban, and particularly female population, do not readily dismiss these claims. Other demands, regarding polygyny and high *lobola* (bridewealth) prices have also been considered.

However, so far the Government has given these proposed changes a very low priority: this too should be seen partly as an effect of wishing not to alienate the extensive, largely male, body of support which is very resistant to changes in women's status. It should be emphasised, however, that such policy decisions are not only the outcomes of the demands of various interest groups, but also result from structural, economic factors. Were women to have full legal equality with men, this would give them greater freedom of movement and might eventually affect the nature of their responsibilities in the rural areas.

The ZANU Congress Report has given some consideration to 'women's' issues. However, generally the tendency is either for women to be left out of policy-making, or, where issues are defined as pertaining to women, policies are often fraught with ideological and political contradictions. We emphasise that we do not see this tendency as peculiar to Zimbabwe, or even to Third World societies,[20] although the ideologies elsewhere may take somewhat different forms. Specifically, we take up two areas crucial to the determination of women's lives: those of production and work; and of biological reproduction, fertility and contraception. We then go on to analyse a particular type of state action relating to women: that of the 'clean-ups' or 'round-ups' which have taken place in Zimbabwe and in other African countries.

WOMEN'S PARTICIPATION IN PRODUCTION

As in other societies, women's contributions and needs in the sphere of production have not been explicitly recognised. This is *in spite* of the acknowledged importance of drawing women into waged employment. In Zimbabwe, employment in all sectors except agriculture has, historically, been almost exclusively reserved for black men. Unlike South Africa, in Zimbabwe, even the poorest-paid factory workers are men; domestic workers, too, are predominantly male.

The National Manpower Survey (1981) of trained personnel[21] found, for example, that in the manufacturing sector only 8 per cent of professional, skilled and semi-skilled workers were female: this low figure includes European women. Selecting some occupations, the percentages of women and of African women who were trained was found to be as shown in Table 2.1[22]

As elsewhere, women with skills are concentrated in the clerical and service occupations (for example, as medical assistants, nurses,

Table 2.1

Selected occupation group	(1) Numbers in occupation group (male) and female)	(2) % of females in occupation group (% of column (1))	(3) % of African females in occupation group (% of column (1))
Professional & technical	27 031	28.4	16.6
Clerical & Related	56 046	36.4	8.5
Service	23 031	11.0	7.2
Agriculture, animal husbandry & forestry workers	43 171	3.75	2.5
Production related workers	117 723	2.5	1.9
Total (all occupations)	298 361	13.7	5.4

Source: Extracted from GOZ, Ministry of Manpower, Planning and Development; National Manpower Survey, 1981, vol. III, Tables 10.3.14 and 10.3.15.

midwives, teachers, social workers, typists and telephonists). African women were found, much more frequently than Europeans, to be in the lowest-paid, lower-ranking sectors of work. (Thus column (3) as a percentage of column (2) is 39.3 per cent.) These figures are not sufficiently recent to indicate much in detail about the post-Independence period. However, there have been some changes, most notably the opening-up of white-collar positions to African women. But such shifts are unlikely to have greatly altered the social composition of the Zimbabwean working class. Perhaps the most important reason for this is the general economic crisis and rising unemployment, which means that job prospects for women are not likely to improve in the near future. It may also be the case that men, individually and collectively, have an interest in reserving their jobs from competition with women. Such competition is likely to increase in the context of crisis: capitalism in Zimbabwe may find it difficult to 'afford' economic equality for women.

The development of the migrant labour system has meant that most black women reside in impoverished rural areas. Some of these women are formally employed on commercial farms.[23] Although the ownership of many large farms has changed hands so that commercial farmers are, with increasing frequency, black, this is not likely to affect the use of either male or female labour power. Most rural women reside in the Communal Lands (formerly, Tribal Trust Lands) where over 70 per cent of the population is female. Here, their role has been as a largely unpaid labour force engaged in subsistence farming and in reproducing migrant 'worker-peasant' households. Female labour – mainly the unpaid labour of wives – has been widely used in the Small Scale Commercial Farm (formerly African Purchase Area) sector, where about 3 per cent of the population live and where polygyny is very widespread because it is sometimes used as a strategy to obtain labour.[24]

The one major attempt to reform the Zimbabwean agrarian structure lies in the resettlement programme. In these programmes, unutilised or under-utilised, formerly white, commercial farms are purchased by the Government under the Lancaster House Agreement. There are various models of resettlement, of which the two most significant are 'Model B' co-operatives and 'Model A' or individual family resettlements, where settlers are issued permits (to reside, to cultivate) and are allocated 5 hectares (12 acres) with variable grazing rights. Although the resettlement programme is large compared with such programmes elsewhere (for example, in Kenya) the number of people resettled is small compared with those left in the overcrowded Communal Lands. There is no discrimination against women applying for resettlement in terms of formal criteria utilised, but Model A plots are allocated only to 'household heads', who are almost universally defined as male.[25] In any case, women are not usually told by local officials and do not know that they have formal rights to apply. The exceptions to this are widows with children, who are considered to be heads of households. Resettlement may improve women's position, if only because resettled families are likely to be better off economically, but it is unlikely to alter women's status in any dramatic way.

CONTROL OF FERTILITY

Unlike the sphere of production, which is implicitly defined as a male realm, that of biological reproduction/fertility/contraception is defined as *the* female realm. This area is fraught with contradictions concerning women's roles, duties and status, and as such, it is an important site of struggle for Zimbabwean women. The struggles involved are both between women and men and between both gender groups and the state. In the colonial and settler States, contraception was administered by the Family Planning Association, one of whose major concerns was to limit the fertility of black women. Contraception was sometimes prescribed without proper medical supervision or follow-up, and black women were pressurised to use contraceptive methods without adequate information. These practices engendered great hostility among both African men and women. Recently the name of the FPA was changed to Child Spacing and Fertility Association, and the organisation placed under state control.

Abortion is illegal in Zimbabwe, except on medical grounds, and is strongly disapproved of by most people. Women who do have abortions are forced to the 'back streets' with their unhygienic conditions and dangerous consequences. Contraception is more publicly discussed, but is still a contentious subject. Women in Zimbabwe generally wish to bear children and are under strong social pressures to do so. They gain status from motherhood and childless women are very much ostracised. This is probably because children's labour is still economically useful, at least in the rural areas. However, many women do wish to limit the number of children they bear and/or to determine the length of the interval between births. Notably for rural women, poor health often means that there is a high incidence of malnutrition, pelvic infection, and so on, causing sterility or precluding the use of the IUD.[26] Furthermore, insufficient facilities, such as medical services or running water, may also preclude use of methods such as the contraceptive pill and the diaphragm. Men's hostility to contraception often precludes the use of most other possible methods.[27] As in the past, many women who are unable to hide contraception (if it is available) are forced to resort to 'the injection' (Depo-Provera), or to bearing children at shorter intervals than they would wish.

Zimbabwe has one of highest rates of the population growth in the world; in the context of economic crisis, this is seen in some circles as a threat to stability. The Child Spacing and Fertility Association is also subject to pressure from outside, especially US funding agencies which wish to slow down rates of population growth, regardless of the wishes of the local population.

The contradictions within the areas of contraception and reproduction highlight the situation of underdevelopment and of subordination of women in a very concrete way. Caught between the differing demands of preserving their own social positions, of husbands and of state programmes, women have to struggle against men as individuals and against gender-based state policies to make decisions concerning their own fertility.

ROUND-UPS AND URBAN POPULATION CONTROL

The corollary to the marginalisation of the mass of Zimbabwean women in the rural areas is their exclusion from cities. Historically, the control of movement through and within urban areas was a vital instrument in the colonial State's political and economic control over the black population. Controls over women took particular forms. Except for an elite minority, the only ones allowed residence were women who serviced the white community as domestics, or else those in small mining towns and in urban townships, who were encouraged to service the black male workforce as prostitutes. Although the numbers of women allowed to live there as dependents of their husbands did increase during the 1950s, the war of liberation, and at Independence, the stigma of women living in towns being seen as prostitutes has remained.

It is against this background of prejudice that most women have very poor chances of finding employment, especially on a full-time basis. They also have enormous problems in finding accommodation: single women, particularly those without children, generally do not qualify for state-provided housing. The material difficulties they face has meant that some women do work as prostitutes. Although data on this is scarce, it is safe to say that a strong and repressive state apparatus historically has kept their numbers lower than in many African cities.

In Zimbabwe and in many Third World contexts, urban centres have an appeal to both men and women as centres of potential wealth and escape. In Zimbabwe, the migrant labour system is widespread, and migrants are often able to stay with a relative in town. Also, during the war and in post-Independence Zimbabwe, several camps of squatters were allowed to develop where people built temporary shelters. Such popular attempts to seize the opportunities existing in urban areas present very real threats to the governments' attempts to gain stable political support in towns, and attract foreign investments. The growth of unplanned urban settlement and economic activity has presented various African governments with major difficulties. In this climate of informal, and sometimes illegal, change women have often found the space to challenge traditional roles and to earn and control (usually paltry) incomes for themselves. In turn they have also been faced with some of the most vociferous and violent attacks from state machineries delivered to any sector of the population. It is not our intention to deny that men also suffer punitive state action for attempting to survive in ways which challenge official policies, but rather to show that women suffer in additional ways, and that the influence of ideologies about women, especially those suspected of deviating from traditional norms, is a crucial component in actions against them.

Both the urban controls and the clean-up campaigns are by no means unique to Zimbabwe and South Africa, but were enforced throughout colonial Africa and similar actions were taken by governments in Kenya, Tanzania and Mozambique. J. Bujra[28] has described how, in 1969, the Kenyan Government enforced the Vagrancy Act in such a way that fear and vulnerability were experienced by many women in Nairobi, although at the same time there was a prevailing view that prostitutes, as the 'beggars' of society, should be punished. L. P. Shaidi[29] describes the enforcement of a similar Act in Tanzania in 1983 in which women were severely discriminated against. In the same year in Mozambique, 'Operação' Produčão' which was intended to clear the towns of 'excess population', and to provide labour for state farms, also had differential effects on men and women.[30]

ROUND-UPS IN ZIMBABWE

In Zimbabwe no new laws were needed to undertake the programmes of mass arrests and removals entailed in the 'round-ups', as the powers created by the Smith regime in the Emergency Clause added to the Vagrancy Act of 1960, have been retained. The State also has access to relatively sophisticated media. The main newspapers, the *Herald* and the *Sunday Mail*, are not completely state-controlled, but function in large part to transmit official views. They have a very wide circulation and so can be used to generate support with very limited questioning of policies. In September 1983 two media campaigns commenced. One was against 'baby-dumping' and the other against squatting. The 'baby-dumping' campaign, which continued until March 1984, involved sensational reporting of women who induced abortions or who abandoned new-born babies. It reached a crescendo on 23 November 1983 with an editorial in the *Herald* entitled 'Kill the Beasts'. An extract reads:

> The grisly discovery of 13 babies at Chitungwiza[31] raises a powerful question: have some of our women become possessed by the devil?

Mothers, aunts or sisters should have known or at least suspected that the girls were pregnant, aborted or given birth. Yet they engaged in a complicity of silence and continued to cohabit with murderesses and abortionists.

(*Herald*, 23 November 1983)

Very few letters or articles critical of such labelling were published, and so an atmosphere hostile to young women generally and a consensus of opinion blaming women for social problems was successfully fostered.

Parallel to this press campaign the Government launched a propaganda offensive against squatting. It first promised to upgrade the oldest and longest-established illegal settlement at Epworth (outside Harare) which dates back to 1976. The Minister for Local Government and Town Planning, Enos Chikwore, agreed that the genuinely landless should be given places on resettlement schemes, but added,

The rest must go back to rural areas and start preparing for the rainy season . . . they do not want to pay rents nor for services. They have become a social menace by enjoying a life of squatting and the Government will always be ruthless with them.

(*Herald*, 8 October 1983)

On 30 October it was reported that the police and army arrested 500 families from one of the oldest townships in Harare, Mbare Musika, and an unknown number of 'beggars' elsewhere. On the same day, the *Herald* stated that women in Harare alleged to be prostitutes were being rounded up by plain-clothes policemen.

The campaigns, which were linked, had economic roots: given the existing social and economic structure in Zimbabwe, the campaigns were necessary to control the movement of people to towns and to preserve the role of women, especially rural women, as unpaid domestic and agricultural labour. However, they should not be explained only in economic terms: ideological and political factors played an important role. The campaigns appear to have arisen partly out of a desire by the Party leadership to change the face of Harare, literally to 'clean it up', in order to create a well-ordered, modern city with no obvious social problems and certainly with no people visibly in difficulty or distress. This was achieved by the bulldozing of squatter camps, the arrest of squatters and by the removal of large numbers of hawkers and beggars. Such reasoning also applies in part to the campaign against prostitution. However, since the majority of women arrested were not prostitutes and did not conform to any stereotypical behaviour of prostitutes[32] some additional explanation must be found. We argue that the campaign against 'prostitution' was, as well as being a 'clean-up' exercise, aimed at controlling women in general.

The first, and main campaign against 'squatters, vagrants and beggars' which took place from October 1983 into early 1984, was characterised by late night, or dawn, raids by the police and/or army; and usually one or two days' warning were given. The round-up was accompanied by statements which branded those arrested as cheats attempting to avoid payment for the benefits of town life. Such statements also claimed that 'vagrants' should be assisting the country through working on resettlements. The Division of Physical Planning stated in February 1984 that the bulldozing of illegal urban settlements – which occured in several well-established areas – was part of a broader policy to reverse the flow of rural people to towns and cities.[33] The campaign later widened out to encompass rural squatting. However, this is beyond the scope of this paper.

The second campaign against squatters, which occured in January and February 1985, was notable particularly for its stress upon 'cleanliness'. Again it was preceded by statements in the media, such as one in the *Herald* towards the end of December 1984. It was reported that, 'Scores of people reappear [each night] . . . to litter the sheltered shop fronts of the city centre . . . These are Harare's scourge, the vagrants.' This dramatic description set the tone for several reports on the lifestyle and arrests of vagrants over the next two months. Throughout this period, statements made in the press and by State officials tended to condemn not so much the *illegality* of the vagrants/squatters/vendors, but their *uncleanliness*. For example, a *Sunday Mail* report (of 30 December 1984) read: 'their children, soot-black with dirt, can be seen begging or scavenging from rubbish disposal bins'. Moreover, after the campaign, the success was at first presented by the Municipal Authority thus: 'Physically, the city is cleaner than a month ago (*Herald*, 10 January 1985).

Another campaign, which was launched in February 1985, was specifically aimed at food vendors. For the first time the Government explicitly made a connection between the illegal cooking and sale of food and the spread of disease. There were no public announcements of the numbers arrested, but arrests appear to have been confined to those engaged in technically illegal activities. It is notable that the definition of 'illegal' under the Emergency Powers Act has come to include some of the main means of income-generation for women.

The 1983 round-up of women accused of prostitution was broader than either of those against vagrancy because in the former, women of various groups, classes and even races, were picked up. Arrests came in two waves: one was centred on Harare and was concurrent with the arrests of squatters; whilst the other occurred across all urban centres in Zimbabwe.

In the initial round-up the raid on 'The Avenues' area of Harare was of central importance. This area is notable in that it was once occupied by Europeans, but is now mixed and is occupied by young professional people, some of them being single black women. We understand that while some women arrested were prostitutes, many young women picked up were not. They felt they had been arrested *because* they were young, single, and showed evidence of earning their own living.

Elsewhere in Harare, in the high-density suburbs (areas which used to be reserved for blacks) and in other towns, women were arrested even while going about their daily business, for example, while waiting at bus stops, walking home from work or shopping. Later it became apparent that many had been arrested and taken away to prison in Harare or in other towns or else to Mushumbi Pools. (a camp hundreds of miles from Harare in a resettlement area in a very hot and humid part of the Zambesi Valley). They were given no opportunity to inform relatives or, in some cases, even to make provision for babies or children at home. It is perhaps significant that during this swoop, most prostitutes working in expensive hotels with higher-status clients were not disturbed. On 13 November and again on 21 November 1983, further mass arrests were reported, under similar conditions.

There has been much speculation about the numbers of people arrested in these campaigns. Although we have been unable to arrive at a confirmed figure, 3000 is commonly quoted as the number of men and women taken to Mushumbi Pools. The Minister for Home Affairs, Cde. Mubako, stated total numbers to be '6316 women from main centres, 2047 men and women in Harare and 2623 from other centres'.[34]

Shortly after the arrests, a Women's Action Group (WAG) was formed, which, at that time, consisted of white and black Zimbabwean and expatriate women, as well as several men. One of its most important achievements at the time was cataloguing many harrowing individual tales of unfair arrest. It also successfully publicised criticisms of Government actions.[35] The newspapers also carried, especially between 13 and 21 November, an increasing number of complaints about the manner in which arrests were made. From the articles, it appeared that there was support from nearly all but nightclub owners for arrests of real prostitutes, but a growing resistance to the random, careless way which raids were carried out, and to the fact that many women who were not prostitutes were arrested. This prompted a statement by a 'spokesman' for the Government on 16 November regretting 'any inconvenience caused'[36] and another by the Minister for Justice and Legal Affairs, E. Zvobgo, a few days later[37] affirming the rights of women to move about publicly and unaccompanied. Such statements did little to allay the fears of many women who chose to remain at home rather than to risk arrest by travelling, nor did it bring comfort to those who 'lost their jobs, homes, salaries or had their marriages broken', as WAG later reported.[38]

Combined with these processes was an amendment in the emergency clause regulations, which strengthened the powers of rehabilitation officers, lengthened the time a prisoner could be detained without being brought before a magistrate, and further limited a prisoner's right of appeal. On 8 December the *Herald* carried a long speech by Mugabe himself which justified this tightening of the law, but which also apologised to the innocent who had been arrested. The Government then, was seen publicly to 'back down' over the excesses of the campaign against prostitution. It may be that the Party leadership was not in full control of all arms of the state machinery, most notably the police, who appear to have been the major progenitors of the mass arrests of women. Alternatively, it could be that the leadership overestimated the tolerance of the urban population for such open violation of human rights. The Ministry of Community Development and Women's Affairs was also moved to protest. However, such protest has not prevented the Government from using its full powers again, as demonstrated by the January–February 1985 round-ups. The continued violation of human rights in Matabeleland also attests to an increase in the exercise of repressive power since Independence.

We have argued that the campaign against 'prostitution' should be seen as being linked to those against vagrants and squatters and to the extension of the new state's control over other, impoverished and weakened groups. Nevertheless, we argue, it was directed against women as a gender group, whilst the campaign against vagrancy was not specifically directed against women or men. The campaigns all had economic, political and ideological causes, but that against prostitution had an additional component in men's collective and individual attempts to control women and their sexuality. We argue that the campaigns should be viewed in the light of overall State policies, in particular, the relative lack of change in women's position and the general move towards the use of a more repressive State apparatus. Women have not been the only group marginalised and stigmatised. However, the component of sexual stigma attached to women suspected of deviancy provides a particularly powerful vehicle in a process whereby all the physical and ideological forces available to the state are marshalled. Women in particular, especially those suspected of independent action, have become scapegoats for the frustrations and tragedies typical of dependent and underdeveloped Africa.

Notes and References

1. For an analysis of why this might be so and of struggles within the Ministry, see G. W. Seidman, 'Women in Zimbabwe: Post-Independence Struggles', *Feminist Studies*, 10, 3 (1984).
2. B. N. Ong, 'Women in the transition to socialism in sub-Saharan Africa', in B. Munslow (ed.), *Africa's Problems in the Transition to Socialism* (London: Zed. Press, November 1985).
3. This is not meant to imply that there is a wholesale acceptance of Soviet and East European policies or philosophy, merely to state that it is from here that the roots of policies towards women can be traced.
4. Hence women in the USSR still bear a 'double burden' of paid employment and domestic work. See for instance, M. Buckley, 'Women in the Soviet Union', *Feminist Review*, no. 8, pp. 79–106.
5. P. Roberts, 'Feminism in Africa, Feminism *and* Africa', *Review of African Political Economy, (ROAPE)*, no. 27/28, p. 183.
6. *Zimbabwe African National Union Central Committee Report*, presented by President of ZANU, Cde. R. G. Mugabe, to the Second Congress of the Party, 18 August, 1984, p. 16.
7. For debates concerning the definition of 'production', or 'socially productive' work, see, for instance, M. O'Brien, *The Politics of Reproduction* (Boston: Routledge & Kegan Paul, 1981) and F. Edholm, O. Harris and K. Young, 'Conceptualising Women', *Critique of Anthropology*, vol. 3, no. 9 (1977).

8. All references to 'preliminary research' and to 'our research' refer to fieldwork undertaken separately by the authors during the period September 1983–September 1984.

9. See, for example, J. May, *Zimbabwean Women in Customary and Colonial Law* (Edinburgh: Holmes McDougall Ltd, 1983) and N. Makamure, 'Women and Revolution: the Women's Movement in Zimbabwe', *Journal of African Marxists*, no. 6 (1984) pp. 74–86.

The many references from the daily Zimbabwean newspaper, the *Herald*, and the weekly *Sunday Mail* which are relevant here are too numerous to be cited thoroughly, but exmaples will be given. Longer and more careful debates about women's legal status are to be found in two Zimbabwean journals, *Social Change and Development*, no. 4 (1983) pp. 16–18; no. 6 (1983) pp. 21–22; no. 8 (1984) pp. 22–24; and *Moto*, no. 28. (1984) pp. 4–8.

10. T. Ranger, 'Thirteenth Review of the Zimbabwean Press, March 16th–April 12th, 1985' (unpublished), p. 9.

11. *Herald*, 9 April 1985, cited in' T. Ranger, 'Thirteenth Review', p. 9.

12. Ibid., p. 17.

13. N. Makamure, 'Women and Revolution', p. 83.

14. For discussion of the definition of 'tradition', see, for instance, articles by R. Milroy in the *Herald* of 31 October 1982, 27 February 1983.

15. J. Mpofu, 'Some observable sources of women's subordination in Zimbabwe', Fundamental Rights and Personal Laws Project, University of Zimbabwe, Harare, April 1983. Mpofu cites evidence from a nationwide survey which conforms with evidence from our own research.

16. Ibid.

17. J. Kazambe, *Social Change and Development, (SCAD)*, no. 8 (1984) p. 22, stated that 'cases which are presently being brought before the Primary Courts are usually being won by the women': this was not confirmed by our own research.

18. This judgement is discussed in an article in *Moto*, no. 28 (1984) pp. 4–5 and 7.

19. For example, the Minister of CD & WA, T. R. Nhongo, in the *Herald*, 30 December 1983, said 'Women can look forward to a declaration of women's rights and customary law reform bills. A quota system to reserve a certain percentage of jobs. . . for women. . . A declaration of women's rights to property in cases of divorce, legal separation or death.' Then on 15 November 1984, she also said her Ministry was concerned with the delaying tactics that had been adopted in making changes in the taxation system where it discriminated against women.

20. See, for instance, E. Wilson, *Women and the Welfare State*, (London: Tavistock, 1977).

21. This survey does not include unskilled workers.

22. Government of Zimbabwe, Ministry of Manpower, Planning & Development, *National Manpower Survey* (1981) vol. III, Harare, extracted from Table 10.3.14, p. 197 and Table 10.3.15, p. 198.

23. D. G. Clarke, *Agricultural and Plantation Workers in Rhodesia*, (Gweru, Zimbabwe: Mambo Press, 1977) p. 28. Clarke noted that in 1977, 23.3

per cent of agricultural workers were women, mainly employed on a casual basis.

24. A. P. Cheater, 'Women and their participation in commercial agricultural production', *Development and Change*, p. 355. Cheater reports that in the area she studied, Msengezi, less than 18 per cent of farmers were polygynous. However, five other Purchase Lands were much higher, and ranged up to 43 per cent of farmers – nearly half the population. See also, A. K. H. Weinrich, *Women and Racial Discrimination in Rhodesia* (UNESCO, 1979), p. 29. Weinrich reports that husbands in Purchase Areas exert strict control over their wives, and that junior wives often appear to be treated virtually as labourers.

25. For a more extended version of this argument, see S. Jacobs, 'Women and Land Resettlement in Zimbabwe', *ROAPE*, no. 27/28 (1984) pp. 33–50.

26. S. Fawcus, 'Letter from a European doctor in Zimbabwe', *International Campaign for Abortion, Sterilisation & Contraception Newsletter*, April 1981.

27. Ibid.

28. J. M. Bujra, 'Postscript: Prostitution, Class and State', in C. Sumner (ed.), *Crime, Justice and Underdevelopment* (London: Heinemann, 1982) pp. 145–161.

29. L. P. Shaidi, 'Tanzania: the Human Resources Deployment Act 1983 – A Desperate Measure to Contain a Desperate Situation', *ROAPE*, 31, pp. 82–7.

30. A public functionary, interview with one of the authors.

31. This discovery was later admitted to be a fabrication. In an article in the *Herald*, 25 November 1983, the Acting Minister of Labour and Social Services, Mr Shava, is quoted as saying, 'Investigation by the police and sewage workers prove that the allegation is untrue'.

32. Women were arrested whilst carrying babies on their backs, walking with husbands or boyfriends, and even in cinemas accompanied by men.

33. D. Patel, 'Squatting : A Problem, or a Solution', *SCAD*, no. 7 (1984) p. 5. It is interesting that the integrity of squatter families was acknowledged: statements were made to the effect that squatter families were not to be split up.

34. S. Mubako, *Herald*, 8 November 1983, cited in T. Ranger, 'Thirteenth Review', p. 6.

35. One of the authors was a member of the WAG during her residence in Zimbabwe in 1983/4, and gratefully acknowledges the useful discussions and conversations with other members. However, she personally accepts responsibility for the views contained in this article, which do not necessarily resemble those of WAG. A detailed description of the formation of WAG may be found in *SCAD*, no. 9 (1984) pp. 22–3, and in an article written by several members about the plight of men and women arrested, in *Moto*, no. 19 (December 1983/January 1984).

36. 'A Government spokesman', cited in the *Herald*, 14 November 1983.

37. *Herald*, 19 November 1983.

38. *Sunday Mail*, 11 December 1983.

To the authors' knowledge, there is no discussion in the Zimbabwean press as to the differing effects of the imposition of customary law upon Shona, Ndebele and Tonga societies. All of A. K. H. Weinrich's work, however, carefully considers the different positions of the three groups in different settings. Of particular interest to the readers may be her analysis of divorce. See, for example, A. K. H. Weinrich, *Women and Racial Discrimination in Rhodesia* and A. K. H. Weinrich, *African Marriage in Zimbabwe* (Gweru, Zimbabwe: Mambo Press, and Edinburgh: Holmes McDougall, 1982). In the article by J. Mpofu, (see n. 15 above) useful points are made about the historically different property rights of women within these different groups.

3 The State and the Regulation of Marriage: Sefwi Wiawso (Ghana), 1900–40

Penelope A. Roberts

INTRODUCTION

> If one marries a woman with all the customary payments, and then divorces, the wife has a share of the property, but not if the case is concubinage . . . because Kwame Tano I wanted to stop bad women (Sefwi Wiawso Native Tribunal, 8 July 1948).[1]

With these words, the senior spokesman (*okyeame payine*) of Sefwi Wiawso State recalled a period of crisis in gender relations, particularly in marriage, twenty years earlier. Between about 1925 and his death in 1932, *omanhene* Kwame Tano I and the Sefwi Wiawso State Council passed several amendments to customary law relating to marriage. Further amendments were made in the subsequent decade.

The attempted reforms arose from the conditions of cocoa production, a crop introduced into Sefwi Wiawso some two decades previously. Cocoa production had led to an increased need for women's farm labour. This affected marriage as an institution through which men obtained access to the labour of wives. Property relations in marriage, however, did not secure the rights of wives in the product of their labour on their husbands' farms. Women's economic security was gained through enterprises separate from those of their husbands. By the end of the 1920s new opportunities for such enterprises were present. European-owned gold mines were re-opened, bringing male migrant labour into Sefwi, the construction of roads and of new market towns. To these, women were drawn to trade and, as it was invariably believed, for the purposes of prostitution. These events coincided with the collapse of the cocoa price leading to a crisis in the farming economy. The immiseration of cocoa farmers was com-

48

pounded by symptoms of a 'moral crisis': the spread of venereal disease and the appearance of new anti-witchcraft cults to deal simultaneously with disease and economic disaster.

Sefwi Wiawso State (*oman*) responded to these circumstances, in its capacities as legislature and judiciary, by various means. First, it attempted punitive measures to combat prostitution. Secondly, it tried to restabilise marriage by imposing new sanctions against divorce and against what it regarded as the increasing prevalence of 'concubinage'. Subsequently, the State sought to control the rising costs of obtaining a wife.

This chapter argues that the interventions of the State should be understood as efforts to guarantee the allocation of women's labour through marriage and therefore to ensure the ability of peasant households to enter into production. There is an increasing volume of literature exploring the interaction between the commodification of West African economies, the sexual division of labour and control over the productive and reproductive capacities of women. Women's labour, engaged through the obligations of marriage, was required for the production of male-controlled cash crops and/or for the maintenance of the subsistence sector. New demands for labour, including future labour, affected the expectations of women's reproductive lives. At the same time, increased trade in foodstuffs – which women monopolised in some parts of West Africa – gave some women greater potential independence from marriage, which had formerly provided them with access to the means of production. The principle of the separation of the economic enterprises of husband and wife favoured, under some circumstances and for some women, earlier separation from husbands to reduce demands on their labour and reproductive services. The convergence of sexual, reproductive and productive obligations in marriage, however, could lead to the representation of women's material alternatives as the removal of constraints upon their sexuality. Some recent studies have particularly drawn attention to the role of lineage elders or of the State (traditional or modern) in affecting to ensure, through law, the reproduction of gender relations.[2] The disciplining of sexuality, reproduction and labour services has been pursued by measures to restore the moral order or, for example, to reform property relations between spouses, or both. None seem to demonstrate that the State has been unequivocally successful in sustaining the patriarchal basis of marriage.

SEFWI WIAWSO

Sefwi Wiawso State is in the forest zone of western Ghana (see Figure 3.1). There are three Sefwi States, Sefwi Bekwai and Sefwi Anwhiaso being very much smaller than Sefwi Wiawso, which occupies all the land from just east of the Tano River to the present Ivory Coast border. They have historically been independent of each other but speak a common language, Sefwi, which is a branch of the Anyi languages spoken in south-west Ghana and south-east Ivory Coast. Sefwi Wiawso became a tributary state of Asante in the early eighteenth century. Its political, legal and social institutions were similar to those of the other matrilineal Akan States before colonial conquest.[3] The head of state (the *omanhene*) was selected from the male members of the royal matrilineage (*abusua dihyie*) and occupied the royal stool at Wiawso. He ruled in association with the leaders of military divisions bearing the rank of *safohene*, the heads of subordinate royal lineages and other hereditary and elected officials. Following colonial conquest and under the regulations of the Native Administration Ordinance (1927), all these officials were designated the State Council of Sefwi Wiawso, which was granted derived legislative and judicial powers. These included the codifying and reform of customary law and the hearing of cases on appeal at the Native Tribunal, composed of representatives of the State Council. Their jurisdiction covered such civil cases as marriage, divorce and land disputes. Civil disputes normally went first to arbitration conducted by elders of the families involved in the dispute and following customary procedures. Any person, however, was entitled to swear the oath of the stool of a *safohene* which placed the dispute within the jurisdiction of his court. Alternatively, or following the hearing of a case at such a court, a person could swear the oath of the royal stool which brought the case within the jurisdiction of the Native Tribunal. A great deal of the time of the Tribunal was spent on hearing marriage cases and its officials were very well placed to observe heterosexual relations and the consequences of the conditions – economic, social and demographic – which affected them (Vellenga, 1983, p. 150). As a legislature, the State Council was entitled to pass bye-laws to alleviate and resolve the conflicts as they saw them.

Sefwi Wiawso was, and is, one of the least densely populated parts of southern Ghana: at the time of colonisation large areas were virtually uninhabited. Most of the population was to be found in two

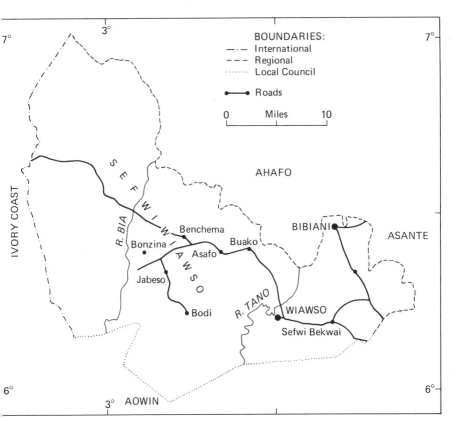

Figure 3.1   Map of Sefwi Wiawso

areas. The first was round the foothills of the capital, Wiawso. These surrounding villages were quite large, some settled with slaves and their descendents, and produced crops, meat and fish for the royal court. A second centre of population lay around Asafo, on the trade route from Asante to the present-day Ivory Coast, also the seat of a branch of the royal matrilineage.

The pre-colonial economy was based on farming, hunting, gathering and gold-production. Farming, mainly carried out by women and male and female slaves, was largely for the production of food-crops for consumption. Women specialised in the collection of snails, which were smoked and traded, and produced a range of household and trade goods such as soap, oil and bark-cloth. In the last decade of the nineteenth century Sefwi Wiawso became a centre for the collection of wild rubber. Among local people, the trade was often enough carried out by husband and wife(ves) teams. Both sexes collected and carried rubber, each person receiving payment for their proportion of the crop, but women in particular invested their earnings in the purchase of river fish which they smoked and traded in the rubber-buying centres further south – some even as far as the coast – returning with other varieties of fish, salt or trade items for local resale. Old women remember this time with great delight, recalling disconsolately that cocoa, which succeeded the rubber trade, caused them 'to settle down', requiring them to spend a greater part of the year farming, and reducing their opportunities for income from trade. The gold rush of the first decade of this century led to the exploitation of new deposits by large numbers of women and men, while European companies employed local and immigrant labour in their concessions along the Bia River.

The rubber trade collapsed and the gold mines closed down at the beginning of the First World War. The local economy, slowly and with considerable difficulty, adapted to cocoa production. The outstanding problems were the shortage of labour, lack of road or rail transport and the low prices for cocoa which from time to time discouraged producers from maintaining or extending their farms. Although by 1925 Sefwi cocoa had 'long enjoyed a reputation for its quality' (Holtsbaum, 1925, p. 76), the bulk of it had until then been produced in Sefwi Bekwai and Sefwi Anwhiaso, within relatively easy reach of the railhead at Dunkwa. For producers round Wiawso and further west, transport problems were not to be alleviated until the first lorry road reached Wiawso in 1925.

Nevertheless, cocoa production began in the areas round Wiawso and Asafo a few years before the First World War. At this period, production seems to have been largely initiated by chiefs and depended substantially upon the labour of their large households or settlements of slaves who were set to work to clear forest, establish farms, maintain carrier routes and headload the crop. Seasonal wage labour, however, especially for head-porterage, existed alongside the use of slaves and other household members from the very beginning, though some of it may have been that of slaves and pawns contracted out by their owners who received their wages.[4]

Many of these early plantations were abandoned briefly during the war when the cocoa price collapsed. The Agricultural Department maintained that this was because farmers were too lazy to substitute their own labour for the wage labour they could no longer afford.

This did not take into account the fact that it was probably at this time that the institution of slavery as a direct source of labour collapsed. Labour which left the farms during the war may well have been that of slaves abandoning their owners whose situation, if they were large scale producers, would have been similar to that of the *omanhene* of Aowin, the neighbouring state south of Wiawso. In 1916 he complained that he had had to move his residence away from the capital 'because there are no stool slaves to work for him any more' to his home town where he had large farms, worked by kin and wage labour, which he had to supervise.[5]

Production revived when prices rose sharply after the war and large farmers were able to draw on the labour of local people, previously involved in the rubber trade, who thereafter invested their earnings in cocoa farms. The high prices, though not sustained, remained sufficiently high until the end of the 1920s for small producers, mainly dependent upon household labour, to continue to invest in cocoa – chiefly hindered by the cost of headloading. The cocoa belt gradually moved westwards. The larger plantations of the chiefs were heavily dependent upon the *corvée* labour of their subjects to maintain carrier routes and evacuate the crop. Nevertheless the Railway Survey of Sefwi in 1925 concluded that returns on a railway would be insufficient to warrant investment.[6] Its main reason was that the population was too small to anticipate any rapid increase in production.

It was, then, in the 1920s that the slow expansion of cocoa was established, largely through small-scale, household-based production but using some seasonal and contract labour. Household relations of production were subject to a rapid transformation in the face of the requirements of the new crop. In particular, the mutual obligations of spouses in the provision of labour, of the means of subsistence and eventually of the means of production were under stress. The principle behind the obligations between husbands and wives was the complete separation of their property and economic enterprises. Their mutual obligations converged in the reproduction of children, in the provision of services for the production of subsistence and of each other's mental and physical health. Women moved to their husbands' homes at marriage. In the pre-cocoa economy, a husband was obliged to get enough of his land cleared for each wife to grow food-crops from which to feed herself, her husband, her children and other household members allocated to her kitchen. Husbands supplied fish and meat in kind or made available the means for buying them. A husband was not entitled to take food-crops from his wives' farms and wives were entitled to sell the surplus, although given the restricted market in foodstuffs, women's income derived largely from the type of trading enterprises which we have described during the rubber trade. Food-crop farms were maintained for only two to three years, after which they reverted to fallow. The old farm retained little economic value and new land was cleared.

Initially, cocoa production fitted well with these obligations. For the first three or four years, a young cocoa farm carries food-crops whose maintenance by women was practically all that was required for the care of the young cocoa trees. After this, little food is produced as the trees start to bear, but maintenance in the form of clearing and weeding has to be continued. This rapidly became the main contribution of women to the mature cocoa farm. Their labour in this respect, however, did not produce crops which they controlled, but cocoa, which was the property of the husband. Meanwhile, trading opportunities for women declined during the first full decade of cocoa production as demands on their labour time curtailed long-distance trade and local markets remained restricted. A woman's labour on a mature cocoa farm was, therefore, directly compensated only in the continued obligation of her husband to provide part of her subsistence from his own earnings.

Since cocoa farms continue to yield for over twenty-five years, the amount of land in production and requiring maintenance was much greater than the amount used or needed for food crops. Demands for male and female labour increased. Mikell found that polygyny had increased as a consequence of the introduction of cocoa in the Brong area of Ghana and that 'older Brong males . . . could remember the search for wives which occurred at the turn of the century when cocoa sank roots' (Mikell, 1984, p. 201). Sefwi women's recollections[7] reflect a slightly different perspective on the changes occurring in marriage following the introduction of cocoa. They recall, first, an increase in the frequency of divorce and, secondly, the growing inevitability of remarriage. The first arose from the conflicts emerging between spouses and co-wives which became manifest from the very beginning around attempts by wives to secure some immediate or future interest in the cocoa farms of their husbands upon which they were working. Their attempts seem to have first taken the form of asking that part of a farm jointly cultivated with the husband should be made in the wife's name. Refusal to do so or, as many women described, the belief that a husband was making a cocoa farm for one wife but not another, led to disputes generally signalled by a wife refusing to farm for her husband at all, either returning to her own home or to live with another man. Divorce might follow.

There is no reason to suppose that divorce had ever been uncommon. 'Before cocoa', a young woman might have married twice or more before she succeeded in bearing and rearing children successfully. She would then tend to stay in that marriage until widowhood (when she could accept or refuse to be inherited by her husband's successor) or until she ceased or wished to cease child-bearing. At this point, she might informally separate from her husband, returning to her own family home. Women's perceptions of the change in the patterns of marriage after cocoa was that older women were more likely to divorce, despite having successfully borne children in a marriage, because their husbands refused to allocate them a cocoa farm or divide farms equally between co-wives. On the other hand, they found it more difficult to refrain from a further marriage. They punctuated their life histories with half-laughing, half-bitter comments such as: 'Then I said I would not marry again, but what could I do?'. Women record being persuaded into remarriage when they would have preferred to 'retire' from both marriage and child-bearing and to establish their own cocoa farms on their own land. Therefore, although divorce was more frequent, a woman came to expect to spend more of her life actually married and with labour obligations to a husband. Persuasion to remarry seems to have taken the form of higher payments to the woman's father and an increase in the value of gifts made to the woman herself.

Some women did acquire cocoa farms from their husbands at this period. However, no court countenanced, at the time of divorce, a settlement which allowed a wife's claims to a joint farm made with her husband unless it had been formally transferred to her as a gift previously.[8] Nor did they countenance the claims of a widow to such farms other than under similar circumstances. The problem that women faced, therefore, was that if they abandoned a marriage, they lost any chance of acquiring rights in farms they had worked with their husbands. They might establish their own farms on their own land, having lost years of labour investment to their husbands[9] or they might risk the possibility of another marriage to a more willing husband. On the other hand, if they stayed in marriage, they had some hope that a farm would be allocated to them eventually, providing that the husband did not die before making such a settlement and that his family acknowledged the gift.

When these conflicts were emerging during the 1920s, there were relatively few alternatives for women other than farming for one husband or another. At the end of the decade the rural economy was devastated by the collapse of the cocoa price. Farmers struggled with debt and some left the rural areas to seek wage work elsewhere, deserting wives and children without providing means for their maintenance. By contrast, following the abandonment of the gold standard, mining revived. Market towns were established along the new roads providing opportunities for trade in foodstuffs and other services to the largely male wage-earning population. Wiawso itself, hitherto a mere village, expanded rapidly, attracting women from throughout Sefwi and elsewhere whose activities were disturbingly visible to the members of the Native Tribunal. A new market had been built, brokers and traders set up shops and bars, and these facilities attracted women to establish permanent market stalls, to trade in foodstuffs from the surrounding villages and to prepare cooked food for the increasing population of strangers and schoolchildren. Below Wiawso, the village of Dwinase was developing as the semi-permanent residence of men dealing in the transport of cocoa and for labourers working on the roads. Here women were setting up stalls and building lodging houses for rent. Mining towns were growing. Jabeso was expanding to such an extent that the State Council had to establish a subordinate Native Tribunal within it to hear cases of drunken and disorderly behaviour amongst the miners, traders and prostitutes living there.

Amidst these material changes, the spread of venereal disease was a peculiarly horrible event. Beliefs about the mode of transmission of gonorrhoea and its long-term effects were complex. The transmission of the disease through sexual intercourse was perfectly well understood but converged – as in any culture – with a nexus of ideas concerning the body, sexuality, fertility and, in southern Ghana, witchcraft. The beliefs linking venereal disease with witchcraft have long been recognised. Field concluded that the main causes of the increased preoccupation with witchcraft in south-eastern Ghana were the cocoa industry and venereal disease. Witchcraft was held to be responsible for most of the sterility, still-births and short-lived infants (Field, 1948, p. 173). Witchcraft, as often with gonorrhoea in women, resided, hidden, in the vagina or in articles of dress intimately associated with female sexuality such as waist-beads and loin cloths. Prostitutes (*tutu*[10]) were invariably believed to be carriers of gonorrhoea (*babaso*).

The presence of venereal disease exacerbated the tensions surrounding marriage and, indeed, between women and men in general. One consequence was the introduction of a variety of anti-witchcraft cults to which individuals resorted for the treatment of the symptoms and ultimate causes of the disease. The threat to sexuality and fertility invoked by venereal disease was epitomised in the destoolment of *omanhene* Kwame Tano II in 1935. The first charge against him was that he had been unable to breed with any of his fruitful stool wives. Although the charge was couched in the language of witchcraft, it was generally assumed that he had contracted venereal disease. The treatments he had sought for it, including travelling at great cost to an anti-witchcraft shrine in the north of the Gold Coast, had failed, and the court concluded that his case was incurable. His mother, it was alleged, was a witch and had 'stolen, boiled and eaten his penis'.[11]

The attempted reforms of marriage and its related practices took place, therefore, against this general background. The introduction of cocoa had provoked new conflicts between spouses leading to 'wife-stealing' and desertion by wives. The crisis in the rural economy coincided with an upsurge of opportunities for trade for some women. The association between trade and prostitution and the spread of venereal disease were seen as results of these conflicts. The remedies of the State Council ranged from hysterical proclamations to more measured reform.

MARRIAGE REFORM

It is not easy to describe marriage transactions in the early 1920s although the basic payments are recorded in Tribunal records.[12] Old people, with the experience of arbitrating innumerable marriage and divorce cases and having generally themselves been married and divorced several times, are well able to explain both current practices and the changes that have been made through State Council byelaws. But apart from basic transactions, marriages were surrounded by further payments. The original significance of these could be fudged in retrospect by lack of proper witnesses or convincing counter-claims. The following brief description of the basic marriage payments and the type of marriage they established is unduly simplified, but attempts to bear on those aspects which were at issue in the marriage reforms.

The first payment was *k꜕k꜕* ('knocking fee'[13]), paid by the future husband's father (or his successor) to the wife's father (or successor). It was about 13/- up to the mid 1920s and rose shortly after to about £1. 1*s*. *0d*. It was accompanied by a full bottle of schnapps.[14] *K꜕k꜕* can be described as a betrothal fee if paid when the future wife was still an infant. Under these circumstances, which were common, the future husband had as yet no claim upon his wife's services but was required to contribute to her support in the form of gifts to her parents and part of the cost of her menstruation ceremony. Once the latter was completed, and if both partners wished to continue the relationship the woman could then move to her husband's home. If *k꜕k꜕* was paid after a woman had completed her menstruation ceremonies or for a previously married woman, it immediately entitled a man to her services. A marriage established by the payment of *k꜕k꜕* alone was called *soma gya*.[15] The woman could move to her husband's home, bear his children and make his farms. It did not entitle a man to claim adultery fees (*ayefere*) from her lovers nor to require that she swear (*di amoen*: 'drink the gods') to deny adultery. At divorce, *k꜕k꜕* was not refundable nor any gifts made by the husband to the wife before her menstruation ceremony or during the marriage. However, any loans between husband and wife, or the two families, were refundable.

Soma gya could be converted into full marriage (*egya*) with the payment of *ti nza* ('head rum', sometimes *ti sika*, 'head money') to the wife's father. *Ti nza* was accompanied by a variety of obligatory payments to be transmitted to members of the wife's immediate family and matrilineage and salt and alcohol for the marriage ceremony (*asetena bo*). The total was not a fixed sum, since it depended partly on the prestige of the families, but in the mid 1920s it hovered between £4 and £10. The total cost was lower for a previously married woman. *Ti nza* entitled the husband to claim adultery fees. The procedure was that if adultery were admitted, the husband demanded adultery fees from his wife's lover at a rate determined by his political rank. Full marriage could end in divorce at which the husband was entitled to the return of only 1/- from the *ti nza*, although he was in theory entitled to the refund of gifts made at or during the marriage to his wife.[16]

The obligatory marriage payments were not very high, even if most of them were not refundable at divorce. Most marriages, however, involved further transactions. These payments were asked for at or after the payment of *k꜕k꜕* , were payable by the husband whether

or not he intended to pay *ti nza* (or ever got round to it) and were
never refundable at divorce. They were described by the term *kari-
to-ye* ('a debt on the wife to be thrown away'). It was usual 'for the
parents to mention to the prospective husband that the girl had a debt
which he should pay before the marriage. The amount cannot be
returned and it can never be mentioned at divorce'.[17] The explanation
of this debt varied, probably because there were a number of different grounds on which it could be claimed. In the case of a woman's
first marriage, it was usually described in two ways. First, it was the
equivalent, in the form of a lump sum, of the parents' cost in bringing
up the girl and carrying out her menstruation ceremony if she had not
been betrothed beforehand and, therefore, her husband had not
already borne his part in this. Secondly, it was to serve as the
repayment of a loan on a girl who had been made a pawn (*awowa*),
thus freeing her to leave her owner and move into her husband's
house. In the case of a previously married woman, it was described as
the repayment of the costs a father had incurred in the settlement of
the debts of his daughter's divorce, whether or not the new husband
had 'seduced' the woman away from her previous husband. *Kari-
to-ye* could be quite substantial, but since it was not mentioned in
divorce cases it is difficult to establish what sums were involved.[18]

Items which were refundable at divorce in the case of full marriage
were gifts to the wife herself. These included specified items of cloth
and household goods which were discretionary in actual value but in
which the status of the husband and the wife were reflected. They
also included all gifts made during the marriage and all loans between
wife and husband or between the two families, all of which had to be
witnessed at the time they were made so that they could be reclaimed
at divorce. Divorce could not be declared until the accounts of the
marriage had been made and settled. The gifts could be returned in
their original form or as a cash equivalent. Normally, the wife's
father was responsible for repaying the cash amounts and this constituted the biggest penalty in the case of divorce of a daughter.
Informants, however, were very insistent that 'if a man is good, he
will not claim the gifts he has made to his wife during their marriage,
only if she is very bad, because she had worked for him'[19]; 'a man can
claim all the things he gave to his wife when he divorces her except
adidi sika since part of that he has eaten himself, but if he does so he
will spoil his name and other women will be reluctant to marry him'[20].
Adidi sika ('chop money') refers to the obligation to provide wives
with part of the food prepared in her kitchen. In addition to this, a

man was expected to absorb the costs of medical care for his wife. If these were exceptionally heavy, he could seek assistance from her family, but failure to support a wife in these two respects usually led a wife to seek divorce.

Thus in neither type of marriage were the presentations to the wife's family refundable at divorce, bar 1/- of *ti nza*. In full marriage, the husband was entitled to the return of gifts and loans to his wife, or her family, but under many circumstances his reputation precluded him from demanding them. Thus the difference between *soma gya*, in which gifts were not refundable, and full marriage were less great than appearances might lead one to suppose. In full marriage, however, the notion of fault was present.

Once the accounts had been made, a husband could require his wife to swear that she had not committed any adultery during the marriage which had not previously been admitted. The husband (or his representative) alone could perform the public ceremony marking a divorce, and the wife's father (or his representative) alone could return the 1/-, marking the completion of the divorce. Under no circumstances could the wife perform the ceremony or return the 1/- on her own account. If she had been a good wife who was being divorced for no fault of her own it seems that a husband could be expected to pay her a sum of money called *esiase* ('to put her behind'), a final gift to maintain her (if she was still marriageable) until she remarried. This may have been the equivalent of, or additional to, the right to go on harvesting from the food farms which she had made during the marriage.[21] The ex-husband remained responsible for the maintenance of his children, whether they stayed with him or returned with their mother to the home of her father or of her matrilineal kin.

Failure to conceive or bring forth live children was a common reason for divorce. This was not regarded as a fault on the part of a young woman. Of the other reasons, the arbitrators dealing with a divorce case were principally concerned with the question of fault, since their first job was to try to restore the marriage. This could be done by getting the spouse deemed to be at fault to pay pacification (*mpata*) to the other, thus leading her/him to drop the case. A wife was at fault if she deserted her husband or refused to cook for him [22] or make his farm, unless she could demonstrate his neglect of her; if she quarrelled repeatedly with her co-wives or members of her husband's family or repeated adultery to the point of harming her husband's health. A husband was at fault if he deserted his wife, generally signified by failing to provide *adidi sika* or to make arrangements for its provision in his absence; failing to care for her when she was sick; impotence and quarrelling with her family.

The demand for wives was, during this period, pushing up the sums claimed as *kari-to-ye*. Since these were unrefundable at divorce, and divorce was increasing, the costs of marriage were falling heavily both on men searching for wives and men whose wives sought divorce. At the same time, competition for wives was pushing up the value of the gifts given to a wife at the time of marriage. This was especially true in the case of women being persuaded to remarry, to whom gifts in cash were an important source of income to invest in the new trading opportunities as were, of course, the payments for occasional prostitution. Further, the State Council clearly believed that *soma* marriages were increasingly common, particularly in the case of women's remarriage, because gifts to women were not refundable in these marriages and because there were no specific sanctions against adultery to threaten a wife's health.

It was, first, the control of women who had abandoned their husbands and, secondly, the management of the increasing frequency of divorce, which were the main concerns of the State Council in the late 1920s and 1930s. Its first, and perhaps most startling, intervention was to seek to stamp out the 'free women' of Wiawso: the traders and alleged casual and full-time prostitutes who had abandoned their husbands or who had no known male guardians. The Free Women's Marriage Proclamation, issued in 1929, ordered that such women were to be arrested, locked up in the outer courtyards of the *oman-hene*'s palace in Wiawso and held there until they were claimed by a husband or by any other man who would take charge of them. The male claimant was required to pay a fine of 5/- to release the woman and to prevent her from carrying on her unacceptable activities.

There is no evidence for any particular disturbance preceding this proclamation. State Councils elsewhere in the Gold Coast were also taking similar action (Vellenga, 1983, p. 150). It seems to have originated in the general concern with the spread of venereal disease. However, the more specific offences of these 'free women' to male authority were constantly brought to the attention of the Native Tribunal. One which outraged them was that of 'free women' disposing of their own daughters in marriage or arranging their daughters' divorces. For example, in December 1926 one Madam Ampoma of Wiawso was charged by her own husband with having received k) k) and 'a debt of £3 to be thrown away' for the marriage of her daughter and of having subsequently sent 1/- to her daughter's husband to complete a divorce. The Native Tribunal found Madam Ampoma's husband guilty of failure to keep his wife under his authority! A further problem was the plight of men who had inadvertently committed adultery with women who had told them that they were, or whom they supposed to be, unmarried. The women's husbands brought them to court for refusing to pay the adultery fees. The Tribunal normally found such men guilty on the grounds that it was unreasonable to suppose that any woman could, in fact, be unmarried. However, in January 1933, the Tribunal actually informed a man charged with adultery under these circumstances of a bye-law called 'Ajuaman Ayifere' which required a wife herself to pay the statutory fee to her husband.[23]

Most of the cases concerning venereal disease reaching the Native Tribunal were about the allocation of responsibility for the payment of medical treatment of those afflicted. A case heard in January 1930 involved a man who had contracted *babaso* from a woman who had promised to pay for his cure provided he did not tell her husband that she had the disease. She had failed to pay and the man's mother brought her to court to claim damages. Most of the cases, however, arose from divorce settlements during which disputes had arisen about whether the husband's costs for curing his wife of venereal disease could be regarded as fully and legitimately his responsibility if the wife had been at fault in any way. What seemed to have concerned the State Council in particular was the enormous costs that could arise for medical treatment which were escalating the unreclaimable expenses incurred by men during marriage. In a case heard in March 1933, for example, a man described how, as a consequence of apparently contracting venereal disease, his wife had become barren. He explained:

I sent her for medical treatment but shortly after she was sick again. I sent her to a fetish priest who ordered me to give rum to the fetish Kukuro and the soul of my wife's late father which I did. She was sick again and I gave her to another fetish priest. Her brother then sent her to another and I paid his expenses of 7/-. She was sick again and her uncle told me to send her to a native doctor at Afere. She said the medicine would not cure her and came back. I sent for another native doctor and I paid him £1.1s.0d. 1/- of gunpowder, one bottle of gin and 1s.6d. food per day. He said he would put medicine on his penis and have intercourse with her. I agreed. Later my wife's uncle told me that the doctor had done this and showed him the sickness he had taken from my wife's womb. I was angry than I had not been called to see. The doctor said that there was another sickness near the heart. The doctor gave her medicine to drink and she got a little better and then sick again. I told my wife's parents and they told me to send her to the native doctor to perform fetish custom. He examined her but she did not recover. I took her to the doctor again and he said there was no love between me and my wife. I said I loved her but my wife brought her properties to me so I may divorce her if not she will commit suicide . . .

The more measured response of the State Council to the escalating, non-refundable costs incurred by husbands and to the increasing frequency of divorce in which fault on the part of one or the other partner could be manifestly established was to tackle the problem of 'settling the accounts' at divorce. They sought to do this by clarifying the concept of fault to ensure, in particular, that husbands' reputations were not tarnished if they demanded the return of gifts and other reclaimable marriage expenses. Fault was clarified in relation to desertion, to adultery leading to wife-stealing in circumstances under which a husband could not claim adultery fees and to the obligations of husbands in *soma gya*. The solution was a new bye-law[24] which set a fixed sum constituting compensation payable to the injured spouse. This was set at £10 under *omanhene* Kwame Tano I and raised to £15 by his successor. When payable to the wife, the sum seems to have been quite distinct from the notion of *esiase* in that it was compulsory rather than discretionary. When payable to the husband, it seems to have been unprecedented except in so far as a husband had previously been entitled to pacification in a marriage dispute which had been *prevented* from concluding in divorce by the arbitrators.

The first case dealing with the new bye-law reached the Native Tribunal in August 1930. Thereafter an increasing number of divorce cases reached the Tribunal on appeal, reflecting difficulties in managing the provisions of the bye-law at arbitration and lower courts. Of eighteen divorce cases between April 1930 and April 1934, eight referred specifically to the new bye-law. Of these, three were found in favour of the wife and five in favour of the husband.[25] Those found in favour of wives were all concerned with unjustified desertion. In August 1930, for example, a woman who had had three children by her husband claimed that she had been deserted because 'he has not given me cloth and he has not given me food so I had to work on my brother's farm to eat and he did not pay funeral expenses of 3/- when my grandmother died'. The Tribunal awarded her '£10 compensation Omanhene's bye-laws'.

Of the cases found in favour of the husband, three were concerned with unjustified desertion and two concerned desertion elaborated by alleged adultery. In a case heard in September 1933, the husband claimed 'amendment *omanhene's* bye laws £15 as customary fee in marriage affairs'. The husband had paid *k) k)* and part of the *ti nza* but the whole amount demanded had been £15 and having 'begged for time' he had never got round to paying it during the twelve years of his marriage. Recently his wife had returned from her mother's village with a 'round vaccination on her chest' which had been taken as evidence of adultery with the priest (*|k)mie|*) who had performed it 'contrary to Bye-laws on marriage'. The adultery case had been settled but his wife continued 'never to pay him any respect' and therefore he had sought to divorce her. Her father had refused to pay the £15 compensation because

> the woman has helped him make five cocoa farms and had two children with him and (the husband) says he will give me the children and take all the farms without giving any to the wife and she bought her own cutlasses and hoes.

The father's witness (chosen somewhat carelessly, one must suppose), stated that

> the bye-law is that any woman who commits adultery (and wants to divorce) should pay £15 and she is liable . . . But the bye-law should not usually apply if the woman has been married without head rum (*ti nza*) for more than five years . . . However, Plaintiff is right in his claim.

The Tribunal decided that the wife was at fault because

> the Bye-law was made to cover just such cases when the head rum was not paid but adultery by the wife committed and she wishes divorce.

In other words, the bye-law was intended as a disincentive to *soma gya* in that a woman who had committed adultery and was seeking a divorce was required to pay compensation to her husband regardless of whether, as in this particular case, she was not judged to be at fault on other grounds. The husband was eligible for compensation in lieu of being able to claim adultery fees.

The apparent open-mindedness on the part of the State Council in being prepared to agree to compensation to an injured wife as well as to an injured husband under this bye-law mitigates the more wild efforts to curtail 'free women's' freedom and penalise them for it. However, the next attempt at marriage reform reveals a distinctly stronger male bias in its attitudes. At some time between 1934 and 1939,[26] this bye-law lapsed and was replaced by one which sought to contain the initial costs of marriage rather than regulate the settlement of accounts at divorce. The resolution of the Sefwi Bekwai State Council was as follows:

> the customary expenses in connection with native marriage in the State are too high when compared with the economic affairs . . . and, thus, such marriage expenses should be mitigated *to suit the convenience of male suitors*, and in order that its encouragement may tend to decrease the high rate of both roving bachelors and spinsters, and to eliminate the spread of venereal disease by illicit unions [my italics].[27]

The bye-law limited the cost of marriage payments for a previously unmarried woman to three pounds, which was to be composed of one pound, comprising all the payments associated with *ti nza*; and two pounds limiting the amount 'given to the girl . . . against the cost of her wedding requisites'. The payments were limited to two pounds in the case of a 'second-hand woman' (a divorced woman) of which ten shillings comprised the *ti nza*. However, in addition fathers were given the right to claim 'special dowries' (the *kari-to-ye*) not exceeding four pounds.

The intention of this bye-law was to ease the financial obstacles to obtaining a wife. First the cost of *ti nza*, payable to the woman's father and distributed amongst her close kin, was to be reduced. Thus, the lower costs of *soma* marriage were virtually matched, enabling men to obtain wives in full marriage with its greater entitlement to control women. However, fathers disposing of daughters were still to benefit from the *kari-to-ye*. The discretionary gifts to a future wife, refundable at divorce but at a cost to the reputation of a husband, were to be reduced. Since these payments (increasingly in money form) often provided the basis for a woman's entry into petty trade, this can be understood as an attempt to restrict women's capacity to pursue their independent economic enterprises. The bye-law, therefore, potentially eased men's access to wives and reduced wives' alternatives to labouring on their husbands' farms.

There can be no evidence that this bye-law had any success whatsoever. It did not keep down the cost of marriage. Although *ti nza* remained much the same for the next twenty years, the restrictions on *kari-to-ye* and on gifts to a future wife were ignored (Mensah-Brown, 1968, p. 75). There is no way, in any case, of measuring whether the frequency of *soma* declined since its prevalence before the introduction of the bye-law is unknown. New forms of 'illicit unions', however, did occur which ignored prior marriage payments entirely. A decade later the State Council was wrestling with the problem of 'seduction' of never-married women and pregnancy outside marriage. It soon became established that fathers were entitled to compensation for 'damage' to a daughter for whom no marriage payments had been paid, while the woman was entitled to *esiase*, a substantial cash sum plus a sewing machine to provide her with financial security independently of marriage. There were other informal relations which involved financial expectations between spouses but no payments to the woman's father or family. These unions certainly eased men's access to women's labour but at a price which women exacted. In these relations, women were developing stronger claims to pursue their own economic enterprises to the detriment of labour services to their husbands. Such alliances were and are strongly favoured by women (Lowy, 1977, p. 22). The disadvantages lie mainly in the fact that, even in long-established relationships of this kind, men often succeed in avoiding support of the children, leaving this to the mother or her family. This issue has been the most enduring struggle of Ghanaian women since they first organised to protect their interests through the law in the 1950s (Vellenga, 1983).

CONCLUSION

We have argued in this chapter that the reforms concerning women's sexuality and marriage originated in the transformation of the rural economy and the redevelopment of petty trade. They were concerned to restrict women's sexual autonomy and their alternatives to the provision of labour services to husbands. They did not measurably succeed in doing so. The State's power was ineffective, through such methods, in dealing with the conditions in which gender relations of production were becoming increasingly embedded in commodity production. Women do, of course, continue to provide farm labour services to husbands but the conditions of this are gradually being transformed by a struggle not yet won but increasingly effective. As we described earlier, almost as soon as cocoa entered the rural economy, wives tried to secure some immediate or future interest in the cocoa farms of their husbands. Since the 1950s, their rights in parts of these farms are more frequently being acknowledged. These rights are not claimed on the grounds of traditional marriage obligations but in recognition of the changes in women's labour contributions to the farming household.

Notes

1. All case material in this article is drawn from the invaluable records of the Sefwi Wiawso Native Tribunal and cited by the date of entry.
2. For recent examples of such studies, in areas other than Ghana, see Elwert, 1984; Richards, 1982.
3. For further details, see Roberts 1972; 1983.
4. Slaves were purchased from northern markets until 1900 and probably later. No estimates of the slave population in Sefwi exist. Perrot (1983, p. 159) has estimated that in the neighbouring state of Indenie around 1911 the slave population might have been one in five or one in seven of the population as a whole. Pawns (*awowa*) were mortgaged by their families to raise money: their labour to their owners paid part of the interest of the debt.
5. Accra Archives, ADM/11/1/671. Enchi (Aowin) Native Affairs 1918.
6. Public Record Office, London. CO/96/656. Western Province Railway, 1925.
7. The following section is based on interviews with old women in the villages of Kojokrom, Benchema and Nkatieso in 1969–70.
8. Okali's recent study of women cocoa farmers in Ghana points out that husbands may be reluctant to make a gift of a farm because this might anticipate divorce. Wives' access to the means of production enables them to establish themselves independently of marriage (Okali, 1983, p. 120). Sefwi women were not allowed claims to farms which they had jointly farmed with their husbands in divorce settlements until the 1950s.
9. Labour service to husbands has been generally established as one of the chief reasons why farms established on their own account by married women tend to be smaller than those of men and started later in their lives (Oppong, Okali and Houghton 1975; Okali, 1983, p. 144).
10. *Tutu*: 'red' or 'hot', especially of female sexuality.

11. For further details of this destoolment case, see Roberts, 1983.
12. The only published account of Sefwi marriage practices known to the author is that of Mensah-Brown, 1968.
13. Translations in brackets are those most commonly used in the Native Tribunal records.
14. All legal transactions require the presentation of alcohol: this is not mentioned on each occasion.
15. d'Aby (1960, p. 144) elaborates the different forms of *soma gya*, in the Anyi States of the Ivory Coast concluding that the type described here constituted fully-recognised marriage with all the accompanying rights and duties. This does not appear to have been entirely the case in Sefwi Wiawso.
16. Mensah-Brown (1968, p. 75) points out that the very small amount refundable at divorce distinguishes Sefwi practices from Asante.
17. Author's field notes, 1970. The *krontihene* of Sefwi Wiawso.
18. Two cases heard in the Native Tribunal in the late 1920s record amounts of £3.
19. Author's field notes, 1970. Interview with a woman, about 50 years old, divorced four times.
20. Author's field notes, 1970. The *gyaasehene* of Benchema.
21. Informants were not absolutely agreed that *esiase* was a customary payment. A divorce case heard in the Native Tribunal in 1926 recorded a claim for *esiase*.
22. To cook for and to have sexual intercourse with a husband were inseparable. Mensah-Brown (1968, p. 82) mentions that failure to give sexual satisfaction was grounds for divorce.
23. No other reference to this concept of *ajuaman ayifere* has been found. It seems to have been an extraordinary reversal of the principles of adultery fees.
24. A full wording of this bye-law could not be located. Its purposes have been deduced from references in the judgements of the Native Tribunal.
25. No conclusions are being drawn from these figures.
26. The Records of the Native Tribunal between 1934 and 1939 could not be found.
27. Cited in Mensah-Brown, 1968, p. 73. Sefwi Wiawso State Council passed the same bye-law but the regulations from the neighbouring state of Sefwi Bekwai are quoted for convenience.

References

Unpublished sources
The Records of the Sefwi Wiawso Native Tribunal. The Magistrate's Court, Sefwi Wiawso
The Public Record Office, London
The Accra Archives

Books and articles
d'Aby, F. J. Amon (1960), *Croyances Religieuses et Coutumes Juridiques des Agni de la Côte d'Ivoire* (Paris: Editions Larose)

Elwert, G. (1984), 'Conflicts Inside and Outside the Household: A West African Case Study', in J. Smith, I. Wallerstein and H-D. Evers (eds), *Households and the World Economy* (London: Sage Publications Ltd)

Field, M. J. (1948) *Akim-Kotoku: an Oman of the Gold Coast*, (London: Crown Agents)

Holtsbaum, F. P. (1925), 'Sefwi and its People', *Gold Coast Review*, vol. I, no. 1, pp. 76–94

Lowy, M. J. (1977), 'Establishing paternity and demanding child support in a Ghanaian town', in Simon A. Roberts (ed.), *Law and the Family in Africa* (The Hague: Mouton)

Mensah-Brown, K. (1968), 'Marriage in Sefwi-Akan Customary Law: A Comparative Study in Ethno-Jurisprudence', *Presence Africaine*, vol. 68, pp 61–86

Mikell, G. (1984), 'Filiation, Economic Crisis and the Status of Women in Rural Ghana', *Canadian Journal of African Studies*, vol. 18, no. 1, pp 195–218

Okali, C. (1983), *Cocoa and Kinship in Ghana* (London: Routledge & Kegan Paul)

Oppong, C., C. Okali and B. Houghton (1975), 'Woman power: retrograde steps in Ghana', *African Studies Review*, vol. 18, no. 3

Perrot, C. H. (1982), *Les Anyi-Ndenye et le Pouvoir aux 18ᵉ et 19ᵉ Siècles* (Paris: Publications de la Sorbonne)

Richards, P. (1982), 'Core, Periphery and Urbanity: The politics of settlement in the Okitipupa region, western Nigeria, 1870–1950', Paper for the African Studies Association Conference, Birmingham (unpublished)

Roberts, P. A. (1972), 'The Teacher and the Community in a West African State', Ph.D. thesis, University of Cambridge (unpublished)

―――― (1983), 'The Sefwi Wiawso Riot of 1935: the deposition of an Omanhene in the Gold Coast', *Africa*, vol. 53, no. 2, pp 25–46

Vellenga, D. D. (1983), 'Who Is a Wife? Legal Expressions of Heterosexual Conflicts in Ghana', in C. Oppong (ed.), *Female and Male in West Africa* (London: George Allen & Unwin)

4 Women, Marriage and the State in Iran
Haleh Afshar

The Islamic ideology regards women with a mixture of fear and paternalism, and sees them both as the source of all evil and as the most vulnerable member of the household, in need of constant surveillance and protection. The policies of the majority of Muslim States are framed accordingly, often equating women with children and the insane.

Islam, which literally translated means 'total submission', is not merely a belief system, but also a way of life and Muslims are expected to run their lives according to the Qoranic injunctions. In many respects the teachings of the Qoran are quite specific, for example Muslims cannot disinherit their descendents,[1] and even the exact proportions inherited by the spouse and children are stated in the relevant verse. There are, however, other poetic and ambiguous injunctions in the Qoran which are open to different interpretations, and much of the teachings concerning women fall in this latter category.

The *Shiia* sect of Islam as practised in Iran interposes the *Mojtahedin*, religious leaders, between the Qoran and the people. The *Mojtahedin*, being wise and learned men, have the authority to explain the teachings of Islam to the *Shiia* Muslims. So long as the clergy were in opposition in Iran, their role as intermediaries between the word of God and His followers enabled them both to offer protection to those persecuted by secular law,[2] and to provide a degree of flexibility and bring the religious dicta into line with secular practices. At the same time as there was a tacit political truce between some leading members of the clergy and the state about the Shah's rule, Iranian women were able to use this temporary peace and obtain a degree of religious approval for the slow and difficult progress towards sexual equality. Thus, during the 80 years preceding the Islamic revolution, Iranian women fought for and gained access to education (1910), the abolition of the veil (1936), the vote (1962), a curb on the unequivocal male right of divorce and the right to contest for the custody of children (1973), free abortion on demand (1974)

70

and a ban on polygamy and the right to maintenance after divorce (1976). Although equal opportunities were still a long way away, the women's movement had great expectations of success in the 1970s.

LEGISLATION AND INEQUALITY

The conviction that women are biologically and intellectually un-equal has led to new legislation which excludes women from many legal rights, while making them equally subject to the harsh treat-ment of the current Islamic laws of retribution *qassas*. These laws demand exact retributional justice, taking an eye for an eye and a life for a life, though the latter is more rigorously applied in the case of murdered men than women.

Within months of his takeover in March 1979, Khomeini issued a decree dismissing all women judges and barring female students from attending law schools.[3] Subsequently, he closed the Law Association, *Kanouneh Vokala*, and replaced secular courts by religious ones, often presided over by theological students with one or two years' religious training.[4] The laws now implemented do not admit women's evidence unless it is corroborated by men, and have allocated to women half the blood money, *diyat*, given to men. *Diyat* is blood money paid in cases of murder by the murderer to the relatives of the murdered person[5] in lieu of retributional justice. A man who murders a woman can only be punished if his descendants receive his *diyat* from the relatives of the murdered woman.[6] Furthermore, a father who murders his children is 'excused' from punishment provided he pays *diyat* to the inheritors;[7] but no specific *diyat* is stipulated for children. Mothers, however, do not benefit from this right to life and death over their offspring.

Women's evidence is not accepted by Iranian courts, unless corro-borated by that of a man. Women who, nevertheless, insist on giving evidence without male corroboration are assumed to be lying and liable to punishment for slander.[8] Even sexual intercourse between lesbians which, like sodomy, is punishable by death, if it occurs more than four times, cannot be proven unless the women admit to it or the act is witnessed by four men.[9] This refusal to accept women's evi-dence is a contradictory interpretation of the clear Qoranic statement which accepts women's evidence, but equates that of two women with the words of one man 'Call in two male witnesses from among you, but if two men cannot be found, then one man and one woman whom you judge fit to act as witnesses' (2/82).

The exclusion of women from the legal and public domain has been justified in the Iranian press through numerous interviews with leading religious figures. The arguments are entirely based on the 'God given' nature of women. Men have been given a status above women[10] and authority over them[11] by the Qoran. The Iranian clergy explain that this superiority is an inherent right of men who are endowed with a 'calm and orderly nature'. Their 'wisdom, judgement, integrity and farsightedness' enables men to 'control and curb the hiatus caused by the unruly passion of women'.[12]

The 'natural' and 'biological' inferiority of women is described as a fundamental law governing all social and political activities. Ayatollah Hashemi Rafsanjani, the *Majlis* (parliament) speaker, who is a leading member of the clergy, denounced the West for 'overreacting' to feminist demands and creating total anomie as a result. In his view Western women have been 'forced to abandon their natural talents, as created by God and endorsed by men'. They have been pushed out of their 'natural and humane domestic environment' and 'propelled from school to offices and subjected to the harsh demands of factories and work places' and 'obliged to adopt shameless and dishonourable roles which go against their gentle and sensitive nature'. The unnatural 'displacement' of women has, according to Ayatollah Hashemi Rafsanjani, imposed the double burden of domestic and waged labour on the women, against their own interest. The result has been the failure of many to fulfil their holy duty of motherhood or, in some cases, even to deny this very instinct: 'this has resulted in the birth of an unloved and uncared-for generation which lacks the fundamental basis of mother love and tenderness, and which has become an alienated and disrupted society'.[13]

Ayatollah Hashemi Rafsanjani is convinced that this enormous social cost has brought no benefit for women at all. 'Despite all the efforts of the so-called liberated women . . . Western women have never had any impact on the political or military destiny of their countries.' It is a remarkably myopic world view which can so easily dismiss the impact of Victoria's imperialist rule, Elizabeth I, Catherine the Great, Maria Theresa, Joan of Arc, or Margaret Thatcher, to name but a few. But the *Majlis* speaker expressed a deeply-held view of the Iranian religious establishment when he qualified this statement by saying: 'Even in those countries where apparently women are in charge, we know that they are no more than the mouthpieces of their menfolk who control these women and dictate their every decision.'[14]

HEJAB *return of veil*

Iranian women have become the reluctant standard-bearers of the public face of the Islamic regime. The republic's fragile honour can now be threatened by the mere appearance of women. National honour is now secured by women covering themselves at all times, except in the privacy of their husband's bedroom. Iranian women have been understandably reluctant to accept this heavy responsibility and have made several attempts to prevent the imposition of *hejab*. The first directive requiring women to don the veil was issued in March 1979, less than two months after Khomeini's return. There followed numerous protests and large-scale demonstrations by women, but the regime has continued its official and unofficial harrassment of those women who are still refusing its decision to make themselves publicly invisible. Shops, restaurants, cinemas and all public places are instructed not to serve women who are not wearing the *hejab* and all Government offices now have individuals responsible for checking that women are properly covered. The open defiance of *hejab* and appearance in public without it, is punishable by 74 lashes,[15] and officials who apprehend such women do not need to take them to court 'since the crime is self-evident, the punishment will be immediate'.[16] The members of the 'Party of God' the *Hezbolahis*, usually fanatical Government supporters, ensure that the regulations are enforced in the street. Women who are considered inadequately covered are attacked by these men with knives or guns and are lucky to survive the experience. The *Hezbolahis* also indulge in frequent 'spontaneous' demonstrations protesting against the 'shameless nakedness' of women who 'trample on the blood of young men who gave their lives to the revolution and died a martyr's death'.[17]

Hejab has been identified by the regime as the very cornerstone of its revolution. It is described as 'basic to Islamic ideology'[18] and prescribed by God himself as a 'duty' for women.[19] The many muslims abroad who appear unaware of this godly duty are denounced by the regime's representatives as ignorant. Mrs Gohar Dastqeib, who attended an educational conference in Cuba reported proudly: 'I was the only woman there with an Islamic appearance. Of course, there were sisters from Malaysia, Pakistan and Egypt, but their appearance showed quite clearly that they were not at all familiar with Islam'.[20] Dastqeib remained convinced that Iranians alone had a clear understanding of God's will, despite her travels to other Islamic countries. She stated placidly that the Burmese 'though familiar with the Qoran, have not realised that it stipulates the *hejab* for women'. It must be noted that the relevant verses in the Qoran require women to 'cover their adornments'[21] and instruct women who are related to the Prophet 'to draw their veils close around them'.[22] Few Iranian women can claim to be descendents of Muhammad, the rest do not conceive their arms and legs to be 'adornments'.

The Iranian clergy, however, have determined that women must cover everything except for the face and hands. This shrouding of the body is supposed to bestow respect and dignity on women. It is said to denote 'deliverance from the yoke of imperialism' and to represent 'a symbol of liberation, and resistance to capitalism, and revolutionary aspirations'.[23] Thus, women who will refuse to don the *hejab* and 'flaunt their naked bodies in the streets' are denounced as 'corrupt, seditious, dangerous and destructive of public honour and chastity'.[24] These 'wayward women' are said to be instrumental in the foreign-inspired plot to undermine the revolutionary puritanism. The voice of the clergy calls on the nation to oppose this internal enemy 'with the same vigour as we oppose other terrorists who have sought to sabotage our revolution'.[25]

As early as June 1979 women were bearing the brunt of revolutionary chastity and being executed for endangering it by acts described as 'seditious, corrupt' or 'prostitution'; it is important to note that these attributes are granted freely to women but not to their male 'accomplices'.

Behind the rhetoric of honour and sedition there lies a deep conviction, not of the vulnerability of women, as publicly stated, but of the fragility of men. It is because men are thought to be eminently susceptible to 'female lures' that the regime insists on making women invisible. This conviction about men's weakness makes it imperative for women to wear the *hejab* in order to 'eradicate' both 'adultery and sodomy'.[26]

The stated assumption of the regime is that the only fundamental threats to male sanity and rationality are anger and sexual arousal; the latter caused exclusively by women. The mere presence of women is said to undermine men's better judgement. It is not only a woman's body, but also her face, her movement, the tone of her voice and even the colour of her garments which can arouse men.[27] Women can be so easily dangerous, and are so feared, that Tehran University has felt obliged to instruct its female members not to talk nor walk 'in a speaking (*zabandar*) manner'.

The imposition of *hejab* is hailed as a timely check imposed on 'loose women', apparently to 'check their dishonourable ways' and 'shield their honour'.[28] But in reality this 'trench of modesty' is imposed, not to protect women, but to prevent the endangered male species from total anihilation at the mere sight of women.

THE LAW, IDEOLOGY AND MARRIAGE

Men's sexual weakness can become a tower of strength within marriage. The Iranian clergy see marriage as a desirable institution which enables fathers to transfer the control of their alluring daughters to strong husbands. This process is said to prevent both 'corruption' and to stave off all threats to 'revolutionary morality'. Husbands will be able to 'curb' the women's irrational tendency to 'appear naked in public and make themselves conspicuous by using artificial make-up'.[29] So important is this institution in securing public morality that men are encouraged to marry more than one wife, allegedly 'to protect young women from moral degradation', but more probably in order to protect men from the ever impending threats of 'loose women'.

Islamic marriage can be, at its best, a flexible contract between two consenting adults. Women are required to stipulate a consummation price *meher*, which they are entitled to receive at marriage and before sleeping with the groom, though usually this is paid to women on divorce. Although in an unequal relationship, married women can expect to be kept in the style to which they have been accustomed and they can demand to be paid fees for suckling their babies. When marriage breaks down, divorce is a matter of the husband making a statement to that effect and repeating it three times before two male witnesses. Although men have the unequivocal right of divorce, women can obtain the right by stipulating it in the marriage contract. Divorced men and women can freely re-marry, but women who have not reached the menopause must wait for up to three months between each marriage.

Iranian women had fought successfully to curb much of the power that marriage bestowed on men and had even gained the right, already enjoyed by men, to prevent their spouse from accepting any job which they said would 'dishonour' the family (in practice everything ranging from teaching to belly dancing could be so described).

Minimum age of marriage for girls was raised to 18, polygamy banned and divorce and custody made subject to the decision of the family courts. Furthermore, over and above the *meher*, mothers who gained custody of their children on divorce were entitled to maintenance payment.[30]

In its haste to re-establish male supremacy in public and private spheres, and protect 'the adolescent from immorality' the Iranian theocracy revoked all these measures before the first post-revolutionary *Majlis* elections. By October 1979 men could have four permanent and innumerable temporary wives, and were given the exclusive right to divorce at will (the only exceptions were women whose marriage contracts stipulated that they had the right to initiate divorce proceedings). Fathers and paternal ancestors also regained the unquestioned right of custody, sons at the age of two and daughters at seven. The age of marriage came down to thirteen for girls and husbands regained the authority to bar their women from getting paid employment. Middle-class women, however, are not easily dissuaded from their latterly gained feminist convictions and the regime has launched an extensive media campaign to persuade this group to embark on marriage. The press, for years the mouthpiece of government in Iran – though more so now that the Ministry of Ideology has the formal right to exercise 'guidance' – has made a curious intellectual turnabout. In 1972 the Iranian papers were publishing articles which depicted marriage as a positively dangerous occupation for young women. The director of the Tehran School of Social Work, Satarea Farmanfarmayan was quoted as saying that 70 per cent of suicides in Tehran were by women aged between eighteen and twenty-five who were in the first years of their marriage.[31] Hardly a desirable fate for prospective brides. By contrast, in 1984 the unmarried are equated with terrorists. Ayatollah Moussavi Bourou-jerdi, a leading member of the High Council of the Judiciary, claims that most political prisoners are unmarried. 'Freedom from marital responsibilities has made these young people vulnerable to false ideas and led them to murder and treason.'[32]

The regime's appropriation of marriage is backed by many long-running series of articles endorsing marriage and denouncing those who refuse to participate. As an indication of the success of its propaganda campaign, *Zaneh Rouz* a leading women's weekly magazine published a letter from an 'old' spinster. A 28-year-old professional woman had written a long and anguished letter stating that she was educated, gainfully employed and ideologically 'pure and committed' yet no man had asked her to marry him. 'Where is my wasted youth?' she is quoted as saying.

> What is left for me in this life? I have saved my purest and most beautiful moments for a man to spend them with him and have his child. Yet the men prefer to marry pretty young girls and leave me to suffer the unbearable longing for motherhood and to shed my tears in solitude. I am the casualty of the men's obsession with beauty and fear of intelligence and intellectual women.[33]

Those women who struggled against the oppressive institution of marriage and regarded it as a final downfall, find it hard to accept that such a fundamental change could occur in the mentality of women in such a short time, particularly since the prescribed marriage is far from a partnership between equals. *Zaneh Rouz'* response to this letter included the stern admonishment that 'too much education has made you too highbrow, that is why 13 years after the proper age of marriage you are still single'.[34]

Nevertheless, the combination of propaganda and the bleak reality of the oppressive public sphere, may in the end push young girls to accept the prevalent ideology of domesticity.

A series on Ethics of Marriage written by Hojatolah Abasqoly Akhtari, a well-known cleric, and published by *Zaneh Rouz* called on the young to embark on marriage regardless of their economic situation and told them that though very difficult at first 'it will all work out for the best'.[35] The articles described marriage as a religious duty which cures almost all social and personal problems. 'Marriage improves the psychology and physiology of the spouses and makes them physically and socially healthier' and 'those who marry accomplish two-thirds of their religious duties and gain comfort and solace'.[36]

SEXUALITY

The 'comfort' gained through marriage is that of the husband and the 'solace' is also his. Marriage is there to satisfy male sexual urges. Wives are there to quench the 'ever blazing fire of lust' and placate the 'obsession' with 'sexual urges' which renders the youth 'desperate' and overrides all their dignity and better judgement. Ardour is the preserve of men, women are merely required to 'give them-selves unquestioningly to their husband' and 'obey their every command'.[37]

But there is a major problem for 'obedient' women; the stated ideology of the regime prescribes total innocence, chastity and mod-esty for young girls, who are expected to cover themselves from top to toe, cast their eyes down at all times and be shy and retiring. Yet as soon as the brief marriage prayer has been pronounced, these puri-tanical creatures are expected to turn into lusty lovers and ensure that their men find nothing more pleasurable 'in this world and the next' than their sexual services. Even the Qoran has declared that 'it is delightful to enjoy sexual pleasure from women'[38] and bedding a pretty wife has been prescribed by one of the Shiia Imams as 'the best cure' and a 'cheerful virgin's laughter and joy' is said to 'alleviate all his pains'.[39]

Instantaneously, women are supposed to abandon modesty 'their greatest asset' and 'when alone with their husband take off their garments and exhibit all their beauty'. They are also required to 'be generous with giving themselves to him and satisfying his every desire'. In fact, they are told not only 'to seek and satisfy his desire, but also to augment his lust'. A wife is instructed to 'seek out his secret fantasies and by enacting them gain hold of his heart. She must never be careless where his desires are concerned lest she loses her grip on him.'[40] Suddenly the innocent young girl finds that 'the worst wives are those who when alone with their husband refuse his advances and deny his pleasure and do not submit to his will and do not forgive his sins' and that 'the worst wives are those who are dry, unproductive, dirty, stubborn and disobedient'.[41] At the same time, however, these desirable sex objects are expected to revert to their previous modesty as soon as the man is satisfied. 'When the man leaves then the wife should put on her garments of modesty and cover herself from the eyes of the strangers'.[42] It is not clear how young girls can go through these repeated metamorphoses at such short intervals.

POLYGAMY

The regime's legalisation of polygamy and its encouragement of young marriages has, not surprisingly, resulted in an epidemic of often short-lived polygamous marriages; frequently involving older men taking a younger bride for a fling and retaining the old one for work. The Family Courts, which are empowered with ratification of polygamous marriages, appear to be merely concerned with the man's ability to pay housekeeping for a second wife. *Sigeh*, temporary concubinage, is a *Shiia* practice which needs no Court approval at all, and can be for as short a period as five minutes or as long as any stipulated number of years. Men can marry innumerable wives in temporary concubinage, but women can only have one husband at a time and must keep a waiting period, *eddeh*, of about three months between each marriage. Concubinage, unlike permanent marriages, does not impose a religious duty on the man to provide for the upkeep of the woman; it is merely a prayer said to validate the satisfaction of male sexual urges. Children resulting from concubinage, however, are entitled to full inheritance.

Women whose husbands have taken other wives are crowding the Family Courts to try to curb the tide of polygamy, but as a *Zaneh Rouz* reporter stated, 'the courts continue to ratify an average of six requests for polygamous marriages per hour. Just think how many polygamous marriages that makes in a week.'[43] As to the first wives, they have no legal power to prevent their 'protector' from taking on many others. The religious establishment has sought to justify polygamy both on historical and religious grounds. Women are told that the practice of polygamy in Iran and Arabia long preceded Islam. All the Qoran has done is to ratify this process and curb it by insisting that men should treat all wives equally. It is stressed that in times of war polygamy is the only viable solution for protecting young widows and female orphans who, in the absence of a welfare state and non-availability of paid employment, would clearly not be able to fend for themselves, domestic creatures that they have become. Failure to marry many wives would unavoidably lead to sedition. The well-known Iranian preacher, Morteza Motahari, has claimed that 'in the religion of Christ polygamy has been permitted; the failure of polygamy to take root in the Western countries is not because of religion but because of social perfidiousness and moral terpitude which harbours improper and haphazard affairs and ousts marital relationships'.[44]

In the eyes of the clergy, the deaths and mutilations of hundreds of thousands of young men in the Iran–Iraq war, made a similar social 'perfidiousness' imminent and has made polygamy all the more essential. Young women are exhorted to marry disabled servicemen. The government provides a small dowry for such brides and the marriages are given a great deal of publicity.[45] The State is unable to provide an adequate pension for war widows, and merely provides a small dowry and a lot of encouragement for them to remarry. Men are urged to 'show excessive generosity', *issar*, and marry war widows, albeit polygamously, to 'protect' their honour and that of society.[46] What the Islamic clergy rarely, if ever refer to, is the injunction in the relevant verse in the Qoran to 'marry only one' wife[47] because 'try as you may you cannot treat all your wives impartially'.[48] These qualifications do in fact make polygamous marriages difficult to justify on religious grounds and at least one leading cleric has been willing to publicly admit this. Ayatollah Moussavi Bojnourdi, something of a favourite with women's magazines, told a *Zaneh Rouz* reporter that the courts should look beyond material means and see whether a man could with justice have two wives? The Ayatollah appeared to think that this was not possible. Nevertheless, he was convinced that 'the Qoran permits men to take more than one wife'. In his opinion polygamy places too heavy a financial burden on men and could become 'economically ruinous'. Moussavi therefore thinks that polygamy is not the best way of preventing young girls and widows from falling into the trap of prostitution. It is the considered opinion of this Ayatollah that the best solution all round is for men to take numerous wives in concubinage since these brief encounters do not place any financial demands on the men and enable them to 'prevent women from being led astray'.[49] The division between morality and immorality for this Ayatollah is clearly in the private pronouncement of a short legitimising verse in Arabic by the man to prevent the woman from being corrupted.

Wives on the whole are justifiably much more worried about polygamy than concubinage, which many still equate with prostitution – despite the religious establishment's pronouncement to the contrary. In either case, however, women have no legal control. Women are said to be 'too emotional' to understand the issues. 'Frequently women refuse to consent because of their feelings, without considering their social obligation to the revolution, therefore we have imposed the wisdom and judgement of our religious courts in the matter of polygamy.'[50] As stated earlier, this wisdom and judgement is merely a matter of estimating whether three can live on the income that had paid for two; that is, a judicial decision that the first wife should have less so that the second gets an equal share. Given the total 'control' of the husband over the family income, there is little that the first wife can legally protest about.

Women's magazines are full of tales of woe and, curiously enough, although they publish interviews with the clergy justifying the practice of polygamy, they also carry stories of the sorrows that befall the wives. 'I have been happily married for seven years and have three children' wrote one woman,

> three weeks ago my husband met this women and married her on the same day. Since then he has sold everything I ever had; all my gold and jewellery has gone to pay for presents for her. Now he wants me to leave the house and take my children off his hands so that he can start again in our home with his new wife.[51]

Despite the Ayatollah's claim to the contrary, in practice polygamy seems not to provide protection for more women, but merely to displace mothers and children to make room for other potential mothers. 'My father married seven wives' states another letter 'he just threw us out when he married the next one. My mother, her daughter and her son, have had to fend for themselves. We were left on the streets and have never had a home since.[52]

It is not only the first wife and her children who are traumatised by the experience; young brides often fare equally badly. One such wrote to *Zaneh Rouz* saying that her father-in-law is for ever telling her husband that she is past her best and it is time for him to have another one 'I live in fear of being turned out' she wrote. Another eighteen-year-old wife wrote to *Zaneh Rouz* 'we have been married for eight months, I am six months pregnant and he has thrown me out'.[53] Another letter from a seventeen-year-old schoolgirl tells of her polygamous marriage to a forty-five year-old man:

> My parents married me off against my will. He kept me for three months. During this time I never felt like a wife settling in her new home. All he wanted was to use and abuse me; he played with me like a doll and did as he pleased. I cannot bring myself to tell you the things he did to me; all I can say is that I was a cheap toy to him. This man trampled over all my dreams and heartlessly tore me apart in his headlong pursuit of lust. Now he has left me without anything in this life. My eyes had never known tears before but all I can do now is cry for my lost youth.[54]

DIVORCE

The Islamic Utopia in Iran has once more empowered men to divorce their wives at will. Since the majority of women have marriage contracts which have not specifically given them the right to initiate divorce, they are unable to benefit from the potential flexibility of Islamic marriage and divorce their husbands.

In theory, women who experience mental incompatibility or religious disaccord or 'marital problems' can appeal to the Family Court to ask for a divorce. But they need to convince the male clerics who preside in these courts that 'the marriage has imposed an unbearable burden and an unacceptable demand on the wife';[55] given the current ideology of marriage and domesticity, it would be difficult if not impossible to present such proof. In practice there are only three acceptable grounds for divorce initiated by women: male impotence, male sterility and desertion. Impotence remains a relatively simple matter, it must be certified by a doctor and is generally accepted as valid grounds for divorce. Male sterility requires not only a doctor's evidence, but also a five-year trial period of the marriage for the man to prove conclusively that he is incapable of having children. Desertion was also subject to a four-year waiting period, which has finally been removed. Now five days' absence without good cause by the husband is sufficient grounds to allow the wife to initiate divorce proceedings.

Desertion has long been commonplace in Iran. This is in part because, strictly speaking, muslim men can divorce their wives in the presence of two other men without necessarily informing the women concerned.[56] In the 1960s and 1970s, desertion was identified as the primary cause for prostitution in Tehran.[57] There is no reason to think that the situation has changed, despite death sentences meted out to many prostitutes. Although it is now possible for deserted wives to obtain a formal divorce, in the absence of a husband there is no-one to pay the *meher*. Islamic laws stipulate that deserted women should receive a widow's pension, but the Islamic Republic has been more eager in its legislation of harsh and retributive Islamic laws than in taking any step towards constructing the welfare measures required by Islam.

The Government appears to have concentrated on draconian measures which are now implemented at the expense of justice. This is clearly illustrated by many of the decisions of the family courts. One example is the granting of the right of custody to all fathers at all times. An article in *Zaneh Rouz* justified male custody by explaining that it made divorce more difficult. 'We know that divorce imposes a heavy burden of child rearing on the man. The man caught in the infernal trap of a bad marriage, fired by the wrongdoings of an evil wife, and the harsh prospect of bringing up his children' will, according to Abasali Akhtari, a leading cleric, choose to keep the bad wife rather than have custody. But even when these fallacious statements are proved conclusively false, the regime remains determined to continue this practice. *Zaneh Rouz* published the case history of a man who had a long record of domestic violence and clearly lacked the competence to take care of his children. Nevertheless, the courts rejected the mother's plea and gave him custody; he preceeded to kill all three children. When Ayatollah Moussavi Bojnourdi, a well-known member of the judiciary, was asked to comment on this case, he replied 'according to religious and legal requirements the father is entitled to have custody of his children after the stipulated age. The courts can only implement the law.'[58]

CONCLUSION

The Islamic Republic in Iran has created two classes of citizen; the male who benefits from the provisions of Islamic law and justice and the female who does not. With the sole exception of the right to vote, Iranian women are in all other respects formally recognised as second-class citizens who have no place in the public arena and no security in the domestic sphere. The husband has become an absolute ruler, entitled to exercise the power of life and death in his home.

Ironically, the effect of Islamic legislation has been to make women legitimate sex objects, excluded from most paid employment and chained with ever increasing social and ideological ties to the uncertainties of Islamic marriage. Iranian women have little to lose and everything to gain by opposing the regime and its dicta concerning women. Thus despite the draconian measures, many women still refuse to don the veil, many others continue to fight for their jobs and some even try to initiate divorce preceedings and leave their homes. Although the resistance is still fragmented, many intellectual women who had initially welcomed the Government are now forming secret societies in Iran, publishing material and working to undermine the regime. Although they have been labelled as seditious, corrupt and servants of foreign powers and dealt with mercilessly when caught, a substantial minority of women struggle against the Iranian theocracy. Many have joined the resistance groups, some are fighting alongside the Kurds and the Turkomans. There are still, however, substantial groups of slum-dwelling women who have remained faithful to Khomeini. To some extent their allegiance is bought by the regular provision of rations and modest food supplies. Furthermore, the war is providing sufficient explanation for the regime's failure to provide improved housing, sanitation and electricity for slum-dwellers. But even these women are growing impatient for the promised Utopia which appears to recede ever further into the future. The drudgery of badly paid, informal work for women and unemployment, other than as soldiers at the fronts, for the men, has rendered the promised domestic dignity less and less attainable for these women, who are beginning to lose faith in the Islamic republic.

Notes and References

I am most grateful to Maurice Dodson, Raana Gauhar and Patricia Jeffrey for their helpful comments on earlier drafts of this paper.
    A more extended version of this chapter appeared originally under the title 'Women, State and Ideology in Iran', in *Third World Quarterly*, vol. 7, no. 2 (April 1985) pp. 256–78.

1. The Holy Qoran, Ayeh 4 Surah 2.
2. L. P. Elwell-Sutton, 'The Iranian Revolution', *The International Journal*, vol. XXXIV, no. 3 (1979) pp. 392–4.
3. A further decree on this subject was ratified by the cabinet on 5 October 1979.
4. For further details see H. Afshar's, 'The Iranian Theocracy', in H. Afshar (ed.), *Iran, a Revolution in Turmoil* (London: Macmillan, 1985) p. 220–44.
5. *Diyat* Laws, 11 July 1982, article 1.
6. *Qassas* Law, 9 September 1982, article 6.
7. Ibid., article 16
8. Ibid., article 92
9. Ibid., article 158
10. The Qoran, 2/228
11. Ibid., 4/34
12. Hojatoleslam A. A. Akhtari, *Akhlaqeh Hamsardari Eslami* (ethics of Islamic marriage) serialised in *Zaneh Rouz*, 28 July 1984.

13. Address to women members of the Islamic party reported in *Kayhan*, 26 July 1984.
14. Ibid.
15. *Qanouneh Taazirat* (Secular code concerning matters not specifically stated in the Qoran, which are subject to the decision of the judge, *Hakemeh Shahr*) 29 June 1983, note to article 102. Article 101 of the same act apportions 99 lashes for people of the opposite sex who are not related by marriage, including daughters and fathers and brothers and sisters, seen kissing in public.
16. Ayatollah Moussavi Bojnourdi, interviewed by *Zaneh Rouz*, 18 August 1984.
17. *Kayhan*, 26 July 1984
18. Ayatollah Moussavi Bojnourdi, *Zaneh Rouz*, 18 August 1984.
19. Ayatollah M. Emami Kashani, *Kayhan*, 8 July 1984.
20. *Zaneh Rouz*, 27 July 1984
21. The Qoran, 24/31
22. Ibid., 33/59
23. *Kayhan*, 23 July 1984
24. *Kayhan*, 14 March, 1983
25. *Zaneh Rouz*, 18 August 1984
26. Ayatollah Moussavi Bojnourdi, *Zaneh Rouz*, 18 August 1984.
27. *Zaneh Rouz*, 11 August and 18 August 1984
28. *Zaneh Rouz*, 18 August 1984
29. *Zaneh Rouz*, 18 August 1984; and H. Afshar. 'Khomeini's Teachings and Their Implications for Iranian Women' in Tabari A. and Yeganeh N. (compilers) *In the Shadow of Islam* (Zed Press, 1983) p. 97.
30. Family Protection Law 1976
31. *Kayhan International*, 10 June 1972
32. *Zaneh Rouz*, 28 July 1984
33. *Zaneh Rouz*, 11 August 1984
34. *Zaneh Rouz*, 18 August 1984
35. *Zaneh Rouz*, 14 July 1984
36. Ibid.
37. *Zaneh Rouz*, 18 August 1984
38. The Qoran, 3/24 and 3/15
39. Hojatoleslam Akhtari, *Akhlaqeh Hamsardari Eslami, Zaneh Rouz*, 14 July 1984.
40. Dr A. Beheshti, *Andar Maquleyeh Zibayi* (on the Subject of Beauty'), serialised in *Zaneh Rouz*, 21 July 1984.
41. Akhtari, *Akhlaqeh Hamsadari Eslami, Zaneh Rouz*, 21 July 1984.
42. Ibid. For an illuminating discussion of fear of women's sexuality see F. A. Sabbah, *Women in the Muslim Unconscious* (London: Pergamon Press, 1984).
43. Report on the Family Courts, *Zaneh Rouz*, 14 July 1984.
44. *Zaneh Rouz*, 21 July 1984
45. For example, see *Zaneh Rouz*, 2 September 1982.
46. Bojnourdi, *Zaneh Rouz*, 14 July 1984
47. The Qoran, 4/3
48. The Qoran, 4/129

49. *Zaneh Rouz*, 14 July 1984
50. *Zaneh Rouz*, 21 July 1984
51. *Zaneh Rouz*, 14 July 1984
52. *Zaneh Rouz*, 21 July 1984
53. Ibid.
54. *Zaneh Rouz*, 2 September 1984
55. Ayatollah Saneyi, the Public Prosecutor, quoted in *Kayhan*, 29 March 1983.
56. For a detailed discussion see H. Afshar, 'Khomeini's Teachings'.
57. Report on the survey conducted by the Tehran School of Social Work, *Kayhan International*, 10 June 1972.
58. *Zaneh Rouz*, 7 July 1984

Part II
State and Population Policies

5 Family and State in Malaysian Industrialisation: the Case of Rembau, Negeri Sembilan, Malaysia

Maila Stivens

Malaysia has recently experienced a significant growth in industrialisation. This chapter looks at a case study of changing patterns of 'family' among Malays, with special reference to arguments about the emergence of a nuclear family form in Malaysia, the effects of a remittance family economy and rising levels of female employment. It argues that the political economy of contemporary Malaysia, in particular state policies encouraging overseas investment in manufacturing, is having a profound effect in restructuring patterns of dependence within the extended family and discusses these findings in relation to arguments about the family as both an instrument and object of state policy. It finishes with a discussion of recent moves by Malay politicians in the government to abandon family planning policies and strongly encourage a return to motherhood, and the effects such moves might have both on women's situation and the family economy in which it is embedded.

The chapter draws on an extended period of anthropological fieldwork (in a rural area of Rembau, Negeri Sembilan, Malaysia) and later more brief return visits to Malaysia aimed at a more macro view of developments.[1] It is intentionally somewhat empirical the cultural and historical specificities of the development process are extremely important. Although the main study is based on a small community at the rural end of the migration process, it can, I hope, provide useful insights into that process, even if we cannot generalise from the experiences of some hundreds of Malays to Malaysia as a whole.

FAMILY, STATE AND THE CAPITALIST DEVELOPMENT PROCESS

Family and capitalism

The recent upsurge in work on the history of the western family has strongly challenged the alleged relationship between capitalism and the nuclear family form. Many of the arguments, however, have lost their way in a confusion of 'households' with 'families' and an essentialist identification of the elementary family as the basic unit of kinship. As feminists have pointed out, the concepts of 'family' and household are highly developed social constructs which have not always been recognised as such in social science (Thorne and Yalom, 1982). Kinship is not a 'thing in itself' but should be deconstructed into the social practices constituting it in specific contexts; we cannot assume a *priori* what these practices will be.[2]

Such a deconstruction prevents the simplistic association of 'family' and economic forms that marks many of social science's models of the development process. According to these, the growing dependence on the individual wage, overall growing commoditisation of the economy and demands of labour mobility are all assumed to strip away ties of economic dependence among kin. Kinship as an object simply disappears from many studies of 'development'.

I have argued elsewhere that the concrete conditions of capitalist development do not in fact pare kinship relations down to a basic elementary family form but tend to produce a range of modified extended family forms which are often female centred (Stivens, 1984). I suggested there that the development process in recent years has domesticated kinship relations; as kin-based production relations decline, kinship becomes concentrated on the reproductive tasks maintaining household and family relationships that the sexual division of labour ascribes to women. This inevitably leads to some degree of female centredness in kin ties, especially where the extensive male out-migration of particular phases of capitalist accumulation leaves women in *de facto* control of the household economy. Such relationships often act as a kin-based welfare system in the absence of state provision, an issue which I explore further below. As I try to demonstrate, at least in this Malaysian case, some of the reproduction of labour power takes place in kin groupings wider than the 'nuclear family' and has not been narrowed down to such units.

Family and state

The role of the state in the development of such family forms is a contentious issue. A great deal of writing on the capitalist state and gender has not only been highly ethnocentric but has also assumed the effectiveness of the state in securing the social conditions of reproduction – the state is seen as structuring women's subordination within the family, albeit in an indirect way. According to McIntosh, for example, the state intervenes less conspicuously in the lives of women, often in fact denying them protection given men. 'The state frequently defines a space, the family, in which its agents will not interfere but in which control is left to the man' (1978, p. 257).[3] Such historically specific interpretations of the history of the (western) family however cannot easily be transposed to other entirely different contexts; in my study area at least this male control is far less certain. A central argument of this chapter will be that the Malaysian state cannot be characterised simply as 'patriarchal', intent on the subordination of women to the family. The development of family forms and women's situation in them is the outcome of a highly complex and contradictory historical process.

We should be wary of generalising from the development of the western family when discussing the evolution of family patterns in the third world; although European patterns can provide interesting comparisons, the relationships between state, economy and family in the contemporary industrialisation process arise in contexts marked by very different historical conditions.

The development of 'family' among Malays

The Malay family should not be considered as an essential reified entity, but deconstructed into the practices that have formed it historically. Many anthropological accounts of 'family' and 'kinship' in the peninsula have not done this, treating kinship as a relatively unchanging core of relationships; but kinship and family have their own history, the effects of a continuous social process of construction through state legislation, economic changes, political action, the rise of social practices like welfare and public health measures, and class action.[4]

In colonial and post-colonial Malay(si)a there have been a number of highly significant state interventions in the 'family' through the legal process. Early in the colonial period, attempts to codify the customary law governing kinship and land tenure played a part in reconstituting the famous 'matrilineal' system of Negeri Sembilan state and to a lesser extent the customary law of other areas.[5] At the same time there were successive legislative shapings of Islamic family law, which set up a competing discourse about the conduct of family life and inheritance. (Chung and Ng, 1977).

These legal precepts and practices of course established a framework for social practices but did not in any way restrict them to the narrow boundaries thus set up. As I have stressed, the evolution of family patterns arises out of a complex interaction of many such interventions; the state can in no way be seen as determining family form. While family has often been an explicit object of policies, the effects of such policies have often been piecemeal and highly contradictory.

Moreover, throughout this process family forms are highly contested. For example, there has been considerable debate about polygamy provisions in successive reforms of family law in the non-Islamic communities in Malaysia. Similarly, successive legislation has attempted various reforms in divorce and maintenance procedures in both the Islamic and non-Islamic communities, again stirring up controversy in the process. Most recently, the reversal of the family planning programme has led to intense public debate about state manipulation of family size.[6]

Malaysian industrialisation

Industrialisation has recently expanded enormously in Malaysia, after the arrival in the 1960s of large-scale industrial capitalist investment. This process has been strongly supported by the post-colonial state, with a central aim of 'restructuring society in the context of an expanding economy'; this has led to active promotion and coordination of industrial development, especially 'labour-intensive resource-based, including agro-based export-oriented and high technology, industries' (Malaysia, TMP, p. 319). The involvement of transnationals has been a central feature.

Historically, merchant and plantation capital had long dominated the Malayan economy. The colonial social process produced an ethnic division of labour with concentrations of Chinese in business and wage work, a smaller number of Indians in plantation wage labour, and Malays in peasant agriculture and fishing. Colonial land legislation was one of the principal agents in this structuring of ethnicity; the creation of Reservations, ostensibly to protect Malay land and produce an 'eastern yeomanry', has been seen by many commentators as a key factor in the subsequent problems of poverty faced by rural Malays. While the extent of Malay proletarianisation in the past is little documented, it was probably greater than is usually suggested; but they probably formed only a fragmented mainly rural labour force, although commodity and wage forms had long predated the colonial period.

It was only after the growth of the industrial sector that large numbers of Malays have entered manufacturing. For example, the percentage of Malays employed in manufacturing rose from 19.6 per cent in 1957 to 36.1 per cent in 1976. More marked still has been the rise in female labour force participation for all the ethnic groups; this rose from 16.7 per cent in 1957 to 41.3 per cent in 1976, falling back slightly to nearly 39 per cent in 1979 (Malaysia Economic Report 1982/83: 14, table 1). In 1970, for example, there were 41 electronics firms employing 3200 female workers. By 1976 there were 138 firms employing 47 000 workers. The numbers of female rural–urban migrants rose from 1000 in 1970 to 80 000 in 1976 (Jamilah Ariffin, 1982).

From a situation of relative economic dependence (although they were clearly important as domestic labour) young women have emerged as a significant source of economic support for the Malay rural family economy. The concurrent rise in urbanisation has meant some growth in the 'housewife' as a social form; as I point out in greater detail below, this model of women as housewives has received considerable state-level ideological support in public pronouncements about 'women's place'. This has been allied to a growth in imported models of femininity, well documented in studies of the management of the famous electronics factories, which reveal a vast ideological edifice of beauty pageants and other aids to learning 'femininity' (Lim, 1978; Cardoso and Khoo, n.d.). Such constructions have not gone without challenge, particularly from Islamic quarters, who decry the rise of the independent factory 'girl' with great zeal, and from local feminist academics.

THE STUDY

The setting

As I noted above, I carried out the rural end of this research in three adjacent village in Rembau, a district of the state of Negeri Sembilan in Malaysia famous for its pre-colonial matrilineal system. This system today, as I have argued elsewhere, is no pristine 'traditional relic', but was at least partly reconstituted by the British colonial authorities at the end of the nineteenth century, with legislation codifying matrilineal land tenure (Stivens, 1985a).

This chapter is concerned with the period from the mid–1960s, when the village economy had been facing increasing problems of production. These can be seen partly as the end product of a long process dating back to the colonial period; in particular, state controls on output and replanting restrictions which prevented the effective reproduction of the means of production in small holding meant that many village rubber trees were at the end of their lives, producing little useful income.[7] Although the post-colonial state implemented a number of schemes to help smallholders (replanting grants and other measures) these were only of limited effectiveness; the situation in Negeri Sembilan generally of static or declining productivity and rural impoverishment meant that many villagers were very willing to migrate out to expanding urban capitalist sectors. By 1976, 950 of the estimated 1400 or so members of my study villages had left[8] and up to a third of rice and rubber land was uncultivated.[9] By 1982, most rice production in the villages had ceased altogether, due to labour shortages.

In common with other parts of Malaysia, migration from Rembau has been rising sharply in the last decade or so. Malay men in Negeri Sembilan were famous in the colonial period as policemen and soldiers, and Rembau especially has long been known for providing a sizeable number of officials for the civil service, schoolteachers and clerks; this seems to have been partly a result of a high valuation of education at least for males (Norhalim, 1976). But today other very different groups are becoming involved in wage labour, most notably young women who rarely entered the labour force before the 1970s. Present-day villagers have migrated out to work in a range of both white-collar and blue-collar occupations, including clerical and administrative, factory and domestic service jobs.

Most villagers gain a livelihood from cultivating rice (on very small plots), rubber and a little fruit. A few have pensions as migrants; a number are beginning to retire back to the village, which is usually the wife's, for residence is still predominantly uxorilocal. A few also earn wages or salaries, for example as teachers, clerks or labourers, in nearby small towns. A large number, however, would find it very difficult to manage on village income without the help of migrant kin, usually adult children, both adult and married. The relative collapse of the village economy and the patterns of kin dependence this has produced, are one focus of this discussion. The ones who can get by best on village income are usually a youngish married couple who can work hard at extracting a livelihood from a combination of village enterprises; but such households are in the minority in the villages. Nearly half the households are headed by women – widows, divorcees or women with migrant husbands away. The extent of out-migration is shown by the fact that few adults under the age of 40 are resident in the villages at all.

I would not characterise this rural area as a reserve of labour for the capitalist sector, in spite of the fact that it could be seen as functioning as such in the contemporary period. The relationship between the rural and wider economy cannot be simply accounted for in such a functionalist way; in many ways it makes a lot more sense to see the remittance economy as reproducing the peasant production process. I have suggested that the colonial state interventions codifying matrilineal customary law and limiting rubber production reconstituted a 'matrilineal' peasantry characterised by non-capitalist agrarian relations of production.[10] Space forbids a discussion of this relationship between 'peasant' and dominant capitalist sectors: the point that the uneven penetration of capitalism into non-capitalist enclaves like this one is a highly specific process and that capitalism does not directly account for the social forms present does not need to be repeated here.

There are growing class differences in Rembau society, but these do not arise out of accumulation in the village society, but from relationships imposed externally by the post-colonial class structure. There are some differences in village landholdings, but only three households have holdings as large as 8–9 acres of rubber land and only one other has 28 acres; these 'concentrations' mostly came from the purchase of land with outside salaries rather than from the generation of surplus internally.

Family and kinship in Rembau, Negeri Sembilan

The future of matriliny

Negeri Sembilan society differs from the rest of Malaysia in that its wider kin groupings are allied to a developed ideology of matrilineal kinship which portrays a system of clans and lineages dating back to the fourteenth century. This ideology today is a product of complex historical processes – pre- and post-colonial ideology, colonial administration and social science – which have all created successive discourses about what it means to follow this 'matrilineal system' (*adat perpatih.*)[11]

A number of social forces generated by the colonial political economy acted to perpetuate aspects of Negeri Sembilan matrilineal ideology and practices, including wider kin relationships of dependence cast in terms of matrilineal ideology, land legislation (whereby women who previously had usufruct rights to ancestral land were given individual grants passing from mother to daughter) the political subsumption of the clan system into the state constitution, and the reconstitution of descent group ideology. At the same time other aspects of family life including marriage, divorce and arrangements over children were administered by the Islamic authorities, setting up a competing discourse about how family life should be conducted.

Most modern comment about 'matriliny' in Malaysia suggests that it is under threat – from Islam and 'modernisation' particularly – and that its dissolution through economic forces at least will mean a decline in extended family ties. Many of the villagers I talked to shared these worries about the future of family life and their matrilineal 'custom'. How far are they right to see a decline in this 'custom'?

Formal matrilineal kinship practices clearly have declined, with open transgression of the clan exogamy rules and a decline in many ceremonials. Young people have very little knowledge of kinship matters – many cannot even tell you what clan they belong to. This is not simply a lack of interest but often an active hostility that attaches itself to other countering ideologies, like Islam, modernity and *adat temenggong*, a term covering the basically bilateral kinship practices of the rest of the peninsula.[12]

This opposition to matriliny has been expressed both at the individual level in attempts to avoid kinship rules (like marriage prohibitions) and at a more general political level in the form of attacks on *adat perpatih*. Some men are openly buying land in towns, they say to avoid matrilineal inheritance rules. As well, there is supposedly some illegal trading in mortgages on ancestral land. The most overt attacks on *adat* took place in 1951 (discussed by de Josselin de Jong, 1960) when attempts were made unsuccessfully by the Religions Affairs Section of the Rembau Branch of the United Malays Nationalist Organisation to abolish matrilineal laws of land ownership; according to its critics, matriliny was against Islam, unfair to men and impeding economic development.

Since then there have been a number of further attacks on matriliny mostly by senior state officials in Negeri Sembilan. While this opposition often adopts Islamic ideology in its arguments, we cannot attribute the decline in matrilineal practices to religious ideology alone even if the recent upsurge in Islamic fundamentalism has fuelled a long-standing opposition between them; Islam and 'matriliny' do conflict, especially over family law, in which Islamic law mostly prevails. For example, most Rembau Malays would not feel married without customary rituals as well as the required Islamic *nikah*; but other non-matrilineal Malays also value such customary practices.

The main source of the present discontent with 'feudal' matriliny is better sought in the decline of the village economy and the industrialisation process. Migration in particular has progressively weakened the local substructure on which the ideology of kin relations is based. Modernisation ideology is readily apparent in a growing individualism that is seen as incompatible with matrilineal extended kin relations. As well, growing levels of commoditisation in the village economy have led to greater atomisation of productive units and less cooperation in agriculture. Formerly, this coöperation was based both on ties of locality and kinship. In practice, too, clan interests in inheritance have become less and less important. Land has been treated more and more as individual property, which the British granting of individual land grants to women of course fostered.

We can see from this very brief account so far that it is possible to picture a number of social forces simultaneously conserving and dissolving aspects of the formal matrilineal ideology of the reconstituted peasant society. How far have the individualising forces described above restructured kinship practices, and in particular, produced a 'nuclear family' form?

The rise of the nuclear family?
The Malaysian state in its official publications takes it for granted that

this process is well under way: 'The emergence of the nuclear family system in place of the extended family will further increase pressures on the projected supply of housing during the (Third Malaysia) Plan period' (Malaysia, TMP, 197, p. 146). A growth in the number of households is seen as direct evidence of such a process; there may be more households, but the sociological determination of household composition always involves more than statistical enumeration. Arguments about the emergence of a 'nuclear family' form raise difficult methodological and theoretical issues as already noted. The formation of separate migrant *households* does not necessarily mean that the elementary family has become a dominant *kinship* form. This confusion between the concrete residential group and the abstract entity of wider kinship relations has been heightened by the fact that the elementary family has often been a dominant Malay residential grouping in the past; none the less both developmental cycles of families and specific historic/economic conjunctures create many other household forms.

In contemporary Malaysia, however, there are a number of forces encouraging this 'modern' household form: first, there is the state-led industrialisation process itself and the growth of waged labour in manufacturing which increases economic individualism. Many rural land settlement programmes, again under the aegis of the state, also assume an elementary family household model in their selective procedures, and institute a 'family' household as a productive unit; in this the male is assumed to be the head of the household and the wife to be a housewife and dependant; although her labour outside the house is also taken for granted, a wife's farming background is not credited in the settler selection process (Shamsul Bahrin and Perera, 1977).

At the same time there is as I have noted a growing individualist modernist ideology which places value on independence, privacy, being '*moden*' (modern) and escaping some of the constraints of family and kinship. Even in the Rembau villages, one can see evidence for this in the changing forms of domestic architecture, closed off bedrooms and the private lockable rooms being demanded by some of the young.

Free choice marriage

This desire for freedom has been most obvious in the changing patterns of marriage. In the past, marrying outside the clan was one of the central rules of Negeri Sembilan kinship and transgressions were rare. Today questioning of the rules has become a central point of ideological conflict between the generations. In fact, though, pressures on customary marriage are coming more from the increasing tendency for out-migrating Rembau Malays to choose their own marriage partners from other Malaysian states. Within the villages, too, free choice marriage probably accounts for up to half of all marriages.[13] Many seem to feel that an arranged marriage is inferior, an admission of failure to attract a spouse. But the 'traditional' payment from the groom to the bride's family, far from lapsing, has become enormously inflated, so much so that in some cases the bride is secretly helping the groom out with her earnings to produce the sum to be presented formally to her family.

These conflicts between old and new forms of marriage were acted out in a number of disputes during my fieldwork. In one case, support for the new ways – marrying a fellow matrilineal clan member – was sought in arguments that the couple were following Islam, and anyway 'people don't follow *adat* (matrilineal practices) these days'. The sadness of some of the young couple's elders at this transgression was expressed poignantly when a woman remarked that 'Maila will go back to England and say that we don't follow *adat* any more.'[14]

It would be easy to connect this growth in free-choice marriage to the semi-proletarianisation of young migrants; earnings in the industrial sector have definitely increased the autonomy of both sexes in relation to their families, but have also given them new responsibilities – many young people are the main economic support of their village families. This is certainly behind the rapidly rising age at marriage: in 1980, 49 per cent of women aged 20–24 had married, compared with 59 per cent in 1970 (Malaysia: General Report of the Population Census, 1980, 1983, p. 39). It is significant that parents wanted daughters in the past but now also want sons, because they bring money home. Parents willingly allowed children to defer marriage, and some young women are even swearing off marriage altogether, saying that they are happier working.[15] The elaboration of romantic ideology, always present I think but fostered by the Indian and western media, has also played a part in these changes in marriage patterns.

It is clear then that young people have complex motivations to migrate: economic factors play a major part, but the desire to escape the personalised control of parents, to seek their own partners in the relative autonomy of the urban environment is also important. Such individualistic concerns, and a new materialism produce extensive conflict with their elders, especially for young women; parents are very anxious about their 'moral welfare' in the city and this concern is highlighted in pronouncements by the state and media.

These new ideologies, especially among the expanding Malay middle classes, directly conflict with the value placed on sharing with kin. But, as argued below, this central contradiction is partly resolved by the new forms of structural dependence among kin produced by the industrialisation process, what I term the remittance family economy.

The remittance family economy

It would seem clear then that at the political, economic and ideological levels there are considerable pressures encouraging the development of elementary family households, especially in the urban context. But, in the recent past, most Negeri Sembilan women did in fact maintain their own households, albeit within a single compound with their mother or sister(s). As residence was uxorilocal, women formed the kinship core, men marrying in.

Migration, however, has changed this process of household formation considerably. Although most younger migrants set up a new household on their own in the urban area (neolocal residence), many women come back to the village to give birth and a proportion live in their home village while their husbands are away working or in the army or police force. The mother's compound has thus become the site of reproduction in all the senses of the term; it is not only the place which women come back to for birth, but also the site of denuded middle-aged households and other complex residential patterns involving the domestic care of grandchildren, the elderly and other dependants.

New households do not mean a new dominance of the nuclear family form, as noted. City and country household are linked by a complex web of support including chain migration of relatives to the city, the provision of help for migrants in the form of housing (often in clusters of kin related through female ties) finding work and childcare. Most importantly, single and married children make extensive monetary contributions to their original families in the form of remittances, although they are not unambivalent about providing this help. In return, parents and other older kin contribute a great deal of domestic labour to the extended family economy. Wage levels in the city and the cost of housing are such that many migrants send their children back to the village to be looked after by the (maternal) grandparents. Such fostering was not rare during the colonial period but these patterns are much more general; grandmothers and other female relatives have become responsible for a significant part of the rearing of migrants' children. Village facilities like schools, water and electricity increase the attraction of this course, although there are dissatisfactions; the young complain about the dullness of village life and their grandparents complain about all the extra work.

It can be argued therefore that the migration process and its structuring of the remittance economy encourages a range of wider kin ties to maximise the welfare role of kinship. At the economic level the elementary family can be seen as at least partly embedded in kin relations, not structurally separated out. Clearly, some at least of the reproduction of labour power for the capitalist sector is occurring within relationships wider than the nuclear family. It is even possible that the dependence produced may intensify rather than reduce kin attachments. As I have already suggested, these ties seem to tend towards the female side, not only because of the continuing force of matrilineal ideology, but also because the domestication of kinship in the migration process means that kinship relations become more focused on the helping 'reproductive' tasks that are women's in the Rembau social construction of gender.

One of the main mechanisms securing the embeddedness of the elementary family is a highly developed moral code enjoining kin to help each other. Although, as I shall suggest, this code is not uniformly effective, it is strongly sustained through a core of female solidarity; this is expressed at a number of levels, including the overtly political, the community and the domestic. It is one of the major forces maintaining a body of ideology that is represented as matrilineal (although much that passes for matrilineal is not necessarily very different from other Malay patterns).[16]

This remittance family economy is by no means a 'private' family matter; the Malaysian state has been very active in its pronouncements about the direction of changes it perceives. Contrary to its exhortations to be 'modern' and develop (and to some of the implications of its new family planning policy as I shall show below) the state has overtly coopted the sense of moral obligation to kin in many of its policies. It is only too clear that the state's unwillingness and presumed inability at this level of development to provide an adequate welfare system produces this somewhat contradictory situation. The Malaysian media are not always direct mouthpieces of the state (although they are very subservient) but it is significant that the volume of articles extolling the virtues of family life and in particular the 'Asian family' over the western model grows ever larger. Less overtly, the failure to provide anything more than skeletal welfare forces dependence on families and kin even if the intent of other elements of policy is very different. I have already pointed out, however, that such kinship practices do not necessarily provide a real measure of protection against the pressures of urban living and work.

I have suggested then that a major effect of the state-led industrialisation process for my informants in Rembau is a restructuring of kin relationships of dependence among kin, strengthened in part by a continued emphasis on a morality of kinship enjoining duties to kin. The remittance economy is clearly implicated in producing radically different household structures and cycles from those of the recent past. The new importance of female labour in industrialisation, especially, has had profound implications for the family economy.

Young women's entry into the urban labour force has of course been more dramatic than the young men's. Young Malay women in the past rarely worked outside the home apart from some 'help' in agriculture, but in Rembau at least this participation was not extensive. They have moved from this 'protected', indeed sequestered, existence to one in which they have become subject to alien work schedules, production lines and social controls in the work situation and an ideology which associates such work with moral licence.

An important question for any discussion of their family role is the extent to which their decision to work and their wages are controlled by parents. Some of the rhetoric associated with social science's discovery of female labour (Malay and non-Malay) in world market factories in Malaysia has assumed a uniform level of subordination to parental and social demands; and tended to ascribe all the social characteristics of these workers like docility, low levels of activism, etc., to their sex, without taking into consideration the painful history of the Malayan working class since the Second World War (cf. Pearson and Elson, 1984). In fact in my experience the situation is a little more complex: there are, first, ethnic differences in family structure that are highly significant; second, in Rembau, both parental and children's responses to the possibility of such work were very variable; some parents put pressure on their daughters to work and some refused to let them go, because of the supposed moral dangers. But some daughters defied them. Conversely, some women refused to go, saying quite rationally that it was hardly worth their while once they had paid their lodging and other costs. Several preferred to get some kind of work locally if at all possible. Of course at the time of the study very little was available, although now the government policy has shifted towards rural industrialisation, with very mixed 'success'.

The extent of parental controls on young women because of their sex can be overdrawn as young men equally are expected to be dutiful children and help their parents; age as well as gender differentiation is an important factor. But men are much freer to 'hang out' in the village, while young women often have a heavy burden of domestic labour. None the less the embeddedness of these women's decisions to work in an integrated family strategy increases the tendency for female labour to be seen as supplementary and secondary, not least by the women themselves.

Young women's position within the new family forms produced by the remittance economy, then, can be particularly contradictory; they are caught up in tensions between drives towards individualism and the structural constraints generating kin dependence. These latter have a long history, as noted; this includes not only the personalised authority of parents but women's own political action within the community to protect their position as the keepers of 'matriliny' and to secure a form of economic autonomy. The increasing value placed on freedom, privacy and individualism by young people, male and female, represents a kind of struggle for new forms of autonomy – autonomy that holds some threat for the remittance family economy.

The 70 million policy and the remittance family economy

In terms of this remittance family economy, 'family' has only been an indirect object of policy. Although the existence of the extended family is an important plank in state ideology, the nature of the connections between the rural family economy and city households is not explicitly recognised officially except obliquely.

I noted earlier the more direct state interventions in 'family', like successive marriage and divorce legislation, development plans for health and welfare and educational policies. The recent moves by the government to reverse the family planning policy, however, have direct implications for the future development of the remittance family economy I have been describing and for family forms generally. The direct intervention of the state in the most intimate aspects of family life and the whole process of family formation represents a situation where 'family' becomes a direct instrument of policy.

Until recently the post-colonial state laid great stress on lowering the Malaysian birth rate; in common with other third world countries Malaysia subscribed to the population policies promoted by international aid agencies like the World Bank who see unchecked population growth as a cause of poverty and underdevelopment. Consequently, Malaysian women became subject to increasing pressure to control the size of their families. Whether it was the programmes or other factors which reduced the crude birth rate from 46.2 in 1957 to 30.6 in 1976 (Nor Laily Aziz and Tan, 1978) is open to debate. Certainly in the villages I studied there is some doubt about the effectiveness of what appeared to be a pills-only policy. Large numbers of village women had been listed as acceptors but large numbers of them had not actually taken the pills. For example, one 45-year-old woman had been prescribed the medication, she said, without any examination, and it had made her 'too weak to work in the rice fields', turned her skin 'brown and blotchy' and she was 'worried about heart attacks'; she threw them away. Village women were very worried about such side-effects.[17]

In an extraordinary reversal it was announced as part of the Fourth Malaysia Plan Mid-term Review in March 1984 that the family planning policy was to be discontinued and Malaysia was now aiming for a population of 70 million by the beginning of the twenty-second century. The rationale has been that a development policy with industrialisation as a central plank needs a large domestic market, hence the pronatalist about-turn. Cynics note that while the Chinese and Indian minorities have made something of a demographic transition, the Malays have done so to a far lesser extent, and seem likely to further outstrip the other communities.

In essence, the new policy represents an attempt by the state to secure the conditions of reproduction of a greatly expanding industrial labour force and presumably an expanding home market. But pronatalism and its associated stress on women as mothers and housewives is in any case as I have suggested based on a faulty analysis that takes little account of the realities of the remittance family economy in which some of this reproduction takes place in units wider than those envisaged by official ideology.

In the wide discussion that has followed the announcement of the policy, there have already been many pronouncements about a 'woman's place'. The origins of this official ideology seem to me obscure; we could follow other western feminist analyses in seeing this as yet another instance of the state confirming men's dominance in the household. Certainly, the latest moves and rhetoric would seem to suggest this; but the history of the ideology at state level still needs to be investigated: is it merely a model of womanhood recently imported by some of the educated bureaucracy, or a historical product of a process beginning in the colonial period or earlier? Whatever its origins, such an ideology seems extraordinary in a society where women were rarely restricted to domestic work until recently.

This is not the place to discuss the complex issues of population, development and women's rights; but some possible effects of maternalism becoming a dominant ideology both at the level of the state and social practice should be noted: first, women might be freed from some of the pressures of neo-Malthusian population policies, but at the cost of a 'return to the home'. Not only do women form a significant proportion of industrial and urban workforces but women of the new middle classes have been avid employees, backed up by domestic arrangements of kin, servants and childminders.[18] (The maternal deprivation thesis in its western form does not yet seem to have gained a strong hold in local ideology, although the new policies could have the same effect in restricting childcare facilities.) Any female withdrawal from the labour market will obviously seriously undermine what independence earning gives women of all classes. In reality of course women in the urban work force are often the poorest of all workers in terms of individual earnings (Lim Teck Ghee, 1983). As already noted, their embeddedness in 'family' encourages them and society to see their wages as supplementary; working often 'only makes sense' as a part of a combined family strategy.

Also, the loss of female earnings, an important factor in generating new forms of kinship, could be very serious. If pressures for women to marry and stay at home intensify the remittance family economy would have lower levels of disposable income. This in turn could seriously affect the volume of remittances and exacerbate the crisis in rural production.

CONCLUSIONS

As Rapp *et al.* (1979) have argued persuasively, many discussions of family history and formation have artificially separated family from the wider society in which it is embedded. This chapter has focused on a case-study of the family economy in Malaysian industrialisation trying to show some of the processes forming family and kinship, especially some of the links between the family, state and economy. I have argued that there is no simple causal relationship between labour mobility demands arising out of industrialisation on the one hand and the elementary family on the other. Transformations brought about by the colonial and capitalist development process, I have argued, have not necessarily dissolved wider family ties but have restructured new patterns of dependence between family members; these have included the important part remittances play in reproducing village households and production processes, and extensive help exchanged between city and countryside; I have particularly highlighted the dramatic emergence of young female labour and its relationship with the family economy. While these patterns are relatively undifferentiated in terms of class at present, it seems likely that they will become somewhat more so in the future, with welfare dimensions being stressed among the poorer sections and the new middle class emphasising transfers of wealth and the reproduction of their class situation.

Much of my discussion has been concentrating on the extent of state intervention in the reproduction of labour power. I argued that the appropriate unit of analysis of this reproduction process was the remittance family economy rather than the elementary family household. Western feminism has made much of the separation of domestic and wage labour during industrialisation and state support for particular (elementary) household forms; but while this separation is visibly emerging in urban areas in Malaysia at this juncture it is by no means clear that such a separation is functional for capitalist accumulation or indeed desired by the Malaysian state (cf. Molyneux, 1979; McIntosh, 1978), the ideology of some of the state agents notwithstanding. As I have been at pains to emphasise, the development of present family forms has been a complicated historical process determined by a multitude of factors.

This case I hope illustrates some of the complexities involved in discussing the relationship between family and state in industrialising Malaysia; the links are far more complex and contradictory than functionalist accounts of the nature of the state would suggest. I suggested that the colonial and post-colonial states had played a decisive role in setting some of the parameters of family and kinship in Rembau; I listed some of these as the reconstitution of matrilineal kinship, the political economy of land legislation, family law and state intervention through economic and welfare policies like health service provision, education and wage legislation; family planning and the new pronatalism have had, and will have, sizeable effects. But these parameters, as I have stressed, have had contradictory effects, both conserving and reconstituting aspects of 'traditional' kinship and family practices and dissolving other aspects. There is a particular contradiction today between the state's historical reconstitution of 'matriliny' and its reliance on the welfare dimensions of kinship on the one hand, and on the other its encouragement of economic forms that put pressure on such relationships by encouraging individualism and materialism.

Clearly the state by no means determines kinship and family forms, even if it has set some of the parameters of these relationship; historically 'family' has been a highly contested area with multiple determinations, not least the family's own political actions in its defence. The force of these contests can be illustrated by mentioning the succession of both local and national struggles (and the word is not too strong) over the defence of 'matriliny' in Rembau in 1951 noted earlier (cf. Josselin de Jong, 1960), over definitions of 'youth's' proper role in the family and society in contemporary Malaysia, over definitions of women's role, highlighted in the recent '70 million policy' and in debates about young factory women, and over the defence of 'traditional' family values. Such defence of 'family' and kinship is complicated by the fact that it draws on competing definitions of how family life should be conducted – in Rembau these definitions have polarised into something of an opposition between Islam and 'matriliny'. The defence of family and kinship in Rembau should not be seen as a simple conservative reflex; for example, it has been significant in resisting capitalist development as it did in 1951 and subsequently. Conservative 'traditional' kinship values are often seen by local critical ideology as deriving from the village community viewed through a somewhat romantic if not 'feudal' haze; but they are also a way of familialising resistance to state policy and capitalist development; 'family' as such sometimes acts as a way to resist policy – as it did when my informants resisted the pills dished out to them. In many ways families not only have, but make their own, histories.

Notes

1. This research was carried out in three neighbouring villages in Rembau, Negeri Sembilan, Malaysia from July 1975–September 1976 and supported by an SSRC (UK) Studentship in the Department of Anthropology, LSE. Further visits were made in 1982 (funded by the Hayter

Fund), 1984, and 1985. The main focus of the original research was gender and the evolution of the agrarian economy. The return visits focused more on macro changes, especially industrialisation.

2. Kinship in anthropological discourse has been beset by the reification of kin relations. I discuss this more fully in Stivens (1983). The most popular approach to kinship in 'modernising' societies has assumed that kinship becomes reduced to a residue of some more complex system (see contributions to Thorne and Yalom (1982)).

3. The definition of the state is beyond the scope of this chapter. See the introduction, and Alavi (1982) for a discussion of problems with functionalist analyses of the capitalist state and Hua (1983) for a Malaysian account and references.

4. Historical studies of the European family particularly have tended to read off family structure from economic determinations of the household as a productive unit (cf. Goody *et al.*, 1976).

5. See Banks (1983) for a summary of Malay kinship patterns.

6. See Chung and Ng (1977), Jomo and Tan (n.d.).

7. See Lim Teck Ghee (1977) and Lee (1973). This brief summary has telescoped a long and complex history. In essence, it is being suggested that political controls led to a crisis in the reproduction of the means of production; peasants were the low-cost efficient producers compared to the rubber estates but were prevented from developing by political controls set in motion by class fractions serving plantation interests.

8. This figure of 1400 measures the proportion of matrilineal descendants of lineage segment heads who would normally be resident in the villages.

9. See Stivens (1985a, 1985b) for fuller accounts of this.

10. Again, see Stivens (1985b). There I argue that while we cannot argue for a simple persistence of 'matriliny', there has in fact been a feminisation of newly acquired land, which has meant a continuing reversion of land to female ownership. (see Fett, 1983 for support for my view.) This has secured a measure of economic autonomy for village women, but the massive economic changes discussed in this chapter threaten to undermine this.

11. The role of colonial reports (like Parr and MacKray, 1910) in recreating matrilineal discourse and a model of 'tradition' is discussed in Stivens (1983).

12. See Hooker (1972) and Banks (1983). *Adat temenggong* is often seen as more in accordance with Islam.

13. Arranged marriage today cannot be seen as a union between discrete kin groups except in an abstract symbolic sense (see Stivens, 1983).

14. This case is discussed more fully in Stivens (1983).

15. Again, see the fuller discussion in Stivens (1985a).

16. Other non-matrilineal Malay societies share many features of Negeri Sembilan culture, including some degree of female-centredness in household and kinship relations. Similarly, so-called matrilineal social practices contain many non-unilineal features, which have perhaps been stressed more in the recent restructuring of kinship.

17. See Nor Laily Aziz and Tan (1978) for a short history of family planning

policy in Malaysia. Jamiah Binti Bador's graduation thesis has explored family planning in one of the study villages (1974).

18. See Noor Laily Abu Bakar and Hashim (1984).

References

Alavi, H. (1982) 'State and class under peripheral capitalism', *in* H. Alavi and T. Shanin (eds), *Introduction to the Sociology of 'Developing Societies'* (London: Macmillan).

Banks, D. J. (1983) *Malay Kinship* (Philadelphia: Institute for the Study of Human Issues).

Cardoso, J. and Khoo, K. J. (n.d.) 'Work and consciousness: the case of electronics runaways in Malaysia, in K. Young (ed.), *Serving Two Masters* (forthcoming).

Chung, B. J. and Ng Shui Meng (1977) *The Status of Women in Law: A Comparison of Four Asian Countries.* (Singapore: Institute of Southeast Asia Studies).

Fett, I. (1983) 'Women's Land in Negeri Sembilan' in L. Manderson (ed.), *Women's Work and Women's Roles, Development Studies Centre*, Monograph No. 32 (Canberra: Australian National University).

Goody, J. *et al.* (eds) (1976) *Family and Inheritance* (Cambridge: Cambridge University Press).

Hooker, M. B. (1972) *Adat Laws in Malaysia: Land Tenure, Traditional Government and Religion* (Kuala Lumpur: Oxford University Press).

Hua Wu Yin (1983) *Class and Communalism in Malaysia* (London: Zed).

Jamiah Binti Bador (1974) 'Rancancan Keluarga Di Kampung Gadung' (Family Planning in Kampung Gadung), unpublished B.A. thesis (University of Malaya).

Jamilah Ariffin (1982) 'Industrialisation, Female Labour Migration and the Changing Pattern of Malay Women's Labour Force Participation', *Southeast Asian Studies*, vol. 19, no. 4 (March).

Jomo K. Sundaram and Tan Pek Long (n.d.) *Not the Better Half: Malaysian Women and Development Planning.* (Kuala Lumpur: Integration of Women in Development, Asian and Pacific Development Centre).

Josselin de Jong, P. E. de (1960) 'Islam versus Adat in Negri Sembilan (Malaya)', *Bijdragen*, 116, pp. 158–203.

Lee, G. (1973) 'Commodity Production and Reproduction Amongst the Malayan Peasantry', *Journal of Contemporary Asia*, no. 4, pp. 441–56.

Lim, L. (1978) *Women Workers in Multinational Corporations in Developing Countries – The Case of the Electronics Industry in Malaysia and Singapore*, Women's Studies Program Occasional Paper No. 9 (University of Michigan).

Lim Teck Ghee (1977) *Peasants and Their Agricultural Economy* (Oxford: Oxford University Press).

Lim Teck Ghee (1983) 'Women, economics and the Environment', in E. Hong (ed.), *Malaysian Women: Problems and Issues* (Penang: Consumers' Association).

McIntosh, M. (1978) 'The State and the Oppression of Women', in A. Kuhn and A. M. Wolpe (eds), *Feminism and Materialism* (London: Routledge & Kegan Paul).

Malaysia (1982) *Economic Report* (1982/3) (Kuala Lumpur: Ministry of Finance).

Malaysia (1983) *Population and Housing Census 1980* (General Report of the Population Census. Kuala Lumpur).

Malaysia (1981) *Third Malaysia Plan* (Kuala Lumpur: Government Printers).

Molyneux, M. 'Beyond the Domestic Labour Debate', *New Left Review*, 116, pp. 3–27.

Noor Laily Abu Bakar and Hashim, R. (1984) 'Child care for working women', in Hing Ai Yun *et al* (eds), *Women in Malaysia* (Petaling Jaya: Pelanduk Publications).

Nor Laily Aziz and Tan Boon Ann (1978) *Methods of Measuring the Impact of Family Planning Programmes on Fertility in the Case of Malaysia* (Kuala Lumpur: Lembaga Perancang Kelauarga Negara (National Family Planning Board, Malaysia).

Norhalim Bin Haji Ibrahim (1976) 'Continuity and Change in the Matrilineal Society of Rembau, unpublished M.A. Thesis (Hull University).

Parr, C. W. C. and Mackray, W. H. (1910) 'Rembau, its history, Constitution and Customs', *Journal of the Straits Branch Royal Asiatic Society*, 56, pp. 1–57.

Pearson, R. and Elson, D. (1984) 'The subordination of women and the internationalisation of factory production' in K. Young *et al*, (eds), *Of Marriage and the Market* (London: C.S.E. Books, 1981; reissued Routledge & Kegan Paul).

Rapp, R. *et al.* (1979) 'Examining family history', *Feminist Studies*, vol. 5, no. 1, Spring, pp. 174–200.

Shamsul Bahrin (Tunku) and P. D. A. Perera (1977) *Felda: 21 Years of Land Development* (Kuala Lumpur: FELDA).

Stivens, M. (1983) 'The political economy of kinship in Rembau, Negeri Sembilan Malaysia', Paper presented to Conference on Cognatic Social Organization in Southeast Asia (University of Amsterdam). To be published in *Cognatic Social Organization in Southeast Asia*, ed. F. Husken and J. Kemp (forthcoming).

Stivens, M. (1984) 'Women, kinship and capitalist development', in K. Young, *et al.* (eds) *Of Marriage and the Market* (London: C.S.E. Books, 1981; reissued Routledge & Kegan Paul).

Stivens, M. (1985a) *Sexual Politics in Rembau: Gender, Matriliny and Agrarian Change in Negeri Sembilan Malaysia*, Occasional Paper No. 5 (Centre of South-East Asian Studies, University of Kent, Women and Development in South-East Asia 11).

Stivens, M. (1985b) 'The fate of women's land rights: Gender, matriliny and capitalism in Rembau, Negeri Sembilan, Malaysia' in H. Afshar (ed.) *Women, Work and Ideology* (London: Tavistock).

Thorne, B. and Yalom, M. (1982) *Rethinking the Family* (London: Longman).

6 Gender and Population in the People's Republic of China

Delia Davin

INTRODUCTION

Under the single-child family policy, first introduced to China in 1978, couples are asked to limit their families to a single child. They come under enormous moral and social pressure to comply, and they are also offered considerable economic incentives. Those who defy the policy can be heavily penalised. The policy was introduced in response to what is perceived as the grim threat of demographic explosion. China's population has almost doubled in the past thirty years and could do so again in the next 45 years if families averaged three children each.[1] Surveys in the late 1970s showed that over 38 per cent of China's population was under fifteen years of age, and 65 per cent under thirty.[2] In the next few years, as the bulge generation of the 1960s matures, 10 million women annually are expected to marry and become potential child-bearers.

By the time of the introduction of the single-child family policy, China's achievements in fertility reduction were in fact already remarkable. In the years after the establishment of the People's Republic in 1949, a falling mortality rate combined with a high birth-rate to produce rapid population growth.

In 1950, the year after the establishment of the People's Republic, the birth-rate stood at 42/1000. It remained buoyant, except in the 4 years of economic hardship from 1958 to 1962, until it began its steady decline in the late 1960s. This high birth-rate combined with a falling mortality rate to produce rapid population growth. From the mid 1950s the rate of natural increase was maintained at about 20/1000 until 1974, again with the exception of the four years after the Great Leap Forward of 1958, which so affected birth and death rates that China actually saw two years of population decline, 1959–61. As the economy recovered, birth-rates began to rise again, peaking at 50/1000 in 1963 when the natural increase rate reached a high of

36/1000. These rates should obviously be regarded as compensatory ones following the famine years, and the birth-rate did not again significantly surpass 40/1000, but it remained high enough for the rest of the decade to be the cause of considerable concern.

From the late 1960s the birth-rate began to decline. It stood at 37/1000 in 1970, 30/1000 in 1973 and 25/1000 in 1975 and had fallen to 21/1000 by the end of the decade. The natural increase rate was only 15/1000 in 1976 and thereafter, despite flunctuation, it has been kept well under that level. This reduction corresponds to a decline in the total fertility rate from 5.8 births per woman in 1970 to only 2.7 births in 1978. In 1984 it is hoped that the natural increase rate will be down to 10/1000, an all-time low.[3]

In the official view, however, the impressive fertility decline of the 1970s came too late, and draconian policies are necessary to prevent economic growth held back by population growth. The official figure for per capita arable land in China is one-tenth of a hectare (one-quarter of an acre), lower than any major country in the world except Japan and Egypt.[4] Urbanisation cannot, at least in the short term, provide a solution for the surplus rural population. Rural migration to the towns has been strictly controlled since the 1950s and the decade of the Cultural Revolution actually saw a ruralisation of the population as young people from the cities were sent to the country-side. Since the mid 1970s the urban proportion of the population has begun to grow again, but even by 1983 it only represented 23.5 per cent of the total.[5] It is official policy to provide rural employment by building-up rural and small town industry as quickly as possible, but these measures can only contribute towards a solution. China remains an overwhelmingly agricultural country whose economy is closely tied to agricultural productivity, above all to grain produc-tion. The past thirty-five years have seen a very creditable increase in the productivity of the land but this has been almost cancelled out by population growth.[6]

The State's response to this situation has been two-fold. Under a programme of agricultural reform, peasant families are being offered higher incentives which it is hoped will stimulate rapid economic growth. At the same time a strict population policy has been intro-duced through which it is hoped to reduce, halt, and ultimately perhaps even reverse population growth.

Population policy has very special implications for women, both because they are the child-bearers who assume primary responsibility for child-rearing and because it may give rise to changes in the family, an institution which in China is still of vital importance in shaping and indeed limiting, women's lives. The primary purpose of this paper is to examine the ways in which women's lives are being affected and will in future be affected by the one-child policy, but it begins with a summary of the way the policy is intended to work and the way it appears to be working.

THE SINGLE-CHILD POLICY

Although the one-child family policy is official, is constantly promoted by Central Government propaganda and has been given further credibility by Party documents, it is not yet enshrined in national law. Both the Constitution and the Marriage Law require married couples to practise family planning, but the regulations for the single-child family are issued by provinces and municipalities, counties, communes and enterprises.[7] The regulations therefore vary in detail but it is possible to give a summary of their common points. With a few exceptions, all Chinese couples are told that they should have only one child. Those who promise to comply receive a certificate entitling them to a monthly allowance while the child grows up. Other common incentives are extra paid maternity leave, and sometimes lump sums or gifts. In the countryside where peasant families receive a per capita allocation of private plot land, the single child is allocated a double share, while in urban areas they are entitled to a double allowance of residential space. In addition, single children have privileged access to education and health care free of the usual charges. The parents of single children may be given preference in the allocation of the most sought-after jobs, and the children are sometimes promised similar privileges in the future.

Parents who defy the policy by producing an 'out-of-plan' child – that is, a second child for whom no permission has been granted, or any subsequent parity children – are to be penalised in various ways. If they are wage-earners, the wages of one or both parents may be docked by 10 or 15 per cent monthly until the child reaches a set age – usually somewhere between ten and sixteen. Alternatively a 'social payment' (or fine) may be levied. If an official office-holder, the parent may be demoted. Quite commonly a formal block is set on future promotion. When the policy was first introduced, rural regulations tended to lay down deductions of work-points earned as the major penalty for peasants. Now that in most areas collective accounting has been abandoned and individual families contract for plots of land which they then farm for their own profit, new rules have to be worked out. The recommended penalties are cuts in the amount of contract land and increases in the quotas to be supplied to the State. Birth expenses for an out-of-plan baby have to be defrayed by the parents themselves and maternity leave is unpaid. The child will receive no priority for health care or education and charges will be levied for both.

It is difficult to assess how far this harsh programme of penalties is actually put into effect. There are certainly numerous reports of individuals being subjected to it, but they are often those of whom better would have been expected, such as Party members or cadres. Early versions of the regulations prescribed penalties for the birth of a third child rather than that of the second, and even now it is the third birth which is commonly reported as activating the sanctions. It may be that implementation depends in part on the extent of local acceptance of the programme. The indications are that in many rural areas large numbers of families still produce second children but fewer go on to a third.[8] In such cases it must be difficult for the authorities to treat the production of a second child as deviant, and they may prefer to rely on rewarding the parents of only children and punishing only the exceptionally defiant parents of three or more. Where there is widespread acceptance of the one-child norm, greater strictness is possible and there may even be some community feeling against any family which refuses to make the sacrifice already agreed to by most families.

The implementation of incentives has also posed certain problems. Complaints about the non-payment of allowances are rare, but the allocation of housing space is another matter.[9] Accommodation is extremely short in most Chinese cities and this, combined with the fact that people cannot be expected to move with every change in the size of their families, has meant that per capita rights to housing space were only rarely honoured in the past. If there is no spare accommodation, the only priority that can be given to single-child families is on the waiting-list. The problem has been exacerbated by the success of the policy in the cities, where most young families can now claim single-child privileges. In the countryside, private plot land and land for housing are similarly difficult to use as flexible rewards since they are usually redistributed at quite long intervals. In a move to encourage more peasant investment in the land, the rural authorities have been urged to contract land to the peasants for periods of 15 years or more: a move which will make it difficult to use the allocation of contract land as a meaningful reward (or punishment).[10] Presumably in future rural authorities will be forced to rely more heavily on quotas, fines or levies.

Most regulations make some provision for exemptions which are themselves of considerable interest. For example the Shanxi provincial regulations promulgated in June 1982 included a list of special circumstances in which either urban or rural couples would be allowed a second child and a further list of real difficulties which would exempt only rural couples from the policy.[11]

Special circumstances which may qualify urban or rural couples for exemption

(1) Where the first child suffers from a non-hereditary handicap which will prevent him/her working normally when adult.
(2) In cases where one partner has a child by a previous marriage but the other has not yet had a child.
(3) In cases where the couple have adopted in the belief that they are sterile and the wife later becomes pregnant. (To qualify the wife must be at least 30.)
(4) Both parents belong to national minorities.
(5) Both parents are returned overseas Chinese.

Real difficulties which may qualify rural couples for exemption

(1) The bride is an only child and the young couple have settled with her family.
(2) The couple live in a sparsely-populated area of the countryside where economic conditions are poor.
(3) The husband is the only one of three brothers able to father a child.
(4) The husband is the son of a revolutionary martyr.
(5) One spouse has a major handicap.
(6) Only one son has been born to the family for three consecutive generations.
(7) The spouses are themselves both only children.

Couples whose circumstances fit these categories are not automatically exempt from the one-child rule but they may apply for permission to have a second child. If permission is granted, they must still leave a four-year gap between births.

THE EFFECTIVENESS OF THE PROGRAMME

The incentives and disincentives put great pressure on the family to comply with the policy. A typical allowance of five yuan a month for fourteen years is significant to urban parents who if they are workers or cadres earn an average of around 70 yuan each, less if, like many, they are employed in the non-State sector.[12] Free education and medical care will certainly add to the temptation to take out the certificate as will priority for good schools, entry to which is highly competitive. In the countryside, the value of the benefits varies considerably according to local economic conditions and the level at which benefits have been pitched. One study of a Suzhou commune in 1980 showed that families there could augment their incomes by a quarter or even a third when they took out the certificate.[13] On the other hand, the income of rural families is heavily dependent on the size of the family labour force, particularly since the recent economic reforms made the household the basic economic unit over most of China, so that peasant families will obviously be concerned with the costs of forgoing a second or a third child. Higher rural mortality rates may also make peasants feel that they need more than one child to ensure that at least one survives to adulthood.

The greatest obstacle to the general acceptance of the one-child family is, however, son-preference.[14] Though generally now referred to in official discussions as 'a remnant of feudal thought', the common preference for sons does, unfortunately, have a rational material base. Marriage in rural society is still patrilocal, the bride moving at least to her husband's village, and very frequently to his parents' home or to their compound. In their old age the bridegroom's parents rely on the young couple for both support and care. Pensions are available for peasants only in a few wealthy areas. Inevitably, those whose children are all female worry about their old age. Absent daughters sometimes remit money to needy parents from their marital homes, but their subordinate position as daughters-in-law and their lesser earning power as women, limit the sums they can send. Furthermore, they cannot give the physical care and comfort which an old couple will expect to get from a co-resident son, daughter-in-law and offspring. In urban areas, patrilocal marriage is no longer universal. The housing shortage and job allocation are more important factors than tradition in determining the young couple's residence, but even in cities the fact that men on average earn more, may cause male offspring to be regarded as better potential supporters. At a less practical level, the traditional concern with continuing the family line also plays a part in this widespread preference for sons.

THE CONSEQUENCES OF THE POLICY FOR WOMEN

Females are the victims of one of the most widely-publicised consequences of the single-child policy, which has been the re-emergence of the infanticide of girl babies and of higher mortality rates for infant girls. In the past in China as elsewhere in the world, unwanted babies were sometimes disposed of by infanticide.[15] Most (though not all) of the victims were female. As boys received better care and a greater share of scarce resources, they often also had a better survival rate than girls. Infanticide was specifically outlawed by the first Marriage Law of the People's Republic in 1950 because the Government recognised that the problem, being bound up with the traditional family system, was properly a part of family policy. The near disappearance of female infanticide in the 1950s and 1960s demonstrated that Chinese parents would, if they could afford it, bring up their daughters. Even in the traditional rural economy, daughters performed a useful economic role in most households and after 1949 this role was upgraded as the use of labour was intensified and more women were mobilised for work outside the home.[16]

Reports of cases of female infanticide reappeared in the Chinese press in 1980–1. Some of the claims seem exaggerated, for example, that there are three boys to every two girls in certain communes.[17] These may emanate from those who wish to discredit the policy or, on the contrary, from those who wish to counter infanticide by creating revulsion against it. However, the fact that the Party, the Youth League and the Women's Federation have issued repeated denunciations of the practice indicates that it is recognised as a serious problem even at the highest levels. Some statistical evidence seems to emerge from the results of the 1982 census. Nationally a figure of 108.5 male to 100 female births was reported.

The ratio varies considerably by region. Shanghai, where for socio-economic reasons one would expect son preference to be weak, reported a reassuring 105.4/100. In contrast, the figure for the southern province of Guangdong, where the single-child policy is known to have met with strong opposition, was a depressing 110.5; while Guangxi and Anhui, both provinces with large impoverished rural areas, reported 110.7 and 112.5 respectively. Of course, theoretically, these figures could be explained by the under-registration of female births, since obviously it would be those areas with strong son preference where females would be most likely to be omitted from the census. The problem with this explanation is that the frontier provinces of Xinjiang and Guizhou reported figures of 106.1 and 106.2 respectively, both well within the normal range. The socio-economic characteristics of these provinces are such that son preference should be strong, but because they are sparsely-populated, strategically important and each has a considerable national minority population, many of their inhabitants will have been exempt from the single child policy. It does seem likely that unexpectedly high male to female ratios at birth and the single-child policy are connected.[18]

Nor is the connection hard to understand. In the past, families were on the whole willing to bring up their daughters if they could afford to. Now they face a situation in which to do so means to sacrifice the chance of trying for a son, unless of course they are prepared to accept the considerable official displeasure and economic disadvantage attached to going through with an unauthorised birth. If, on the other hand, they dispose of a female first-born undetected, they are free to try for a son.

Infanticide is the grimmest of the consequences of this situation, but, without doubt, far greater numbers of women are affected by the lesser evils it produces. The vast majority of Chinese mothers must always have gone into labour hoping for a boy who would raise their status in society and with their in-laws. However, a female first-born was at least welcome proof that her parents were fertile and elder sisters were often given names such as 'Leading-in-a-Son'. Now that the first child should officially be the last, such consoling thoughts are no longer valid. It is not hard to imagine the stress which the mother must endure through her pregnancy and labour. Women were traditionally held to be responsible for the sex of their infants and, despite attempts at scientific education, this notion persists. There have been widespread reports of the ill-treatment of mothers who are blamed by their husbands or in-laws for having given birth to daughters; ranging from a refusal to give them the special foods traditionally offered to post-parturient women, through to persistent abuse, violent beatings and even murder.

Again, the problem has been officially recognised and campaigns against infanticide have been coupled with campaigns against the ill-treatment of women.[19] Local Women's Federations have attempted to detect such cases in their own areas and to deal with them in such a way as to deter others. But even if the incidence of violence can be reduced, the tensions, miseries and rows associated with it will continue, and women will continue to be the main victims. This major form of pressure on women, though not actually created by the single-child policy, has certainly been greatly intensified by it.

To comply with Government policy each couple must control their fertility. Women carry a disproportionate share of this burden. In the 1970s, couples were urged to accept sterilisation after the birth of their second child and many couples who felt they had completed their families must have regarded it as the best contraceptive method available. According to the national fertility survey of 1982, 70 per cent of the 170 million women of reproductive age were practising some form of birth control.[20] Of these 25 per cent had had tubectomies, while 10 per cent had husbands who had undergone vasectomies; totalling 35 per cent who were relying on sterilisation. Sterilisation in general has received greater acceptance in the countryside than in the cities. Another somewhat unexpected urban/rural difference is that although female sterilisation is generally more common than male, the difference is greatest in the cities, presumably because the superior medical facilities required for tubectomy are more readily available. Only in the populous province of Sichuan do vasectomies outnumber tubectomies, for reasons which remain obscure to outside observers. In general however, despite some urging, particularly from the Women's Federation, that men should undergo the simpler procedure of vasectomy, it is women who 'pay the price' once more.[21] At least those in registered employment have the consolation of paid sterilisation leave.

Those couples who accept the single-child certificate are likely to rely on contraception. Occasionally even these parents have been urged to accept sterilisation, but the more realistic campaign slogan is: 'After the first birth an IUD, after the second a sterilisation'.[22] Unlike the couples of the 1970s who accepted sterilisation after two or three births, today's parents of an only child must be acutely aware that a single misfortune could leave them childless. They are unlikely to give up all possibility of replacing a lost child. Moreover some couples, while confining themselves to one child at present, still hope for a relaxation of the policy which may allow them to have a second in the years to come.[23] Despite well-publicised efforts in China to develop a male contraceptive based on gossypol, and despite the resolution of the Women's Federation at its Fifth National Congress in 1983 that: 'men should also be urged to take contraceptive measures', the burden of contraception still falls mainly upon women.[24]

The IUD is the most commonly-used contraceptive, relied on by 50 per cent of the couples who practise family planning. This breaks down to 53 per cent for the countryside and 39 per cent for the cities. The pill is used by only 8 per cent of these couples, 6 per cent in the countryside and 19 per cent in the cities. The condom accounts for only 2 per cent of contraceptive use and 'other methods' for 4 per cent.

The IUD in common use in China has no tail and cannot therefore be removed by the user or by an unskilled person. Although officially contraceptive measures are supposed to be voluntary and there have been sporadic official condemnations of forced sterilisations, abortions and IUD insertions, the official assumption is quite clearly that a woman has no right to remove an IUD or to cause it to be removed without permission. There have been many reports of prosecutions of medical personnel or 'quacks' who have accepted payment to remove the devices unofficially. Concern about this possibility may create further hazards to women's health. In some units women have been given regular X-rays (florescopes) to check that their IUDs have not been removed or become dislodged.[25] The use of X-rays tends generally to be more casual in China than in the West in recent years, but by any standards this is surely a misuse of the procedure.

China was comparatively cautious in her approach to the pill. It was not approved for general use for some years after it had become acceptable in the West and in the 1970s it tended to be recommended for short-term use in delaying the first birth or spacing subsequent ones. Prevailing medical opinion is still against the long-term use of hormone contraceptives and considerable effort is made to ensure that users get regular medical check-ups. This, combined with problems of supply, may explain its rather low rate of use in China. Caution however seems to be giving ground to pragmatism in regard to other types of hormone contraceptive. A range of 'visiting' pills, 'morning after' pills and 'one-a-month' pills is available, and China recently accepted aid from the UN Fund for Population Activities to treble its output of contraceptive injections from 1 million to 3 million doses per annum.

As the use of barrier methods is so low in China, reliable contraception must pose a particular problem to women who do not tolerate the IUD well and who do not want a sterilisation. Such women probably account for much of the pill-use, despite unease about the effects of taking it over many years.

Another threat to women's health posed by population policy is the abortion rate. Abortions rose from 21.6 per 1000 women aged 15–44 in 1971 to 24.8 per 1000 in this age group in 1978. In absolute numbers this meant a rise from 4 million to $5\frac{1}{2}$ million abortions – a rate similar to those prevailing in the USA and Singapore.[26] However there seems no doubt that the rate must now be much higher, as with the introduction of the one-child policy official pressure has intensified and fewer young couples can be expected to rely on sterilisation. It is constantly stressed that abortion should not be used as a method of contraception, but only to terminate pregnancies which result from the failure of other methods.

For married women who wish to terminate an unwanted pregnancy abortion poses little problem. Both bureaucratic and technical procedures are simple and a large number of operations are carried out at an early stage. The recording and checking of women's menstrual cycles is an integral part of family planning work so that most women quickly become aware that they are pregnant. No particular shame or guilt attaches to the procedure and women in employment are entitled to some leave to recuperate from it. However, many of the women who undergo abortions may originally have wanted the baby. They become pregnant knowing that the baby, if born, will be 'out-of-plan', because they or their families hope that the pregnancy can be carried through without attracting official attention. Legally, no woman can be coerced into an abortion, she must agree to it. There have none the less been reports of forced abortions, particularly from Guangdong Province, where the campaign seems to be especially strongly resisted. Although such incidents are officially condemned, it seems inevitable that they will continue now that a bonus and penalty system has been built into local cadres' salaries whereby they will lose money if their area exceeds its birth quota. More common than cases of physical force are those where a woman who wants to go through with an unauthorised pregnancy will be worn down by patient, unremitting persuasion which continues for days, weeks or even months until her reluctant consent is finally extracted. In cases like these, the husband or other family members are also likely to come under considerable pressure. Sometimes another family member is identified as being the true source of resistance and attention is focused on him or her. Usually, however, the woman is the main target and she is the one who will inevitably eventually undergo the operation. Where people have held out a long time, late abortion is the result, so that there are instances of abortion in the sixth, seventh and even the eighth month, with obviously painful physical and psychological consequences for the woman.[27] Some families attempt the tactic of sending women away from home to friends or relatives in other areas or in cities to conceal a pregnancy. If discovered such women are escorted back to their home areas by officials of the public security bureau as if they were offenders, and are then persuaded to abort.[28]

In some urban areas the availability of both abortion on demand and amniocentesis may lead women to terminate their pregnancies, either under family pressure or voluntarily, because they are carrying a female fetus. Such abortions will of course be undesirably late. The authorities are aware of this danger and officially the parents are not supposed to be told the sex of the foetus unless there is a possibility of a sex-linked hereditary disease.[29] There are, however, persistent rumours that this practice does occur and the present promotion of private medicine will surely make it harder to control. For the moment at least it will be limited by the expense and technical sophistication of the procedure.

Most regulations on the single-child family are non-discriminatory in the sense that the husband and the wife are held to be responsible for the birth of an out-of-plan child and the penalties apply to them both. However, there are occasional reports in the press of individual cases in which the wife has been more severely dealt with. For example, in a case where a couple in Beijing had a fourth child in 1980, the wife was to be deprived of bonuses for three years and the husband for only one.[30] In Guizhou in the same year a woman who gave birth to her third child lost her post as deputy head of the people's court. But in this instance she was probably more strictly treated than her husband simply because of the seniority of her position.[31] Moreover, the husband, not the wife, was ordered to be sterilised, so it was not a simple case of 'blaming the woman'. There have also been reports of peasant fathers-in-law being fined because a daughter-in-law had had an out-of-plan second baby. This is an interesting reflection of rural realities in which the co-resident rural family functions as a single unit with a common budget controlled by the household head – the oldest working male. In this case the household head was held reponsible for the actions of the household members as he would have been in imperial times.

Given the common household budget, the loss of paid maternity leave for an unauthorised birth is in financial terms a loss for the whole family but it obviously hits women hardest, as they are also likely to lose rest time. If a family finds it impossible to get kindergarten places for children who have no priority because their births were unauthorised, it is again, in practice, their mothers who are likely to suffer directly.

Many of the exemption clauses in the provincial regulations display a strong concern for the male line of descent which seems more inspired by respect for tradition than by notions of sexual equality. The exemptions from the one-child rule which, as we have seen, are granted in the Shanxi regulations to the only fertile son among three generations fit this pattern. On the other hand, most regulations, like those for Shanxi province, include strong encouragement for uxorilocal marriage, traditionally only a desperate resort for families lacking a male heir. Uxorilocal marriage can definitely be regarded as favourable to women in its effects.[32] The inspiration for this encouragement is, however, pragmatic; the Government rightly sees the breakdown of patrilocal marriage custom as helpful to the population campaign and has promoted the idea that in some circumstances husbands should join their wives' families since the early 1970s. It has been suggested that higher benefits for parents who take out the single-child certificate although their first-born is a girl might be beneficial, but this idea does not yet appear to have been included in the major provincial regulations.[33]

The intensification of the effort to reduce births in the 1970s led to criticism of the earlier tendency to leave the promotion of family planning to women and women's organisations. It was recognised that in backward areas where male supremacy was strong and women's organisations weak, this practice led to the neglect of family planning work. The medical aspect of family planning work is now integrated into the health system. The campaign is the responsibility of a whole hierarchy of birth planning committees on which senior officials are supposed to sit to confer prestige. For example, the provincial governor or his deputy should sit on the provincial committee, and an important brigade cadre would be on the production brigade committee.

At the grass-roots level most birth control workers are women. Indeed, their tasks would be considered inappropriate for men, as they keep records of the menstrual cycles of the women under their charge, urge them and their families to accept the one-child certificate, advise on methods of contraception, arrange for abortions,

IUD insertions and sterilisations, hand out permissions to get pregnant and so on.[34] In most cases they have already had experience of working with women as Women's Federation activists, or as cadres with special responsibility for safeguarding women's rights. Their work would then have included, for example, intervening on behalf of women who claimed that they had been beaten or ill-treated in the family or were being discriminated against at work. Inevitably these women sometimes suffer unpopularity for their birth-control work and their ability to work effectively in other fields must then be impaired. In rural China there is often a serious shortage of women with the self-confidence, education and determination to work as cadres so that this is a very real loss.

The public reputation of the Women's Federation itself could be adversely affected by the close association of its basic-level officials with the implementation of the one-child programme. Perhaps aware of this danger, the Women's Federation at national level has issued condemnations of coercion and resolutions that women's health should not be put in danger by birth control work.[35]

The generally more active role played by the Women's Federation in the past few years and a recent campaign to promote women's rights should also be seen in the context of the one-child family policy. Problems in implementing the policy have highlighted the continuation of son-preference and discrimination against women. It is no longer possible to dismiss them as phenomena left over from the old society which the mere passage of time will eliminate. It is officially recognised that the implementation of the one-child family necessitates an improvement in female status and earning power.[36] As yet, however, despite the rhetoric, there appears to have been little action in this direction and the Women's Federation, although more active than before, has not recovered the strong image it enjoyed in the early years of the revolution.

The single-child family policy has also produced renewed high-level interest in infant and child mortality. The authorities are aware that the reluctance of many people to restirct themselves to one child stems in part from a fear of being left childless by illness or accident. Despite this concern, infant mortality actually appears to have risen from under 40/1000 in the late 1970s to 48/1000 in 1983, a depressing trend which can probably be attributed in part to the disruption of rural health services which followed decollectivisation.[37] Of course the policy itself may also have contributed, since a rising proportion of total births will now be first births, and thus more liable to complications than subsequent births. Family members apparently show greater anxiety than before about birth. The Shanghai First Maternity and Children's Hospital saw its caesarian rate rise from 12 per cent in 1978 to 16.7 per cent in 1980.[38] Questioned about this high rate, the hospital director explained that 90 per cent of their deliveries were now of first birth babies, so that a high caesarian rate was to be expected. However, she thought that there was also a serious social problem: family members had become so concerned for the child's welfare that they were reluctant to allow a labour of more than a few hours and quickly began to pressurise the doctor to perform a caesarian.

Single children are offered special health check-ups and an unprecedented amount of popular advice material on subjects such as child nutrition, nursing, innoculation, development, 'eugenics' and parentcraft now appears in the media.[39] Parents are urged to choose 'quality over quantity', that is, to bring up one well-fed, well-educated and well-cared-for child. This sort of approach is probably quite effective, at least with urban parents who are ambitious for their children's education and careers. Even in earlier years when frugality was in fashion, Chinese parents lavished attention and income on their children. In the cities now, the children's shops stock a range of expensive luxury items such as leather shoes, fur coats and high quality sweaters which can be bought by those parents whose spending power has been enhanced by limiting their families to a single child.

The Chinese government has already succeeded in reducing fertility to a degree which must have a remarkable effect on women's lives. Few women now give birth to more than three children, the majority have one or at most two. For this new generation of mothers this represents a tremendous reduction in the proportion of their lives which will be spent in pregnancy, lactation and child care. For urban women this transition will mean less interrupted, less harassed careers and less suffering from the double burden of work and home responsibilities. Significantly there were numerous single-child families in the cities before the introduction of the policy, showing that many urban women early sought this relief for themselves.[40] When maternity becomes so much less time-consuming, discrimination against women in employment and promotion (illegal but widespread in China at present) should become more difficult, or at least more difficult to disguise.

Although in the long run the same may hold true, for rural women (or even urban women in tradition-bound families), a troubled transitional period seems inevitable. Much of a woman's sense of worth was gained from her familial roles of mother, daughter-in-law and wife. The single-child family policy threatens the self-image of such women, especially.

The implications of China's population policy are complex. For women, they are both negative and positive. Women in Chinese society have never controlled their own fertility. The timing of marriage, together with the ideal size of a family, were matters in which the elders of the family had a major voice. The State is now intervening in these decisions on a scale unprecedented anywhere in the world. The anger of the family at this development is voiced in the often-heard complaint, 'You control heaven and earth and now you want to take charge of our child-bearing too'.[41] It is the misfortune of women that it is their reproductive power and their bodies which are being fought over in this struggle between the State and the still patriarchal family.[42]

On the other hand, even in the short term, the single-child policy has produced a concern with women's status and rights, with child health and welfare and with education which runs counter to other trends in China today and has helped to protect these areas from the neglect they might otherwise have suffered.

In the long run, if the single-child family policy is implemented or even partially implemented, it will produce great changes in family structure. All the children of the 1980s and 1990s will have 'rarity value'. Patrilocal marriage may come under real challenge, as families whose only child is a daughter will invest heavily in her and will be reluctant to let her leave upon marriage. Even if they do so they will surely encourage her to maintain far closer ties with them than was customary in the past. In general, daughters' obligations towards their parents are likely to become more comparable to those of sons and their status should rise accordingly. In the past social policy in China has relied heavily on the family to care for the old, and sick and the disabled. Now, at least where couples are unable to support two sets of surviving parents, the State will be forced to become more directly involved. The exact consequences of all this change are of course too complex and too remote to predict.

Notes and References

1. Charles H. C. Chen and Carl W. Tyler, 'Demographic Implications of Family Size Alternatives in the People's Republic of China', *China Quarterly*, March 1982, p. 67.
2. Tian Xueyuan, 'A Survey of Population Growth', in Liu Zheng *et al.* (eds), *China's Population: Problems and Prospects*, (Beijing: New World Press, 1981), p. 42.
3. I am here using figures taken from Judith Banister's computer reconstruction of population dynamics, rather than official data (Judith Banister, 'Population Policy and Trends in China, 1978–83', *China Quarterly*, December 1984, pp. 740–1). However, official data would give a similar overall picture. See also Banister, *China's Changing Population* (Stanford California: Stanford University Press, 1985).
4. Tian Xueyuan, 'A Survey of Population Growth', p. 46. This calculation is based on the official figure for China's cultivated area which is probably something of an underestimate, as it is in the interests of lower-level authorities to understate in their reports to Central Government.
5. Judith Banister, 'Population Policy and Trends in China, 1978–83', p. 734.
6. For a discussion which relates the problem of grain production to the recent agriculture reforms, see Andrew Watson, 'Agriculture looks for shoes that fit', in Neville Maxwell and Bruce McFarlane (eds), *China's New Road to Development*, (Oxford: Pergamon, 1984).
7. For a much longer discussion of the regulations see Elisabeth Croll, Delia Davin and Penny Kane (eds), *China's One-Child Family Policy*, (London: Macmillan, 1985).
8. In 1981, only two years after the start of the one-child drive, first-borns made up 47 per cent of total births, births of second children 25 per cent and of third and higher parity infants 28 per cent of live births. Rural fertility was significantly higher than urban fertility. Qian Xinzhong and Xiao Zhengyu, 'An analysis of the one in one thousand sample survey of fertility' (Beijing Economics College, 1983).
9. 'A Survey of the Single-Child Family of West-Side, Hefei, Anhui Province, China', *Renkou Yanjiu*, no. 1, (1981).
10. Central Committee of the Communist Party of China, 'Document no. 1 on Rural Work for 1984', 1 January 1984.
11. 'Shanxi Planned Parenthood Regulations', *Shanxi Ribao (Shanxi Daily)*, 17 November translated in Survey of World Broadcasts, 16 December 1982 (FE/7210/B11/3).
12. Nicholas Lardy, 'Consumption and Living Standards in China, 1978–83', *China Quarterly*, December 1984.
13. Ashwani Saith, 'Economic Incentives for the One-Child Family in Rural China', *China Quarterly*, September 1981.
14. For a detailed discussion see Dalia Davin, 'The Single-Child policy in the countryside', in Croll, Davin and Kane (eds), *China's One-Child Family Policy*.
15. See Bernice J. Lee, 'Female Infanticide in China', in R. Guisso and

S. Johannesen (eds), *Women in China* (Youngstown, N.Y.: Historical Reflections/Reflexions Historiques no. 8, 1981).

16. See Delia Davin, *Woman-work: Women and the Party in Revolutionary China*, (Oxford, 1976) ch. 4.

17. Yang Fan, 'Save the Baby Girls', *Zhongguo Qingnian Bao [China's Youth]* 9 November 1982.

18. Figures for sex ratios at birth are taken from John S. Aird, 'The preliminary results of China's 1982 Census', *China Quarterly*, December 1983.

19. 'Resolutely eliminate discrimination against women', *Renmin Ribao (People's Daily)* 3 March 1983. For a Women's Federation campaign see Elisabeth Croll, 'The Single-child Family in Beijing: A First-Hand Report', in Croll, Davin and Kane (eds), *China's One-Child Family Policy*, p. 228.

20. All the figures on contraceptive use in the following pages are taken from Qian Xinzhong and Xiao Zhengyu, 'An analysis of the one in one thousand sample'.

21. Report of the Fifth Chinese National Women's Congress, September 1983. Survey of World Broadcasts, 12 October 1983.

22. For detail see, Pi-chao Chen and Adrienne Kols (eds), 'Population and Birth Planning in the People's Republic of China', *Population Reports Series J*, no. 25, January–February 1982).

23. As stated to me on trips to China in 1981 and 1984 in numerous personal conversations.

24. See note 21.

25. As shown on Ed Goldwyn's BBC *Horizon* Programme on the Single-Child Family Policy, first broadcast 7 November 1983.

26. Chen and Kols, 'Population and Birth Planning', p. J.593.

27. As shown, for example, in the BBC *Horizon* Programme mentioned above (note 25).

28. John Gittings, 'Communes: new direction or abandonment?', *China Now*, no. 102 (May/June 1982).

29. Information given to the author in an interview with the Director of the Number One Shanghai Maternity and Children's Hospital, March 1981.

30. Survey of World Broadcasts, FE6401, March 1980.

31. *Daily Report* (Foreign Information Broadcast Services) 25 March 1980.

32. For the classic discussion on the disadvantageous effects on patrilocal marriage on Chinese women see Norma Diamond, 'Collectivization, Kinship and the Status of Women in Rural China', *Bulletin of Concerned Asian Scholars*, Jan.–March 1975.

33. Qian Xinzhong, quoted in *Beijing Review*, 28 March 1983.

34. For a detailed description of their work see Elisabeth Croll, 'Beijing', in Croll, Davin and Kane (eds), *China's One-Child Family Policy*.

35. See 'Report of the Fifth National Women's Congress', September 1983.

36. As has been repeated in many articles. Dr Qian Xinzhong, head of the Family Planning Commission has even suggested that women should be given priority in education and job opportunities. Yan Keqing, 'Problems and prospects in population policy', *China Reconstructs*, June 1983.

37. Judith Banister, 'Population Policy and Trends', pp. 760–1.

38. Author's travel notes, March 1981.
39. Elisabeth Croll, 'Beijing' in Croll, Davin and Kane (eds), *China's One-Child Family Policy*, p. 194.
40. 'Urgently take action to reduce the birthrate in our city', *Tianjin Daily*, 4 August 1979, p. 1, translated in *Daily Report*, 19 November 1979 p. 58.
41. For an interesting argument that the Party's family reform policies have actually strengthened patriarchy see Judith Stacey, *Patriarchy and Socialist Revolution in China* (California University Press, 1983).

7 Some State Responses to Male and Female Need in British India[1]

Jocelyn Kynch

INTRODUCTION

This paper sets out a part of the historical background to changes in the well-being of Indian women relative to the well-being of men in situations of hardship.

Two kinds of hardship are considered during a period of fifty years in India. Between 1880 and 1930 there were many famines and scarcities and also recurrent epidemics – including cholera, smallpox, plague and influenza.[2] During both sickness (which occurs in every life-time) and famine (which is a rare disaster) people need relief in the form of medical care or nutrition, which they may not have adequate means to command. Some groups may be particularly vulnerable to loss of livelihood, lack of provision of relief and resultant increases in morbidity and mortality. Here the case of women will be explored. It will be suggested first that State policy during famines, initially favourable towards women *vis-à-vis* men, became less favourable; and second that the State failed to respond adequately to women's general ill-health.

The first section of this chapter presents sources of data and discusses mortality differences between the sexes, including some regional patterns.

The second section is concerned with how, during the period in question, women fared relative to men in terms of tasks and wages on famine relief works. The conclusion is reached that a diminishing provision of famine relief in the form of wage labour was in part due to the perception of women as poor workers – feeble, in bad health and expensive. The evidence, however, does not support the view that they were less cost effective on the works. In order to understand why authorities and men labourers did not like the employment of women as workers, the question of women's health is then explored in the final section.

DATA SOURCES

The women referred to throughout this paper are those who became 'visible' – as workers, as persons on gratuitous relief, as patients attending dispensaries or hospitals, or as dead bodies. The absolute numbers and rates recorded must, of course, be treated with caution. Adjustments have not been made to allow for changes in registration practices, methods of collection or changes in areas because it is the *relative* data for males and females that are the primary object of interest. It serves no purpose to speculate on how the Government might have responded if they had known of the 'true' condition of the people. There is plenty to be said about their actual response to the condition that they had on paper before them.

Mortality is considered below. During famines, reports enumerating those relieved and relevant expenditure were required by the Government of India. Reports were summarised by Commissions of Enquiry for each famine, and sometimes for individual districts or towns. Further information has been drawn from Sanitary Commissioners Reports and statistics of British India collected by the Government of India such as Moral and Material Progress and Condition of India and London, Statistical Abstract for British India. Famine Codes were derived from the recommendations of the Government of India following reports from the Indian Famine Commissioners (for example, Geddes, 1874; Indian Famine Commission Reports of 1880, 1898, 1901). There were regional variations and standards. These are summarised in, for example, Famine Code for Bengal, 1897, Bombay, 1885, 1896, 1900 and 1927, Madras 1895, 1927 and 1937. The provision of medical care and health organisation was also a provincial affair, with Sanitary Commissioners making Annual Reports and Health Officers reporting for the larger municipalities.

Female and male mortality in India 1880–1930

Mortality rates per thousand are available for the period 1880–1930 from the reports of the Sanitary Commissioners and Health Officers. Data are given for the provinces of Bengal (now mainly West Bengal and Bangladesh), Punjab, Madras (Tamil Nadu), and Bombay (Maharashtra and Gujarat), and the cities of Calcutta, Madras and Bombay. The same areas will be used in considering health care later in this chapter.

and cities are shown in Table 7.1. Rates for both sexes rose until 1920, partly because of improved registration, but also due to mortality during the virulent epidemics and famine-related diseases. These did not affect all provinces equally – Madras escaped much of the plague, for instance – but in each area the gap between male and female rates tended to persist. Within this broad framework, it is instructive to consider how rates changed from year to year, and whether males or females received *relative* gains or losses from rising or falling mortality.

For Table 7.2, the annual change in mortality rates for males minus that for females has been calculated. If the result is negative (that is, the female rate has risen faster than, or fallen slower than, the male rate), then this is a male advantage, and if positive, there is a female advantage. If zero, the sexes have fared equally. Table 7.2 shows the number of years of male advantage, female advantage, or no advantage for each of the following: (a) the total period 1880–1930; (b) years of famine or non-famine; and (c) according to the direction of change in mortality. It can clearly be seen from Table 7.2 (a) that in all the provinces and cities, except in Madras province, there were more years of male advantage.[3]

Turning now to the differences between years of hardship (famine or rising mortality) and non-hardship (non-famine or falling mortality), there are two distinct symmetries (which were further confirmed when the data was considered by decade). In the first type, which I shall call F-symmetry, there was more female advantage in years of hardship and more male advantage in years of non-hardship. Examples are Bengal (Table 7.2 (b) and (c)) and Madras (Table 7.2 (c) only). The second type, M-symmetry, is the mirror image, with more male advantage during hardship and more female advantage during non-hardship. This is the dominant city pattern (Table 7.2 (b) and (c)) and also that of Punjab (Table 7.2 (c) only). These symmetries are more marked in the cases of changes in mortality – which approximate to illness or epidemics and their absence. Once again there emerge distinct regional patterns, and a city pattern, as well as obvious differences in the ability of males and females to survive hardships.

Famine and increased ill-health have different characteristics. The former may be understood in terms of loss of entitlements (Sen, 1981), important features being collapse of access to work, migration and relief. Mortality from ill-health is most generally associated with longer-term issues of poverty. During fluctuations in mortality,

Table 7.1 Deaths per 10 000 per decade

	Provinces								Cities					
	Bengal		Punjab		Madras		Bombay		Calcutta		Madras		Bombay	
	m.	f.	m.	f.	m.	f.	m.	f.	m.	f.	m.	f.	m.	f.
1881–90	240	202	312	319	214	197	267	256	419	423	399	391	241	329
1891–1900	338	291	334	354	225	208	359	347	316	419	417	431	424	563
1901–10	362	326	412	472	239	222	346	345	304	436	443	446	503	613
1911–20	323	308	346	388	263	248	361	376	260	402	421	447	348	515
1921–30	257	250	299	312	243	230	262	270	252	419	423	447	249	377

Source: Sanitary Commissioners' Reports and Health Officers' Reports.

Table 7.2 Numbers of years of male and female advantage (calculated from relative annual changes in mortality rates) 1880/1 to 1929/30

(a) *Advantage during total period 1880/1 to 1929/30*

(i) Provinces

	Bengal			Punjab			Madras			Bombay		
	male	*none*	*fem.*	*male*	*none*	*fem.*	*male*	*none*	*fem.*	*male*	*none*	*fem.*
No. of years of advantage (% years)	16 (32)	20 (40)	14 (28)	25 (50)	6 (12)	19 (38)	11 (22)	27 (54)	12 (24)	15 (30)	26 (52)	9 (18)

(ii) Cities

	Calcutta			Madras			Bombay		
	male	*none*	*fem.*	*male*	*none*	*fem.*	*male*	*none*	*fem.*
No. of years of advantage (% years)	21 (42)	13 (26)	16 (32)	19 (38)	15 (30)	16 (32)	22 (44)	10 (20)	18 (36)

(b) *Advantage during famine and non-famine years*

(i) Provinces

	Bengal			Punjab			Madras			Bombay		
	male	none	fem.	male	none	fem.	male	none	fem.	male	none	fem.
Famine years (*% famine years*)	4 (25.0)	6 (37.5)	6 (37.5)	5 (45.5)	2 (18.2)	4 (36.4)	2 (22.2)	4 (44.4)	3 (33.3)	7 (35.0)	6 (30.0)	7 (35.0)
'*Non-famine years*' (*% non-famine years*)	12 (35.3)	14 (41.2)	8 (23.5)	20 (51.3)	4 (10.3)	15 (38.5)	9 (22.0)	23 (56.1)	9 (22.0)	8 (26.7)	20 (66.7)	2 (6.7)

(ii) Cities

	Calcutta			Madras			Bombay		
	male	none	fem.	male	none	fem.	male	none	fem.
Famine years (*% of famine years*)	11 (68.8)	2 (12.5)	3 (18.8)	5 (55.6)	3 (33.3)	1 (11.1)	13 (65.0)	0 (0.0)	7 (35.0)
Non-famine years (*% non-famine years*)	10 (29.4)	11 (32.4)	13 (38.2)	14 (34.1)	12 (29.3)	15 (36.6)	9 (30.0)	10 (33.3)	11 (36.7)

continued on page 136

Table 7.2 continued

(c) Advantage during years of rising mortality and falling mortality

(i) Provinces

	Bengal			Punjab			Madras			Bombay		
	male	none	fem.	male	none	fem.	male	none	fem.	male	none	fem.
Years of:												
rising mortality	4	9	8	18	3	3	4	12	8	9	14	4
no change	3	3	1	2	1	2	0	3	0	0	1	0
falling mortality	9	8	5	5	2	14	7	12	4	6	11	5
(%) years of:												
rising mortality	(19.0)	(42.9)	(38.1)	(75.0)	(12.5)	(12.5)	(16.7)	(50.0)	(33.3)	(33.3)	(51.9)	(14.8)
no change	(42.9)	(42.9)	(14.3)	(40.0)	(20.0)	(40.0)	(0.0)	(100.0)	(0.0)	(0.0)	(100.0)	(0.0)
falling mortality	(40.9)	(36.4)	(22.7)	(23.8)	(9.5)	(66.7)	(30.4)	(52.2)	(17.4)	(27.3)	(50.0)	(22.7)

(ii) Cities

	Calcutta			Madras			Bombay		
	male	none	fem.	male	none	fem.	male	none	fem.
Years of									
rising mortality	11	2	7	13	9	3	17	2	2
no change	2	2	0	0	1	0	2	4	1
falling mortality	8	9	9	6	5	13	3	4	15
(%) Years of:									
rising mortality	(55.0)	(10.0)	(35.0)	(52.0)	(36.0)	(12.0)	(81.0)	(9.5)	(9.5)
no change	(50.0)	(50.0)	(0.0)	(0.0)	(100.0)	(28.6)	(28.6)	(57.1)	(14.3)
falling mortality	(30.8)	(34.6)	(34.6)	(25.0)	(20.8)	(54.2)	(13.6)	(18.2)	(68.2)

The male and female mortality rates per decade in the provinces rather than famine, the M-symmetry is much clearer – suggesting that females, compared with males, were either more susceptible to diseases, or that their condition (for example, poverty) made it more likely that the disease would prove fatal. These possibilities will be explored in the third section of this chapter.

In summary, we have found that regions recorded different, but fairly persistent, absolute and relative rates of male and female mortality. Regions also differed in terms of advantage to one or other sex, with Madras showing greater female advantage overall, and Bengal and Madras having the F-symmetry of advantage to females during hardship. A city pattern of M-symmetry (also dominant in Punjab), with more male advantage in hardship, was found.

THE FAMINE CODES: TASKS AND WAGES

Famines in India were a frequent feature in the late nineteenth and early twentieth centuries and it has been argued that the absence of famines today is due to early Government intervention.[4]

Relief was given in two main forms – gratuitous and in return for work. Various loans or relief from revenue were made, too. Persons (even the feeble) who were able to work, were required to report to relief works, and only very particular classes of person were exempted (these included weavers, 'respectable' men and women, and village servants). Persons were originally exempted as individuals, not as members of households.

Surveillance of rainfall, grain prices, extent of cultivation, mortality of cattle, and migrations of population alerted the authorities to the likelihood of scarcity or famine, and a programme of small or large relief works was drawn up to employ any suffering population should it be required. The system of surveillance and relief was refined throughout the nineteenth century.

Tasks

Under most Codes until the turn of the century, there were four classes of labour. Commonly, 'A' (or an equivalent status category) was professional labour (on earthworks, for example, diggers); 'B' were able-bodied, non-professional labour (usually carriers); 'C' were the able-bodied unused to labour, and 'D' were the feeble, who were given 'healthy work' such as 'patting and consolidating earth'.

Women were eligible but unlikely to work in class A. In the Bengal Famine Code (1897), class A women were to be paid as class B men, while in 1901 the Indian Famine Commissioners recommended that class A women (or diggers) should be given half the male task and the male class B wage. In 1901 it was further explicitly recognised that the new classification into diggers and carriers 'secures the advantages of a sex distinction', one advantage being that a 'sex distinction alone can reduce the extravagance of the rations earned by a family' (pp. 38–9).

The sex distinction was first introduced by the Famine Commission in 1880. It was abolished in 1898 and then recommended again. Women, it was said, were used to receiving lower wages; they had lower 'physiological' needs for food. The fact that they also did household duties did not entitle them to an equal wage, as any such claim for an equal wage was 'refuted by the custom of the country' (p. 39).

The work required of the classes varied by system and province. Usually a task was set, and labourers, in gangs, were paid a daily wage. For instance in the Madras Code (1927), it is stated that 'the recognized coolie load nearly all over India is 50 lbs. Three-quarters or 35.5 lb. . . . would be the load of the class I [A] worker; 25 lb. the load of a class II [B] worker, 12 lb. the load of a class III [C] worker' (Appendix D). This gives relief work in the ratio of 100:70:34 for the three classes. The ratio of work from each class A:B:C in Madras (1895) was 100:75:50; in Bengal (1897) it was 100:85:75. On an earthwork, a carrier would be expected to carry the assigned load 11–5 miles in a day, half the time with the basket empty. In stone breaking, the carrier was expected to carry the load at 60 yards per minute for 7 hours. One method of estimating the gang for a task, was to call one child a unit and work out the total units required to perform a task. In Madras in 1872–3, thus, one man = two women = four child units. In Bengal in 1896–7, one man = $1\frac{1}{4}$ women = 2 large children = 4 small children. Thus, an attempt was made to fit a task and a gang of labourers together.

The use of commercial contracts (especially piece work) on relief works was contentious. Before 1880, where piece work was introduced, women were often under pressure to cease to present themselves for or obtain work. Piece rates could boost men's wages but reduce women's, as in the 1860s in Midnapore, Bengal, where on the introduction of piece work, men's wages rose by 40 per cent, but women's fell by 25 per cent. The Famine Commission in 1880 banned all commercial contract work on relief works (pp. 58–9, section 132), having considered its adverse effects.

Although in breach of the Famine Code, in 1897 Bengal again introduced piece work – although at a higher relative rate for women – and arguments were put forward in favour of paying the piece worker at a rate to include dependants – gratuitous relief on works could therefore be abandoned. In fact piece work was allowed in later Codes specifically in order to test the 'real' need for relief, to drive agriculturalists back to their villages, to reduce the costs of works, and to close the works.[5] I shall consider below whether wages paid to male and female workers reflected those which the *individual* could expect to command if employed off the relief works.

We may conclude that the Government of India did not expect women to execute as hard a task as men. Women faced some barriers (for example, male gangs refusing to accept them, especially on piece works) when they tried to do the more highly paid tasks. The Government tended to accept these barriers and codify them. The supervisors and engineers on the works exercised some discretion, and did not always remain remote from the distressed condition of the persons from whom they were expected to extract work. It was not their responsibility to look after the well-being of relief workers, however.

Wages

The wages on relief works were supposed to lie somewhere between a minimum 'subsistence' (calculated per head until the later notion of a 'family wage' was introduced) and a maximum which sometimes included enough to encourage the labourer to have a little to invest after the famine.[6] The balance between task and wage was such that 'no person would willingly perform [the task] in exchange for the famine wage unless impelled thereto by want' (Bombay Famine Report, 1899–1902, section 48).

After the Punjab famine of 1869, the Government had declared 'the object . . . is to save every life' (quoted in Indian Famine Commission, 1880, p. 19). Taking the high moral stand of this statement literally, in 1873–4 in Behar (Bengal), relief works and high stocks of food claimed to have saved *all* preventable deaths. In 1877, appalled by such apparently profligate expenditure and the surplus grain which the Government of Bengal had had to sell (at a small loss) afterwards, the Government of India announced that the

Table 7.3   Changes in relative wages of unskilled labour, Orissa Canal
1873–1920

Year	Cuttack			Mahandi		
	wage(annas)		*women's wage as % of men's wage*	*wage(annas)*		*women's wage as % of men's wage*
	men	*women*		*men*	*women*	
1873	2.25	1.50	67	2.50	1.50	60
1895	2.75	2.00	73	2.50	1.50	60
1898	2.75	2.00	73	2.70	2.00	74
1901	2.30	1.79	78	2.25	1.41	63
1903	2.50	1.76	70	2.70	1.50	62
1904	2.75	1.76	64	2.80	1.50	54
1905	2.72	1.88	69			
1910	3.24	2.21	68			
1915	3.69	2.81	76			
1920	4.00	3.00	75	4.80	2.60	54

Source: Prices and Wages in India (Department of Statistics, Government
of India, 1921).

'task of saving life, *irrespective of cost*, is beyond their power to
undertake' (Indian Famine Commission, 1880; p. 23, my emphasis).
The Bombay famine of 1876–7 followed the new more cost-effective
guidelines, although Madras did not. The insistence on cost-
effectiveness was an important and severe change of policy towards
suffering during scarcity and famine (see Bhatia, 1963, pp. 271–2).

This switch towards saving life at minimum cost immediately raises
the question of whether certain groups suffered more than others.
Here we will only consider men and women.

Although relief wages were at times acknowledged to be extremely
low (due to misinformation and miscalculation of needs, fines, leak-
ages, or lags in the adjustments to the price of grain or fuel), the
relative wages applying to men and women of the same labour class,
appear to have been, officially, *at least* as favourable to women as
existing non-relief rates. Data on wages for non-relief work are
sparse and inconclusive.

One continuous series for wages of unskilled labour is from the
Orissa Canal in Cuttack and Mahandi, and the years in which there
were changes in any of the wages are given in Table 7.3. On the
Mahandi site women's wages were generally lower both relatively

Table 7.4   Relative wages on famine relief works

Area/code	Year	Women's wage as % of man's wage	Type of work
Bengal (Pooree)	1865–6	83	task
Bengal (Midnapore)	1865–6	80	task
(Midnapore)	1865–6	43	piece
Central Provinces	1868–9	75	task
Punjab (Amritsar)	1869	100	works opened
		60–6	during famine: task
N-W Provinces	1869	100	Ross's system: carriers
Dept of Public Works	1874	66	minimum task
Madras	1891–2	78	task
Bombay (Deccan)	1891–2	89	task
(Dharwar)	1891–2	75	task
Bengal	1891–2	83	piece
	1891–2	75–80	task
Burma	1891–2	80	piece, maximum wage
Ajmere-Merwera	1890–2	60	piece
	1890–2	71	task
Madras	1895	90–95	task
N-W Provinces	1895	89–94	task
	1896	84–93	Blackwood's system: piece
Bengal	1896–7	75–99	Blackwood or 'pit-gang'
Famine Code	1901	87–93	
Madras Code	1927	100	

Sources: Geddes 1874; Indian Famine Commission, 1880, 1898, 1901, various Famine Codes and Reports from Provinces.

and absolutely. There, boys were paid more than women – the reverse was true of Cuttack.

Turning to relief wages, Table 7.4 shows a more favourable policy towards women than on non-relief works.[7] Although the rates adopted after 1901 were frequently close for men and women, the new system of labour classification into diggers and carriers was a sex distinction as noted above on p. 138. This may have reduced the ability of women to obtain relief from famine on equal terms with men. Women labourers formerly able to command a *relatively* high wage of their own were reduced to family helpers paid a dependant's allowance included in the main labourer's wage.

It is reasonable to ask why women labourers should be disliked by labouring men and the engineers on the works. Could we expect them to be weaker, sicklier and thus an expensive form of labour to employ? Despite the prevailing opinions, an estimate of the cost per cubic feet of work done in Bengal 1896–7 shows that relief works employing more women and children did *not* have higher costs. Although greater female morbidity may have been widespread, in 'famine' years in Bengal and Madras female advantage in mortality changes were found (see Table 7.2). Restrictions on women's ability to get work may have formed part of a tendency towards increasing disadvantage relative to men.

WOMEN'S HEALTH AND HEALTH CARE

Bombay 1877–85: migrant women

Women in cities were *expected* to be sickly and attempts to help them were limited. For example, despite the fact that the high rate of tuberculosis in young women (three times that in men in Calcutta) caused great concern, new TB sanatoriums nevertheless provided beds for *men* which added to the inequality of treatment. General sickness in women was often regarded as unavoidable, even when its incidence among men was decreasing.

Because women were expected to add to health and sanitation problems, they were unwanted as migrants, as is shown by the case of Bombay. In 1877, the second year of famine, the usual number of migrants to the city swelled. The Health Officer, T. S. Weir, had expected the famine to follow the pattern of 1862, with excessive deaths of the men who had migrated from the famine areas. The usual winter influx of working *men* from the Deccan and Kutch in search of trade and service returned yearly to their villages. But even then Weir wrote disapprovingly of some, that 'they were encumbered by families and relations' who raised his city's mortality rate (Health Officer's Report, 1877, p. 79). The larger number of migrant women confounded his expectations concerning mortality. Destitutes were turned away and in 1880 all immigration officially stopped.

First, the demographic effect of women migrants was different from that produced by men, who were more mobile on a day-to-day or longer-term basis. In order to get to work, women tended to set up home where a job was available. Secondly, instead of the supposedly healthy outdoor village life, the conditions of work for women 'in cotton mills and wool-cleaning factories' were 'injurious to female life' (Municipal Commissioner's Report, 1884–5, p. 231). These working women were criticised for how they coped with home life. A further fear was that they brought vice.

Despite the Health Officer's conclusion that the influx of women was an intolerable strain on his resources, we may consider that women fairly enhanced their chances of survival by their unwelcomed mobility. This conclusion is supported by the mortality data presented earlier (Table 7.2 (b) and (c)), which indicate that, despite the fact that Bombay city has the expected M-symmetry, Bombay city females gained as much advantage as Bombay provincial females in famine years – and much more in non-hardship years.

However, because of the *condition* of these visible women, they posed a strain on sanitation which could not remain unnoticed, and provoked a restrictive response. That women constituted a majority of the poor was not considered abnormal at the time. Instead, it was city life, it was believed, which had a different impact on male and female health. In 1886, Weir wrote:

> The influences affecting female vitality in this city and diminishing the chances of female life are numerous and in continual operation; the most active are hard toil – much of which is of a nature specially fatal to womanhood – . . . on poor nourishment and amidst conditions of air impurity and pollution – overcrowding and . . . conditions and diseases connected with and arising out of childbirth. . . . (Report, section 9)

In Calcutta also, the unhealthiness of the life of poor women was emphasised, and there was an argument put forward for village life as being healthier (for example by D. F. Wise in Dacca, quoted in Sanitary Commissioner's Report Bengal (1879); and the pathologist Dr Mackellar, Bombay (1880)).

It was not only during famines that mass movements of women received attention. In epidemics similar observations were made – for instance in 1898 a 'plague exodus' of women from Calcutta was noted. There are few observations on movements of women in later years, for instance in the large influenza epidemics. We should recall that the ignorance of the condition of women was considerable. The immigration of women, rather than the arrival of men, gave the Health Officers cause for concern.

Epidemics and ill-health

Some health officers tried hard to understand the problem that they perceived.

There is a detailed report from the 1905 Sanitary Administration in the Punjab concerning the excessive female mortality from plague. This relates female daily activity to the illness. The first report notes the presence of large numbers of women in the sick room, observing that they do the nursing on an insufficient diet, handle soiled clothes, and then gather in even greater numbers when there is a death – 'sit the whole day on the ground inside the houses, generally badly ventilated and badly lighted, in which plague deaths have occurred'. The females fasted, while men stayed outside. Further, the report states that females usually 'do all the menial work of the house', not even letting sweepers inside. They made the fuel cakes from dung, and were more likely to handle infected grain as they did the threshing and grinding. Plague mortality had declined with each successive epidemic, so that 'it seems as if women are learning by bitter experience to take better care in protecting themselves against the infection, or perhaps they are becoming immune' (Section 20). This attempt to investigate the connections between female activities and health contrasts with other areas where high mortality was perceived.

A circumstance of women in India which was used both in favour of the arguments that women could not be helped and that they needed more and special care, was the *purdah*. *Purdahnishin* women were treated with alarm and awe by the almost exclusively male administration of India. (Lady health visitors were grudgingly added to the staff in the 1910s – municipal authorities at first did their best not to employ them.) For example, the Famine Code for Bombay (1897) states:

> Section 43. Respectable women who are debarred by national custom from appearing in public shall always be relieved in their own homes . . . Section 45 . . . spinning cotton is a work most suitable for women to do at their homes and one which is not repugnant to the feelings of any female. . . .

The other Codes had similar clauses.

However, there was an ignorance of the general condition of women. This was excused through equating 'women' with the *purdahnishin*. Non-*purdahnishin* were left to compete with men and were referred to as 'he' or as 'coolies'. These were the majority of women. There is some evidence that *purdah* was confused with the more common problem of poor women being trapped in very insanitary home conditions.[8] A Calcutta Health Officer, H. M. Crake, contrasted the twin reputations of Calcutta: as a Mecca for ill persons because of its fine medical services, but also as the 'Matricidal City'. He blamed the latter on *purdah*, writing:

> Surely the women of India have a right to demand the abolition of a custom which means premature death to so many of them? Intolerably bad as the housing conditions are in many of the slums of Calcutta, it is only when the inmates are constantly exposed to these insanitary conditions that they suffer so severely . . . males can escape during the day. (Health Officer's Report, 1914, p. 56)

In the early part of the century, having failed to come up with any specific theory of health care, the issue of high female mortality became overshadowed by the more visible problem of infant mortality. The dangers of childbirth and childbearing were a factor in high female mortality of course. Undoubtedly, improvements in infant care were not misplaced, but since the death rate of females was not greatest where infant mortality was highest, this was not tackling the problem of *general female ill health*.

So far I have indicated the perceptions of female health held by the health authorities. They thought, often, that women were normally more ill than men. Their reports record fear of migrant women during famines and scarcity, because such women brought disease (this was despite the contradictory stated belief that women labourers were healthier than rich women). Confinement to the home, work in the factory, biology, or ignorance were all blamed for the morbidity of women. Finally, the perception of women as reproducers rather than producers reinforced efforts to concentrate on childbearing as being to blame. I shall now turn to the basic question of whether women benefited equally with men from the health care facilities.

Benefits from health care

One may consider the absolute mortality (the numbers of deaths) to reflect variations of needs. Because different age and sex groups will make different use of medical care one would expect the treatments per head of population to be different for each group. By taking patient treatments per death, a measure can be made of whether a person is likely to receive care relative to need.

Where available, this ratio has been worked out and the results for adults are graphically represented in Figures 7.1.1 to 7.1.7. It is clear that patient care per death increased considerably in every case. The ratio shows the smallest change for children.

The excess of the male ratio over the female was greatest for Bengal adults and children, and least for Madras, again for both adults and children. The relative gap has not decreased as much as it appears because, as noted above, maternity services have been the major area of increase in health care services in this century. Thus, while cases of normal or abnormal labour made up 5 per cent of inpatients in 1900 (in British India), these rose to 20 per cent by 1935. Excluding these cases, one finds, for instance in the major hospitals in Bombay, that the female ratio is still lower than the male (Kynch and Sen, 1983), but declining substantially. Provision of hospital beds has also favoured the males. (These include railway, police and private non-aided hospitals and dispensaries.)

In terms of treatments per patient, the number remained remark-ably constant – in each region female children were highest at about 2.5 to 3, male children came next, then adult females, and adult males lowest at about 2.

In conclusion, this description has looked at two aspects of official response to women's well-being. Changes in the relief offered during famines and scarcities favoured a woman's increased dependency and a loss of ability to maintain herself through wage employment. A second kind of ability – to procure health care – improved consider-ably, but the perception of health in women, and a fear of their innate sickliness affected the supply side of health care. Moreover, the disparity in care between males and females and especially between male and female children, has persisted to the present time. Recent data (see Isely (1981); Miller (1981); Padmanabha (1981); Dyson and Moore (1983); Kynch and Sen (1983); Sen and Sengupta (1983); Mukhopadhyay (1984); Kynch (1985); Jeffery, Jeffery and Lyon (this volume)), provide evidence that there remain very serious forms of bias against the female from the cradle. These affect the ability of women to achieve well-being equivalent to that of men.

Figure 7.1   Ratio of adult patients treated per death

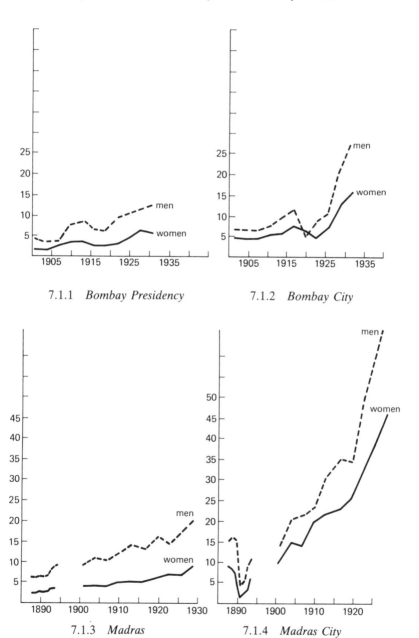

7.1.1   *Bombay Presidency*

7.1.2   *Bombay City*

7.1.3   *Madras*

7.1.4   *Madras City*

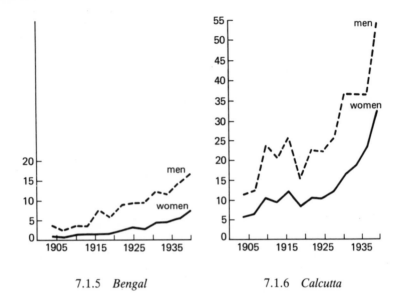

7.1.5 *Bengal*   7.1.6 *Calcutta*

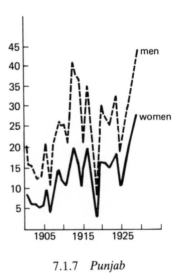

7.1.7 *Punjab*

Sources: Annual Reports and Triennial Reports on hospitals and dispensaries; Sanitary Commissioners Reports.

Notes

1. The author is most grateful to the Leverhulme Trust and the Institute of Economics and Statistics at Oxford which have supported Amartya Sen's project on sex bias in India from which this is a historical offshoot. Development Studies Association women's study group, Amartya Sen, Patricia and Roger Jeffery, and Mike Maguire have made helpful comments.
2. The period forms a part of that on which McAlpin (1985) has produced demographic data, including the relative importance of hunger and illness in mortality.
3. This pattern became established after the turn of the century in Bengal and Punjab, and dominated from 1900–20, especially in Bombay. The pattern in Bombay city was similar, with male advantage concentrated from 1890–1 to 1899–1900 (perhaps because of the policy of the city – see 'Bombay 1877–85: migrant women'). In Calcutta, however, despite the massive differences between the male and female rates (in one ward of the city in the late 1920s, one-eighth of the females, but only one-twentieth of the males, were recorded deceased), the advantage actually swung from the male *towards* the female during the fifty year period.
4. See Sen (1984) and McAlpin (1985).
5. For example in Bijapur, and Sholapur, Bombay 1897 (James, 1897).
6. It is of no concern here exactly how 'subsistence' was defined, nor the relation between work and requirements. (For this difficult problem see Bliss and Stern (1978); FAO/WHO (1973); Garrow and Blaza (1982); and Satyanarayana *et al.* (1978)). As far as famine relief was concerned, estimates of food requirements were made from convicted persons in jail, or reports from district officers – see for example Punjab Famine Report 1878–9, vol. I, p. 212; Cornish (1863) and Lewis (1880). Confidence in these empirical data was not great. In practice, people voted with their feet. For example in Punjab in 1878–9, the West Jumna Canal 'did not succeed in attracting famine labour, because the starving people knew they would not be employed unless they could do a full days work and this was to them obviously impossible' (Punjab Famine Report 1878–9, p. 809). Again, in Bombay, 'In Nasik, Ahmednagar and Poona districts it was noticed in December 1899 that large numbers of people were earning less than 4 annas in a week. . . . The registers showed that when gangs began with fair earnings they continued to do well, but if they began badly, their weekly wages became gradually less until some left the works, while others remained in a very reduced condition' (Report on Famine in Bombay, 1899–1902, vol. I).
7. The proportion of women and children does not seem to affect the average wage paid. An attempt to explain the average wage paid on six relief works over eleven months by the proportion of women, or the proportion of women plus children, produced non-significance. The price of rice proved a good predictor.
8. See for example Pemberton (1946) and Spring Rice (1939, Appendix 2) on women in slums in British cities in the 1930s.

References and Sources

Barker, Surgeon Major J. F., and G. J. Nicholls (1878), *Answers to Questions of the Famine Commissioners prepared for the Central Provinces* (Naipur)

Bhatia, B. M. (1963), *Famines in India 1850–1945* (London: Asia Publishing House)

Bliss, C. J., and N. H. Stern (1978), 'Economic Aspects of the Connection Between Productivity and Consumption', *Journal of Development Economics*, 5, pp. 331–98

Cornish, W. R. (1863), *Reports on the Nature of the Food of the Inhabitants of Madras Presidency, and on the Dietaries of Prisoners in Zillah Jails* (Madras: United Scottish Press)

Dyson, T. and M. Moore (1983), 'Kinship structure, female autonomy, and demographic behaviour in India', *Population and Development Review*, vol. 9, no. 1, pp. 35-60.

FAO/WHO (1973), *Energy and Protein Requirements* (Rome: FAO)

Garrow, J. and S. Blaza (1982), 'Energy requirements in human beings', in Neuberger, A. and T. H. Juke (eds), *Human Nutrition: Current Issues and Controversies* (M. T. P. Press United)

Geddes, J. C. (1874), *Administrative Experience recorded in Former Famines: Extracts from Official Papers containing Instructions for Dealing with Famine* (Calcutta: The Bengal Secretariat Press)

Ghosh, K. C. (1944), *Famines in Bengal 1770–1943* (Calcutta: Indian Associated Publishing Co., Ltd)

Iseley, B. (1981), 'Social Correlates of Sex Differences in Mortality in a Small Area of South India'; Ph.D. Thesis, University of Oregon (microfilm)

James, H. E. M. (1897) *Notes on Tour* (Central Executive Committee, Indian Famine Relief Fund, Office of the Superintendent, Government Printing, India)

Jeffery, R. (1984), 'Sexual differences in child mortality in North India', University of Edinburgh, mimeo

Kynch, J. and A. K. Sen (1983), 'Indian Women: Well-Being and Survival', *Cambridge Journal of Economics*, 7, p. 314

Kynch, J. (1985), 'How many women are enough? Sex ratios and the right to life', in *Third World Affairs 1985* (London: Third World Foundation)

Lewis, Surgeon Major T. R. (1880), 'A Memorandum on the dietaries of labouring prisoners in Indian Jails', Appendix A in *Report of the Sanitary Commissioner for Madras* (Madras: Fort St. George Gazette Press)

McAlpin, M. B. (1985), 'Famines, Epidemics and Population Growth: The case of India', in R. I. Rotberg and T. K. Rabb, *Hunger and History* (Cambridge University Press)

Miller, B. (1981), *The Endangered Sex: Neglect of Female Children in Rural North India* (Ithaca, N.Y.: Cornell U.P.)

Mukhopadhyay, M. (1984), *Silver Shackles* (Oxfam)

Padmanabha, P. (1981), *Survey on Infant and Child Mortality 1979* (New Delhi: Office of the Registrar General)

Pemberton, J. (1946), 'On the Difficulty of Isolating the Nutritional Factor in Disease from other Factors in the Social Background', *Proceedings of the Nutrition Society,* vol. 5, nos. 1 and 2.

Satyanarayana, K., A. N. Naidu and B. S. Narasinga Rao, (1978), 'Nutrition, Work Capacity and Output', *Indian Journal of Medical Research,* 68, pp. 88–93 (Supp.).

Sen, A. K. (1981), *Poverty and Famines* (Oxford: Clarendon Press)

Sen, A. K. (1982), Family and Food: Sex Bias in Poverty', forthcoming in P. Bardhan and T. N. Srinivasan (eds), *Rural Poverty in South Asia* (Columbia University Press)

Sen, A. K. (1984), 'Development: Which Way Now?', Presidential Address, Development Studies Association, September 1982, in *Resources, Values and Development* (Oxford: Basil Blackwell)

Sen, A. and S. Sengupta (1983), 'Malnutrition of Rural Indian Children and the Sex Bias', *Economic and Political Weekly,* 18, Annual Number

Spring Rice, M. (1939), *Working Class Wives: Their Health and Condition* (Harmondsworth: Penguin)

8 Contaminating States: Midwifery, Childbearing and the State in Rural North India[1]

Patricia Jeffery, Roger Jeffery and Andrew Lyon

INTRODUCTION

Childbearing can only be fully understood within the specific social and economic context in which it occurs. In rural India, the pregnant woman and the newly-delivered mother are simultaneously workers and the bearers of the next generation of workers.[2] The high levels of maternal and infant mortality current in North India result in part from the high price paid by Indian village women, as the day-to-day requirements for their labour power often run counter to longer-term considerations for their own, or their babies', health. Moreover, piecemeal maternal and child health programmes will founder if they are based on an inadequate understanding of women's position in society and local evaluations of it.

Most international health agencies now take the view that traditional birth attendants (TBAs) are a valuable medical resource, socially close to their clients, and an important source of assistance towards the goal of 'Health For All by the Year 2000'.[3] Indian mortality statistics certainly indicate that there is plenty of room for improvement in maternal and child health: in rural Uttar Pradesh, for instance, the mortality rate for women in the childbearing years was 4–5 times that for men during the 1970s and neonatal mortality was fairly stable at over 90 deaths in the first month of life for every 1000 live births.[4] Such considerations have recently led the Indian Government to opt for the training of TBAs.[5] But childbirth and women's relationships to the State are not such that a single style of State intervention will have universal benefits in maternal and child health.[6] We address this issue here by considering the role of the *dai*

152

(traditional birth attendant) in rural North India, and State-sponsored attempts to raise the standards of midwifery through *dai* training schemes. We consider that such programmes are unlikely to be successful there, for three main reasons. First, North Indian birth attendants work in a context in which the physiological processes entailed in childbirth are associated with degrading views of midwifery. Secondly, the acceptability of trained midwives is limited because of their connection with a State whose legitimacy was seriously undermined by the sterilisation programme (especially as experienced during the Emergency of 1975–7). Finally, directed attempts to improve maternal and child health in India may well be counteracted by the effects of secular changes on women.

This paper arises from our fieldwork in Bijnor District, Uttar Pradesh, in 1982–3. We were based in two adjacent villages (one totally Hindu and one Muslim) for over a year. The material used here comes from our intensive study of 41 women who were pregnant or had recently given birth when the research began, and our survey of 301 new mothers in 11 randomly selected villages in Bijnor District. We interviewed the *dais* (TBAs) mentioned by these women (25 in all), covering such topics as their career histories, obstetric practices and other types of expertise. This material was supplemented through discussions with the *dais'* clients (especially those in the base villages) about their views of *dais*, the management of childbirth, contacts with the *dai* at times other than delivery, and so forth. In addition, several births were attended in the base villages. Our research was initially hampered by our informants' fears that we were sterilisation workers. Gradually, their anxieties receded and we were, instead, regaled with memories of the Emergency, on which we have also drawn.

MIDWIFERY AND CHILDBIRTH IN NORTH INDIA

Childbearing in human society is socially organised and, consequently, interrelated with wider aspects of gender relationships and social organisation in general. Different societies are likely to be associated with distinctive medical systems, in which midwifery and the TBA have characteristic places. In India, 'elite medicine' (*Ayurvedic* and *Unani* medicine) is highly sophisticated, but the classical texts pay little attention to obstetric and gynaecological issues.[7] 'High-culture' medical practitioners are all male, and local medical arrangements for women are rarely well-developed. Women's access to medical services is generally less than that of their menfolk, because they have limited mobility in public, restricted access to funds, and their complaints may be considered inappropriate to take to male practitioners, especially if they pertain to 'embarrassing matters' (*sharm ki baat*) such as menstruation and childbirth. This must be appreciated when trying to understand the role of the TBA in North India.

In what follows, we focus on local understandings of childbirth and the *dai*'s role in Bijnor District, Uttar Pradesh. We want to show that the role of village *dais* in Bijnor is virtually limited to the removal of childbirth pollution; and *dais* themselves are in a structurally poor position to remedy this. The *dais* we interviewed can be divided into three groups: the village, *desi* or *gaon-ki-dai* (who were 19 of the 25); five 'intelligent' or *hoshiyar dai*; and one woman probably better described as an apprentice medical practitioner. Here we shall concentrate on the *desi dai*. Of these, 11 are Muslim, and 8 are *Harijan* (Untouchable), normally *Chamar*. They are illiterate and very poor; most are widows aged forty-five or over.

First, we want to highlight the *dai*'s role in the management of pregnancy and childbirth. There is rarely any contact between a pregnant woman and a *dai* before the delivery. Many of our informants said that their *dai* would not even have known of their pregnancy, while *dais* say that few women seek their advice. Women normally give birth in their husband's family home, which seems unusual in North India and possibly has some implications for maternal and child health.[8] Once in labour, a woman is generally surrounded by women from closely related households. She will probably be attended by a *dai*, usually untrained, but she may be in labour for some hours before the *dai* is summoned. Generally, her mother-in-law determines which *dai* to call and when.

Once the *dai* arrives, it is evident that she is not considered an expert whose advice should be taken without question. The *dai* usually squats on the foot of the bed and offers her opinion; some *dais* also perform internal examinations to assess cervical dilation, but none possesses special equipment to aid or monitor the delivery. Indeed, rather than the *dai* alone, the labouring woman's female affinal kin – especially the mother-in-law and other elderly women – pass judgement on the management of the labour. If progress seems slow, they may suggest remedies – all well known to the women present – to 'heat up' (accelerate) the woman's contractions. These include giving her warm milk with almonds or tea with semi-refined sugar ('hot' items to counteract the 'cooling' of the contractions); opening locks on grain stores and loosening the woman's plait; circling a sieve containing wheat and one and a quarter rupees round her head and placing it under the bed head; and changing the woman's position from lying on her bed to squatting on a pair of bricks. Some women these days are given labour accelerating injections of oxytocic drugs administered by private or Government-employed male medical practitioners.[9] Here again, the decision to give an injection does not rest with the *dai* alone. She does not possess the wherewithal to give injections and, while she may suggest an injection, her advice is rarely accepted readily and immediately. The issue is debated (often lengthily) and the practitioner who gives the injection is fetched only once the women present agree. Since the *dai* remains at her post, the timing of an injection is not under her control.

Shame and pollution are dominant features of childbirth in rural Bijnor. Shame (*sharm*) means that a woman should deliver in silence, to avoid attracting attention; she gives birth fully clothed, usually lying under a quilt on an old string bed, in the dim light of her hut. The new mother is considered impure (*a-sudh* or *na-paak*) until she has taken a purifying bath some days after delivery. The baby also causes feelings of disgust until it has been properly cleaned. Cutting the umbilical cord, burying the placenta and washing clothing and rags soiled (made *ganda*) by the mother and the baby are regarded as *ganda kaam* (dirty work), in which the *dai* plays a central role.

Once the baby is born, the *dai* delivers the placenta, massaging the woman's abdomen or pulling from inside if this is at all delayed. Then the *dai* places rags against the woman's vulva which she presses in with her heel; she has no means of stitching a woman who tears during delivery and does not examine a woman after giving birth. Then she cuts and ties the umbilical cord using instruments and thread provided by her client's household. She usually applies some medication which they also provide. Next she moulds the baby's nose, 'opens' its throat and anus by inserting her finger, and clears up the placenta, the baby's faeces, and the blood spilt during delivery. The mud floor is chipped or scraped clean, and the placenta is buried in the hut or in the dung pit. The *dai* repairs the floor with new mud, and bathes the baby either immediately or sometime later, depending on the time of delivery.

Childbirth, then, is considered an extremely polluting occurrence.

Much of the pollution is dealt with by the *dai*, whose position is analogous to the *Bhangan* or Sweeper, who removes night soil and is permanently degraded by the work. Indeed, some of the Harijan *dais* are also Sweepers. Performing the 'dirty work' associated with childbirth contaminates the *dai*, and our Hindu informants in particular consider that the new mother should not be touched by the *dai* after the purifying bath, for fear of becoming polluted again. Generally, the *dai* and her client are unlikely to be in contact apart from the delivery and shortly afterwards. The exceptions are *Chamar* (Untouchable) women who are closely related to their *dai*. The management of the labour is not demonstrably in the hands of the *dai* and she is not seen as an expert. Indeed, the obscenities directed at a *dai* when she makes what are considered outrageous demands for payments, and the arguments about how much to pay her (which were observed after all the deliveries attended) suggest that the *dai* is viewed as an inferior menial by her clients – and not as an expert, superior both in knowledge and social status.

Why, then, do *dais* do this work? Only about half of the *dais* reported 'training' received by accompanying a female relative (usually their mother or mother-in-law). Several were drawn into midwifery somewhat by chance, or even against their will. There is certainly a rhetoric that the work is undesirable. But *dais* say that they lack marketable skills and that employment opportunities are scarce. Several do have other sources of income – the *dai* for the village where we lived is a goatherd, and others cut fodder, weave baskets or work as Sweepers – but none of these provides a comfortable living. They say that they deliver babies *majboori main* – out of necessity – and that they can hardly think too badly of work which keeps them alive.

Most village *dais* took up the work after a domestic crisis (generally the death or serious illness of their husband or marital breakdown). Many reported considerable pressure from kin not to do the work. Two women (one a Muslim *Nai* or Barber) said that their own brothers began to refuse to eat food they had cooked. Several *dais* had been prevented from doing midwifery by their husbands, but they had to take it up when they were widowed. If a *dai*'s sons try to stop her, she tells them they should support her properly instead, as she is only working to 'fill her stomach'. Most *dais* say they deliver babies wherever they are called, though a small number of Muslim *dais* deny that they deal with the birth pollution of Untouchables. The veracity of these statements is less significant than the rhetoric

employed, which reflects the ethos of shame which permeates midwifery.

Village *dais* say they generally carry out two or three deliveries a
month. Incomes from midwifery are impossible to estimate accu-
rately, since there is no fixed fee. The *dai* gets nothing if the baby is
stillborn, or is delivered in hospital. Otherwise, fees are negotiated
according to the wealth of the family and the 'happiness' caused by
the birth. Most *dais* say they are paid more for a boy than for a girl
and more for a first delivery than for later ones. Payments rarely
exceed Rs 25 for a boy's birth. Generally, the *dai* also receives one or
two kilos of grain (usually wheat, with a market price of about Rs
2.50 a kilo) and occasionally some cloth (usually old clothing, very
rarely some new cotton for a sari). Several *dais* say that poor clients
often fail to pay them anything. Only delivering the first son of a
wealthy landowning family could provide the *dai* with a surplus to see
her through until she delivers another baby. Unfortunately for the
dais, these are precisely the customers who are beginning to look to
the towns for clinic deliveries.

In other words, midwifery provides an income for desperately poor
women – often quite elderly widows – with few marketable skills. The
work is seen as undesirable and dirty and is generally not eagerly
taken up.

The routine involvement of medical practitioners in ante-natal and
obstetric care is considered unnecessary. None the less, childbirth is
considered a potentially life-threatening event: a woman may haem-
orrhage, the labour may be obstructed, or the baby might die *in
utero*. The *dais* themselves are painfully aware of their own limitations. They say they can deal only with normal deliveries. When
asked about maternal or infant deaths, they give a stock response, 'I
have never lost a mother or a baby'; but we soon discovered that they
withdraw from cases they consider beyond their capacity. A *dai*
might be *present*, then, at a death for which she bears no *responsibility*. One woman reported that she had four *dais* present when she
gave birth: the first three had refused to deal with her, but stayed on
to watch. Generally *dais* say that difficult cases should be taken to a
hospital or health centre. Thus, a vital part of the *dai*'s diagnostic skill
is the ability to assess bad risks, which they basically do by external
and internal examinations to assess whether the presentation is
normal, the baby's head is engaging on the cervix and cervical
dilation is proceeding efficiently. They have no instruments to assess
the baby's condition, but if the mother's abdomen becomes 'cold'

during labour they take this as a sign that the baby has died *in utero*. Village *dais* are preoccupied with avoiding dangerous cases, for they have their reputations, their incomes – and maybe even their lives – to protect.

Most village *dais* play little part in more general gynaecological work. None admits to knowledge of medicines to treat infertility, to prevent miscarriages, or for *seh palat* (creating a boy in *utero*). They all deny performing abortions.[10] Clearly, *dais* might wish to conceal their practices (perhaps particularly abortions), and they might be secretive about medicines they prescribe. We feel justified in asserting this limited role of the village *dai* only when we juxtapose their denials with comments from village women, who probably have less reason to conceal the *dais*' activities. Our informants deny that village *dais* have any expertise beyond delivering babies, they say they do not consult *dais* for their complaints – they go instead to male practitioners or else have no treatment at all – and, further, few village *dais* are reputed to perform abortions.

We should briefly note that five of the *dais* we interviewed did claim involvement in some treatment, although they often rely on male medical practitioners to provide the remedies which they administer. The most obviously differentiating characteristic of these 'intelligent' (*hoshiyar*) village *dais* is their greater wealth and self-assurance. Two Muslim women, for instance, both with living husbands, say that several women in their families worked as *dais* and taught them the work; they consider that midwifery should be highly regarded among Muslims, because the Prophet treated his mother's midwife so respectfully. Their clientele is spread through several nearby villages, and they claim higher rates of pay and more deliveries than the ordinary village *dais*. A sixth woman – a Sikh from Punjab and the only literate woman among them – is developing a medical practice with her husband. She provides a range of treatments, including labour-accelerating injections, post-natal tetanus injections, injections to prevent miscarriages and early abortions using pills or injections.

There are also urban 'intelligent' *dais*, usually in the larger towns, who hold clinics and have widespread reputations. We did not meet these women, but we have material from women in the base villages who had consulted them. These urban 'intelligent' *dais* seem to offer a wide range of remedies, for infertility, for women who have frequent miscarriages or a succession of daughters, or for those wanting abortions or contraceptive treatments. They are apparently the only *dais* locally who act as healers with a wide range of expertise, though we are unsure if their skills are diagnostic only or involve pharmacological knowledge too. However, these women have no base in a specific community, for their clients come from miles around for what are generally once-off consultations. Moreover, it is our impression that these *dais* are not (at least now) birth attendants.[11] They are unlikely to have much enthusiasm for the outreach entailed in health education work, given their already busy and lucrative practices.

These few exceptional *dais* should not, in any case, distract us from the salient characteristics of the ordinary *dais* who serve the villages we studied. Our data suggest that the typical North Indian *dai* is illiterate.[12] She therefore has little chance of access to 'elite' medical knowledge, though illiteracy *per se* need not reduce her ability to accumulate 'folk' knowledge, which may be quite complex and sophisticated. She may have had little midwifery instruction and there is no institutionalised means of collecting, sharing and preserving knowledge. *Dais* are relatively isolated from other practitioners because of their immobility (though they are less tied to domestic responsibilities than most other women) and they compete with their fellows, the younger *dais* waiting to poach the clients of elderly ones who fall sick or die. They tend to explain problems in childbirth or the post-partum period as the working of evil spirits, or 'God's will'. They are thus difficult to persuade to use modern methods, and unlikely to perceive the possibility of control over childbirth. In any case, a trained *dai* would face problems in implementing her training if opposed by the labouring woman's female affinal kin. The dynamics of recruitment are also significant, for villages *dais* distance themselves from their work, employ a rhetoric of involuntary recruitment brought about by poverty, have negative images of their work and generally come to it late (so training will not have long-term benefits). They would probably give the work up if they could. Their clients employ *dais* to remove pollution, do not see *dais* as repositories of knowledge and are resentful when *dais* patrol their village to drum up custom. For them, contact with *dais* should be limited. If the expert *dais* are respected and designated *hoshiyar* (intelligent) by their clients, the village *dais* are written off as mere *naal khatney-wali* (cord-cutters).

We have concentrated on the village *dais* at whom the training schemes have been directed because their characteristics provide some reasons why these schemes are unlikely to work. The village *dai* is socially distant from her clients – an inferior menial to be kept at arm's length, and not someone from whom villagers are likely to accept maternal and child health education or family planning advice. Local understandings of childbirth are only part of the story, however. In the next section we consider the uneasy relationship between the populace and Government personnel and the role of the State in providing maternal and child health services.

WOMEN'S HEALTH AND THE STATE

In India, there have been numerous legislative reforms apparently intended to produce profound changes in the position of women.[13] However, women have remained largely under the control of domestic authorities (males and elderly females) and subjected neither to the direct control nor the protection of the Indian State. Entrenched ideas and interests have rarely been seriously challenged and the direct impact of the State on women has, in practice, been slight.[14] One area which is no exception to this is maternal and child health.

Before 1947, several Viceroys' wives (sometimes in collaboration with Missionary Societies), rather than the State, seemed to feel duty-bound to raise funds for medical programmes to ameliorate the position of women in India. But these early schemes were restricted in their impact. The limited numbers of female medical staff (doctors and also, by the 1920s, Health Visitors) who were trained hampered the expansion of medical facilities for women. Only relatively wealthy urban women could benefit from plans to enable female doctors to visit *parda-nashin* (secluded) women in their homes; while poor urban women could attend the general dispensaries, or the female dispensaries staffed by women, which began to be established in North India in the 1890s.[15]

For rural women, there were merely the attempts to train the *dais* or local midwives. *Dai* training schemes in India are an interesting case of bureaucratic amnesia. Efforts to improve the conditions in which women bear and rear children have been made for over a century and a common component has been the attempt to draw on traditional birth attendants or *dais*. The earliest example we have found from North India is a course held in Amritsar from 1866, still in operation in the early 1880s. Such schemes have been repeatedly re-invented since then.

Several points should be made about maternal and child health facilities in the rural areas. The scale of *dai* training ebbed and flowed and the impetus came from private funds raised by leading British women, not from the State apparatus, although the State helped with funding these schemes. Furthermore, the infrastructure of health services directed specifically at women – female dispensaries, in most District headquarter towns, and the female nurses working in clinics in other sizeable towns – strikingly demonstrate the urban bias of the provision. By 1947, then, there had been no concerted effort to improve the availability of medical services for rural women. Attempts to train *dais* were sporadic, urban-biased and had little noticeable impact on obstetric practice in most of the country.

After 1947, *dai* training courses were somewhat expanded and more Trained Dais were employed, some of whom are still working in rural sub-centres and clinics. The post 1947 expansion of medical provision for women, though, has largely depended on a new cadre of personnel – the Auxiliary Nurse Midwife or ANM, whose training was introduced after 1956, following proposals in the Second Plan (1956–61). Prospective ANMs are required to have at least eight years of schooling; they are, thus, mainly from urban literate backgrounds (often from Kerala in southern India). This in itself sets a barrier between them and their village clients. But the ANM, moreover, has always worked primarily as a motivator for contraception, in spite of a training schedule which covers basic medical care. Indeed, only the urgency provided by the perceived 'threat' of a rapidly growing population made the Government give ANM training any priority. This same urgency has all but deprived the ANM of the time or incentive to deal with more broadly-based maternal and child health work. The population programme, then, contrasts with many other aspects of overt State action, for it has a high profile with people at the 'grass-roots'.

Initially, family planning services were effectively restricted to urban clinics and the programme had little impact. The 1961 Census showed that the Indian population was growing much faster than had been believed.[16] In 1963 a review of the population programme led to a new emphasis on 'extension' – taking services to the clients by using ANMs based at Primary Health Centres, and employing mass education and propaganda techniques to increase knowledge of contraception and persuade people of the attractions of small families.[17] At first, the preferred contraception was the IUCD, first introduced in 1966–7 when 900 000 were inserted; but its side-effects soon detroyed its credibility with the populace.[18] After that, sterilisation (initially vasectomy) was favoured and 'incentives' were introduced for 'acceptors' and 'targets' for family planning workers. But the number of 'cases' declined during the late 1960s – probably (as Cassen argues) because the programme still only reached people near the hospitals and clinics where operations were performed.[19] Numbers only rose again, briefly, in the early 1970s with the introduction of 'mass camps' which created temporary operation facilities in the countryside. But popular resistance to sterilisation led to renewed emphasis on spacing children rather than on ending a couple's childbearing altogether.

However, the Emergency of 1975–7 brought a new attempt to reduce the birth rate.[20] It was, indeed, this facet of the Emergency which met with most widespread hostility. Sterilisation was again the favoured technique but there were some novel components in the programme: the wider range of official personnel given 'targets', the strong political support (especially from Sanjay Gandhi) for those who met or surpassed their targets, and the use of the police by some officials desperately attempting to meet them. People approaching Government personnel for whatever reason experienced efforts to 'motivate' them for sterilisation. 'Family limitation' achieved a salience for the mass of the Indian population, and the State was forcefully felt through State employees, who often depended on motivating enough 'cases' to be paid or promoted. In 1976–7, there were about eight million 'cases', over six million of them men.[21]

Our informants' views on the Emergency revolve around the intrusion of State agencies into 'private' matters, an intervention which is virtually unparalleled in India. Public debate was generated about issues which, until then, would rarely have been discussed even in private by married couples. Many of our informants are outraged by the shamelessness of the Delhi government. But a more significant recurrent theme for people in Bijnor is resentment at the State's audacious attempt to *compel* people to limit their families by *irreversible* means. Infant and child death is part of 'normal' existence in rural North India and this lies behind many people's objections to sterilisation. The household is the basic unit through which the elderly are cared for and labour power is recruited – and the need for at least one son to survive to adulthood is paramount. This was recognised somewhat, for the requirement to be sterilised was waived for couples with no sons. But we heard of couples (no doubt many apocryphal, but none the less important) who had been forcibly sterilised and whose sons or even all of whose children had subsequently died. For rural people, the disjunction between the State's population programme and the conditions in which they and their children live and die was all too painfully obvious during the Emergency.

After the 1977 elections, the new Janata Government pledged to return to voluntarism in family planning matters; proposals pending since 1975 were implemented, introducing Community Health Workers (CHWs) and expanding the *dai* training programme. The ANM is now to spend more time and effort on maternal and child health services, to recruit and help to train *dais* and to maintain a referral network with them for abnormal presentations and ante-natal care. But the population programme revived somewhat in 1978–9 and again in 1980 when Mrs Gandhi returned to power, though vasectomy was no longer the main method being offered: the present emphasis is on tubectomies and on IUCDs.[22]

The *dai* training scheme has almost reached its target of providing one *dai* for every 500 people. However, we doubt that it will have significantly reduced maternal and perinatal morbidity and mortality in much of North India. Only four of the *dais* we interviewed had taken Government training, all in the recent past. Two Hindu *dais* are employed as part-time helpers for the local ANM – and they say this reduces their income, since they attend fewer births now. Two others (both Muslims) are ambivalent about their training, saying they are being undercut by untrained *dais* who accept lower payments; but they do register pregnancies with their ANM, ostensibly so that tetanus injections can be given. Several other *dais* fear that training would make their clients view them as Government employees who no longer need to be paid. And, crucially, ANMs are still under great pressure to produce 'cases' for sterilisation. Most *dais* are wary of close involvement with the ANM, in case they are pressed to motivate 'cases' themselves: indeed, several had adamantly refused training, fearing that their clientele would decline.

An ANM visiting a village is assumed to have a 'case', because similar willingness to come for maternal or child health purposes is rare. Motivating 'cases' is believed to be the ANM's major concern and villagers are unwilling to avail themselves of her ante-natal care. The ANM for our base villages talks of 'all I have done for these villages' (tetanus injections or helping women needing admission to the Government hospital in Bijnor) 'but they haven't given me any cases'. From the other side, we have accusations that she visits daily before a 'case' goes to hospital, but shows no interest once the sterilisation has been performed. Indeed, villagers view maternal and child health services as mere sweeteners, which enable ANMs to pressurise people into being sterilised. Consequently, ANMs are rarely called to attend births. Trained *dais* do not replenish their delivery kits or consistently refer women for care, and the ANM cannot provide continuing training, or be sure that her lessons are being applied.[23]

Briefly, Indian villagers display a shrewd and not misplaced cynicism about the motives of Government health workers – exacerbated by the sterilisation drive during the Emergency – and they and the village *dais* maintain a distance from them. This, then, is a further reason why the recent *dai* training scheme is unlikely to ameliorate maternal and child health in rural north India.

MIDWIFERY IN A WIDER CONTEXT

Now we want to broaden our perspective, for changes in midwifery and maternal and child health provisions *alone* cannot, in any case, be a panacea for Indian women's obstetric ills (let alone all the others from which they suffer). Exclusive concentration on legislation or on other purposeful State action is not very enlightening: we must also consider the impact of the State through the secular changes which ensue from policies which are not overtly related to women. State programmes in all spheres, not just in health, can have an impact on maternity and infancy, by affecting gender relationships in society at large. Clearly, rural Indian women are virtually 'hidden from history' so anything we say must be very tentative. However, viewing midwifery in a wider context adds a further – and necessary – dimension to our assessment of *dai* training programmes.

Many writers have suggested that 'development' has differential effects on males and females.[24] Evidence, though, is often patchy; moreover, women in a stratified system are not uniformly affected by social change. None the less, many of our informants in Bijnor consider that the Green Revolution has fuelled both the escalation of dowry demands and the associated devaluation of daughters, especially among the relatively wealthy and the newly rich. Certainly, demographic records indicate a very marked gender differential in the improvements in life expectancy since 1901. Infant mortality rates for boys and girls in rural Uttar Pradesh have declined in this period, but female rates remained about 16 per cent higher than those for males throughout the 1970s. The adverse sex ratio in Bijnor has been steadily deteriorating to the 1981 level of 850 females per 1000 males.[25] These figures are not out of step with the general picture in North India.[26]

Our comments on the effects of secular changes on village *dais* must be even more circumspect. There is virtually no plausible historical material against which to set our own data. Official documents from the latter part of the nineteenth century onward portray *dais* as illiterate, usually middle-aged or old, with experience their only qualification, and predominantly drawn from Untouchable castes. British doctors were adamant that *dais* endangered their clients, because of their lack of intelligence, their dirty habits, and their incapability of learning new methods.[27] But we cannot legitimately generalise from comments such as these and we simply cannot know if village *dais* offered additional services, such as abortions, treatments for menstrual problems, or massage.

However, three possible scenarios can be outlined. One is that women's knowledge and referral systems elude male historical enquiry, yet an oral tradition can develop valuable skills and methods of initiating novices. Alternatively, some expertise would surely have survived, if it ever existed; but *dais* came from such disadvantaged castes, regarded midwifery as dirty, probably took it up unwillingly, and were thus incapable of effectively transmitting skills to new practitioners. However, in a hierarchical system, a more plausible view is that any category of workers is internally differentiated, which raises the question of how secular changes might affect this.

In Bijnor, women at the bottom of the economic hierarchy (perhaps especially those in female-headed households) seem to have been relatively pauperised by the Green Revolution, as various means of supplementing household incomes have become more unattainable. This might propel more women into midwifery, which may now be more dominated than before by women without links to family traditions of midwifery and with skills limited to cord-cutting. 'Intelligent' *dais* are probably not a new phenomenon, but they are now suffering competition from medical practitioners, usually male. Since 1947, increased rural wealth has created a market for medical services and there has been a dramatic influx of practitioners – private and Government employees, trained and untrained – who provide allopathic, *Ayurvedic* and *Unani* treatments.

Such developments may have brought some benefits, perhaps

especially in the mass programmes to control malaria and smallpox. But optimism needs to be tempered by an awareness of the implications of male-dominated systems of medicine for women. In the realm of childbearing alone, powerful labour-accelerating drugs – available on the open market and administered by men unable to examine their clients properly – will probably worsen the conditions of childbirth rather than enhance them.[28] Similarly, we cannot be sanguine about amniocentesis services to detect female foetuses and abort them.[29] 'Modern' medicine is not an unqualified good for women. Its impact is no less permeated by gender inequalities than are general processes of social change.

Midwifery must be socially located: the lowly village *dai* is symptomatic of other features of social organisation. To be successful, maternal and child health programmes would also require a dramatic shift in women's favour in the gender and age-based power relations typical of the Bijnor village household. This might (among other things) improve the access of women in their childbearing years to food and to health facilities, and re-orientate women's views of the physiological processes involved in childbirth. Put in these terms, the task is monumental.

If our interpretation is correct, though, secular changes are not clearly working to the relative benefit of women. Thus, ideas about childbirth pollution and midwifery are unlikely to be subjected to much challenge. Certainly, too, *dai* training schemes are undermined by people's lack of trust in the State, and by the State's own lack of commitment to their value in their own right, rather than as a carrot for population control programmes. But equally surely, trained *dais* cannot combat maternal and child health problems in the face of often countervailing trends, many of which, indeed, have been generated through Government action. In a different social context, of course, traditional birth attendants could be important agents in State attempts to improve maternal and child health. But we cannot be optimistic about the prospects in rural north India.

Notes

1. This paper is a revised and abridged version of our *Contaminating States: Childbearing, Midwifery and the State in Rural North India*, Indian Social

Institute Monograph Series, no.22 (New Delhi, 1985). The research reported here was funded by the Economic and Social Research Council, to whom we are grateful. Thanks to the generosity of the late Dr Alfred D'Souza we were Visiting Research Fellows at the Indian Social Institute, New Delhi, while we were in India. Kunwar Satya Vira and Dr K. K. Khanna were immensely helpful during our stay in Bijnor, and we should also like to thank our research assistants, Swaleha Begum, Radha Rani Sharma, and Savita Pandey. Many people have helped with comments on earlier versions of this paper: our particular thanks go to Haleh Afshar, Jocelyn Kynch and Carol Wolkowitz.

2. We do not restrict our understanding of 'work' to Census categories (which show very few of these women as workers) nor to views which belittle the considerable efforts expended by women. See further L. Beneria (ed.), *Women and Development: The sexual division of labour in rural societies* (London, 1982).

3. Declaration of the Alma-Ata Conference on Primary Health Care, September 1978 (Geneva: WHO, 1978); 'Traditional midwives and family planning' *Population Reports*, Series J, 22, May 1980; and *Health Sector Policy Paper* (New York: World Bank, 1980). See also S. Cosminsky, 'Cross-cultural perspectives on midwifery', in F. X. Grollig and H. B. Haley (eds), *Medical Anthropology* (The Hague: Mouton, 1976) pp. 229–49; D. N. Kakar, *Dais: the Traditional Birth Attendants in Village India* (Delhi: New Asia Publishers, 1980); G. Greer, *Sex and Destiny* (London: Secker & Warburg, 1984) pp. 15–19.

4. *Survey on Infant and Child Mortality 1979* (New Delhi: Office of the Registrar-General, 1983) p. 701; and *Sample Registration Scheme 1970–75* (New Delhi: Office of the Registrar-General, 1980).

5. See R. Jeffery, 'Medical policy-making: out of dependency?', in M. Gaborieau and A. Thorner (eds), *Asie du Sud* (Paris: Mouton, 1981); and R. Jeffery, 'New patterns in health aid to India', *Economic and Political Weekly*, 1982 (revised version in *International Journal of Health Services*, 15, 3, (1985)).

6. H. and B. Velimirovic 'The role of traditional birth attendants in health services', *Curare*, 1, 2 (1978) pp.85–96.

7. For more detail on this argument see our 'The Medicalisation of Female Illness in North India', given at the ixth European Conference on Modern South Asian Studies, Sweden, July 1983. For more general accounts see C. Leslie (ed.), *Asian Medical Systems* (Stanford: California University Press, 1976).

8. See our 'Childbirth and collaboration amongst women in Bijnor District, Uttar Pradesh', *Journal of Social Studies* (Dhaka) 1984; and 'When did you last see your mother? Aspects of female autonomy in rural North India' (forthcoming). Contrast this with H. Gideon, 'A baby is born in Punjab', *American Anthropologist*, 64 (1962) pp.1220–34.

9. We also interviewed twenty of these practitioners; most were men who had education to 10th grade and then worked in a hospital or for a private pharmacist for a few years before setting up in independent practice.

10. We attempted a number of indirect approaches to ask about abortions

(such as asking if the *dai* was ever asked to do abortions and if so how she responded) but we cannot be sure that alternative methods might not have produced different answers.

11. W. Crooke (ed.), *Islam in India* (Oxford University Press, 1921) p. 25.
12. A. Young, 'The relevance of traditional medical cultures to modern primary health care', *Social Science and Medicine*, 17, 16 (1983) pp. 1205–11.
13. See, for example, Jana Matson Everett, *Women and Social Change in India* (New Delhi: Heritage Publishers, 1981), Joseph Minattur, 'Women and the Law: Constitutional Rights and Continuing Inequalities', in Alfred de Souza (ed.), *Women in Contemporary India* (New Delhi: Manohar Book Service, 1975), Shyamala Pappu, 'Legal Provisions – An Assessment', in Devaki Jain (ed.), *Indian Women* (Publications Division, Ministry of Information and Broadcasting, Government of India, 1975).
14. *Status of Women in India* (*A Synopsis of the Report of the National Committee on the Status of Women*) (New Delhi: Indian Council of Social Science Research, 1975).
15. M. I. Balfour and R. Young, *The Work of Medical Women in India* (Oxford University Press, 1929).
16. R. Cassen, *India: Population, Economy, Society* (London: Macmillan, 1980) pp. 145–8.
17. D. Banerji, *Family Planning in India* (New Delhi: Progress, 1974).
18. Cassen, *India: Population, Economy, Society*, pp. 149–60.
19. Cassen, *India: Population, Economy, Society*, p. 161.
20. M. Vicziany, 'Coercion in a soft state', *Pacific Affairs*, 55, 3 (1982) pp. 373–402 and 56, 1 (1983).
21. *Family Welfare Programme in India Yearbook 1976–77*, (New Delhi: Ministry of Health and Family Welfare, 1977) pp. 82–3.
22. Vicziany, 'Coercion in a soft state'; D. R. Gwatkin, 'Political will and family planning', *Population and Development Review*, 5, 1 (1979) pp. 29–59; C. H. Brown, 'The forced sterilisation programme under the Indian Emergency', *Human Organisation* 43, 1 (1984) pp. 49–54.
23. H. S. Gandhi and R. Sapru, *Dais as Partners in Maternal Health* (mimeo; New Delhi: National Institute of Health and Family Welfare, 1980) gives supporting evidence from Meerut District, Uttar Pradesh.
24. For example, I. Ahmed (ed.), *Technology and Rural Women: Conceptual and Empirical Issues* (London: Allen & Unwin, 1985); L. Beneria (ed.), *Women and Development: the Sexual Division of Labour in Rural Societies* (New York: Praeger, 1982); E. Boserup, *Woman's Role in Economic Development* (London: Allen & Unwin, 1970); M. Mukhopadhyay, *Silver Shackles: Women and Development in India* (Oxford: Oxfam, 1984); B. Rogers, *The Domestication of Women* (London: Kogan Page, 1979); K. Young et al. (eds), *Of Marriage and the Market: Women's Subordination in International Perspective* (London: C.S.E. Books, 1981).
25. See above note 4; see also Census of India 1981, Series-22, Uttar Pradesh, Paper 1 (Provisional Population Totals) (Lucknow, 1981).

26. B. Miller, *The Endangered Sex* (Ithaca: Cornell University Press, 1981).
27. See, for example Balfour and Young, *The Work of Medical Women in India* and J. E. Mistry, 'My experience of the harm wrought by Indian Dais', extracted in V. Anstey, *The Economic Development of India* (London: Longman Green, 1936) pp. 489–91.
28. For an account from Britain see A. Cartwright, *The Dignity of Labour? A study of Childbearing and Induction* (London: Tavistock Publications, 1979).
29. R. Jeffery, P. M. Jeffery and A. Lyon, 'Female Infanticide and Amniocentesis', *Social Science and Medicine*, 1984.

Part III
Ideologies, Women and the Labour Market

9 Women and Handicraft Production in North India
Ann Weston

This chapter aims briefly to describe women's role in handicrafts production in North India and how (if at all) this has changed with the rapid expansion of production for the export market.[1] After an outline of the dimensions of the sector, it considers various hypotheses, found in the literature, about the contribution of handicrafts to women's development (and of women to the development of handicrafts). The focus here is on the effects of the changes in technology and the organisation of production, arising from the commercialisation of handicrafts, on the role of women. It concludes with some ideas on ways women might be more effectively involved in handicrafts production.

BACKGROUND

It may be helpful to begin with a few words about the importance of the handicrafts and handlooms sector to the Indian economy, measured by its contribution to employment and exports, the organisation of production and returns to artisans.

Employment

In 1979/80 roughly 2 million people were estimated to be employed producing handicrafts and another 6 million in handlooms, compared to 1.5 million and 5 million respectively in 1973/4. Further expansion over the next 5 years (to 1985) is expected to provide employment for an additional 1.5 million. The crafts with the largest work force are handprinting (500 000), gem cutting (400 000), carpets (255 000), art metalware (195 000) and woodware (110 000); these figures do not distinguish between those who are fully employed, part-time em-

173

ployed, and underemployed. Surveys of individual products show that underemployment is widespread – employment may fall at particular times of the year as a result of technical reasons (monsoon interfering with work), scarcities of raw material, and in response to fluctuations in demand (peaking domestically at Diwali and in the marriage season, and at Christmas abroad).

Exports

Exports of handicrafts and handlooms now account for about 20 per cent of India's total foreign exchange earnings – with handlooms earning Rs 3500 million and handicrafts Rs 8500 million in 1979/80 – compared to a mere 8 per cent in 1970/1. In other words, growth in handicrafts and handloom exports accounted for about a third of the growth in total exports during the 1970s. By far the largest craft items are gems and jewellery (Rs 6000 million), carpets (Rs 1550 million), art metalware (Rs 640 million), handprinted textiles (Rs 300 million) and woodware (Rs 180 million). Net earnings are somewhat lower, especially in the case of gems and jewellery, at least two-thirds of which is imported in the form of rough diamonds, while imports of wool, silk, brass scrap and chemical dyes are required for the other products, and all use inputs from the organised sector (for example, machine-spun yarn in handwoven cloth).

Handicrafts production is quite concentrated both regionally and within regions. According to one estimate, six northern States account for over 65 per cent of handicrafts exports (excluding gems and jewellery and handlooms) and 75 per cent of production: Uttar Pradesh (UP) – 40 per cent; Rajasthan – 10 per cent; Jammu and Kashmir, Delhi, Haryana and Punjab – around 5 per cent each. Within these States there are several major urban handicraft centres, for example, in UP, Moradabad for brassware, Bhadohi and Mirzapur for carpets; in Gujarat, Surat for diamond cutting; in Rajasthan, Jaipur for semi-precious stones and other items; in Haryana, Panipat for dhurries and household linen. Over 75 per cent of handloom fabric destined for export originates in the south, mainly in Tamil Nadu, and production for export is concentrated in certain centres. Reasons for such concentration include technological factors (some technology is inappropriate for rural production as it requires reliable electricity or water supplies), distribution costs, and managerial constraints.

Organisation of production

Broadly speaking, crafts may be produced in four ways – at one extreme, where low technology goods are being produced for the local market, is simple commodity production, typically involving family labour operating at home, with the goods being sold directly to the consumer without the mediation of a trader. At the other extreme is high volume production of goods for mass consumption in India or abroad, in a factory with extensive specialisation and all wage labour (though it is possible in the case of co-operatively run factories for workers to share in the profits). In between there is household production which may take one of two forms, both logical extensions of simple commodity production, and workshop production. The first type of household production includes wage labour but the original artisan family remains in control of the decisions about production and marketing. The other also involves some wage labour but under a putting-out system, that is, where an outside agent is responsible for supplying raw materials and marketing the end product. Where households specialise in different production processes, the system is said to resemble an invisible factory. Expansion of production in either case has often led to the actual location of production being shifted from the home to a nearby workshed.

Instances of simple commodity production are declining, and virtually non-existent in the case of exports, being more typical of khadi and village industries than handlooms and handicrafts. Factory production is also less common than one might have expected given the substantial increase in the value of production and exports of both handicrafts and handlooms. Of the four products studied in the ODI – IDS project, namely handlooms, handprinted textiles, handknotted carpets and art metalwork, factories are most prevalent in the carpet industry and in handlooms. But even here they probably account for no more than a fifth of the output. Two major deterrents are the fear of organised labour and the costs of complying with factory legislation. Another reason sometimes put forward is that the uniqueness of each artisan's work may disappear if they work *en masse* – this is belied by the preference of many importers for large volumes of identical output. A common way of bypassing the legislation is for the manufacturer to hire out parts of his factory to subcontractors or mastercraftsmen, who are in charge of up to nine workers. This happens in several instances – for example, handprinting (IDS, 1983/3), handloom weaving (IDS, 1983/1), carpet finishing (IDS,

1983/2) and also in garments (Kalpagam, 1981). Workers are still accessible to trade union activities however, and for this reason (amongst others) several factories have been disbanded and production reverted to the small household workshop on a putting-out basis. Thus, while the size of the average handicraft unit has grown slightly in terms of the number of workers, the major change in the last decade has been in the proliferation of the number of units.

Conditions of artisans

Most studies have found that artisans earn low hourly wages, and that the hours worked fluctuated throughout the year, and from one year to the next, according to the demand for the handicrafts. In many cases they are unable to maintain their family income above poverty level, having small sources of secondary income (see, for example, Aziz, 1980; GIDS 1975, 1980; SEWA 1980; Taimni 1979). Low incomes may partly reflect low productivity, and surplus labour capacity (for example, in gem-cutting, where there was rapid entry in response to the growth of exports). There is also evidence that market imperfections exist, especially under outworking, and have kept wages depressed. These include artisans' incomplete knowledge of the value of their work, their limited freedom to sell their work to different buyers (having accepted inputs and credit from a particular merchant or subcontractor), and connected with this their limited ability to refuse arbitrary reductions from their wages on the grounds that their craftsmanship is substandard. On the other hand, in many handicraft centres it is usual for rates to rise in seasons of peak demand, especially when manufacturers/exporters are trying to meet importers' deadlines, and at harvest time.

Wage rates are usually higher than in alternative agricultural or informal activities, and above the national minimum daily wage (though considerably below the level of earnings in the organised sector). For some crafts, notably carpet weaving, which have experienced a steady growth in demand, there appears to have been an improvement in real wages. In the Bhadohi–Mirzapur carpet belt, artisans have been able to buy a few consumer durables (radios, bicycles) and to improve their houses. Some have managed to accumulate savings which they have invested in land, or they have bought raw materials and become small manufacturers subcontracting work to other artisans, or running their own units. According to several studies, however, most new units have been set up by people from outside the artisan community; what is more common is that artisans move up the skill hierarchy to the position of mastercraftsmen.

HYPOTHESES ABOUT HANDICRAFTS

The promotion of handicrafts as providing opportunities for low-cost employment in rural areas, either on a part-time basis, or full-time, compatible with agricultural or other activities, has been advocated since the 1950s (Minkes, 1952/3; and Herman 1955/6). The realisation that there was a potentially vast market for these goods in high income countries (confirmed by the the findings of Little, 1974; and Ho and Huddle, 1976) led the Indian Government and others to view the promotion of handicrafts as an effective way of simultaneously solving problems of rural unemployment (or underemployment) and foreign exchange shortages. Some problems were recognised, such as access to raw materials and designs, and the need to raise productivity in some cases by improving the technology, but it was felt that these could be overcome with (limited) Government support, while the intervention of middlemen could be avoided with the formation of co-operatives. In general it was assumed that craft production was cottage-based (whether independent or as part of a putting-out system) and therefore particularly important for women:

> Promoted by governments or public agencies and combined with appropriate facilities and training, handicrafts and rural industries represent the best method of providing gainful employment for women without disturbing the existing pattern of society. (Dhamija, 1975, p. 465)

Similarly, Littlefield (1979, p. 481) suggests that the reason why many important Mexican crafts depend heavily on female labour is that they can be combined according to their own needs with childcare and household work. Finally, a recent ILO publication on cottage industries and handicrafts (Allal and Chuta, 1982, p. 14) states that

> The role of women in the very small enterprise sector constitutes an additional factor in favour of the promotion of this sector . . . On the basis of the available evidence it would seem that women make an important contribution to the development of the very small enterprise sector. It therefore follows that projects for the

promotion of small production units should be designed to enhance remunerative employment for women in the sector.

There is a growing body of opinion, however, which considers handicrafts production to be a low priority as it is poorly paid – particularly so in the case of domestic handicrafts production. Rodgers (1981, pp. 95–7) blames the inherent low productivity of handicrafts: 'the effect for most women may be to drag them into low productivity jobs rather than to help them find more productive and remunerative employment'.

Others have suggested that the problem is not so much low productivity as the tendency of women to undervalue the labour they expend in the home on non-domestic activities. It is generally maintained that women artisans are exploited by handicrafts buyers (whether they be exporters, manufacturers, middlemen or merchants) who take advantage of women's inability to judge the value of their labours – and reinforce this inability in several ways, for example, by introducing an extreme division of labour into the production system (making it difficult to compare the value of an individual component or process with the value of the final product), fixing rates amongst themselves for particular processes/items, and sabotaging efforts by women to market their goods independently or to set up co-operatives. Dhamija herself by 1981 (p. 15) wrote that

> It is necessary to exercise caution when developing the field of handicrafts. It can be a means of providing a viable income, but it can also be a means of exploitation, serving only to increase the burdens women already shoulder and cutting them off from opportunities to improve their economic and social position.

Mies' work on the lacemakers of Narsapur (1980) and work by the Giri Institute of Development Studies (1975) on *chikan* workers of Lucknow, amongst others, give strong support to this hypothesis, specifically in the case of women. What has happened in lacemaking is that the expansion of production has led to an increased sexual division of labour, with men taking over the entrepreneurial functions. At the top end of the production chain in Andhra Pradesh are about 80 manufacturers/exporters (of which only 15–20 are large) compared with about 30 (6 large) in 1970. They advance supplies of cotton thread (and even wages) to the thousands of women crotchet-makers (200 000 or so in Narsapur alone) via an extensive network of agents. The most notable feature of lacemaking has been the phenomenal increase in the number of these agents – as Mies points out (1980, p. 47), 'there has been a virtual mushrooming of agents, sub-agents, sub-sub-agents, etc. According to one exporter the number of agents could be estimated to be 16 000 to 18 000 in 1978'. While some of the increase may have been necessary to mobilise the volume of goods required for the rapidly growing export market, the question must be asked whether it was excessive – certainly Mies found that it was associated with a drop in artisans' earnings. Another notable feature is the enforced specialisation of production, even though lacemaking involves relatively few processes: the making of simple patterns, which are then joined into flowers, and finally the flowers are sewn together to form a particular item. Instead of producing a complete item, each woman (sometimes each village) specialises in a particular pattern or flower, leaving the final assembly to a few women usually based in the houses of manufacturers/exporters. According to Mies this extensive horizontal and vertical division of labour serves three functions. First, it minimises labour costs by increasing productivity. Second, by dividing up the work process and restricting knowledge about assembly of the final product it atomises labour which also helps to keep labour costs low. Thirdly, the restriction of such knowledge to only a few trusted workers also restricts copying by competing manufacturers/exporters.

In a few instances some women with the finishing skills have attempted to sell their products themselves. But they have been threatened by agents and blacklisted by exporters. Similarly, attempts to organise the women, for example by setting up a co-operative, have been frustrated by the local bureaucracy under pressure from exporters. For example, access to raw materials is a problem as the local market is supplied by only 3 yarn stockists, all of whom have become large exporters.

The GIDS study of 200 *chikan* (embroidery) workers also concluded that the very low earnings of women embroiderers (who accounted for 95 per cent of the work force) was attributable to the several layers of intermediaries. The few women who were self-employed earned considerably more than the majority who worked on pretailored cloth supplied by wholesale merchants, while those who worked for contractors earned the least. In both the latter cases wages were also found to be unreliable, as the merchants or contractors made arbitrary deductions from the payments due, on grounds of poor workmanship. While their low incomes partly arose from low wage rates, it was also due to low levels of employment – on average only 107 hours were worked per month, though most women wanted to work longer. But apparently few women wanted to become self-employed because of problems in obtaining the necessary minimum working capital (estimated at Rs 5 000) and the added responsibilities of obtaining work. The Government has subsequently set up a production centre, but it has been unable to offer full-time employment to all the *chikan* workers in the area.

The third hypothesis about handicrafts production and women is that the expansion of production has displaced many women artisans, or at least not provided employment opportunities for as many women as might have been expected. A report by the ICU (1973) based on over 150 surveys of various crafts in different regions of India, which were carried out by the All India Handicraft Board in the 1960s (and a few in the 1970s) found that even before the rapid expansion in production for export of the 1970s, 'the handicrafts industries provide only subsidiary occupation to the women in most cases and only a very few women artisans are whole time workers' (p. iii). Women were predominantly employed in crafts which were tribal, household-based, and not commercialised. In crafts which were commercialised, men did the more 'crucial' (sic) jobs while women worked only in 'ancillary' jobs, and as a result there were large differentials between male and female wages. But there was a large regional variation – for instance, in the case of embroidery, only 8 per cent of artisans in Jammu and Kashmir were women, compared with 100 per cent in Kerala. But the report concluded that the degree of commercialisation was the key explanatory variable, though the reasons for this were not clear:

> In regions where a craft is developed more in a commercial way and has large market demand, the percentage of women in the craft and their nature of work participation is much inferior to that in the regions where the craft is still in an undeveloped stage. How much of this is due to the different problems of female labourers in the organised sector, e.g. the pattern of their time disposition etc., and how much due to their discouragement in the labour market in face of the tough competition from skilled and trained male labour (government measures for specific training facilities exclusively for women being meagre) etc., is a question that needs to be probed into (p. vi).

One possible explanation for the low participation of women, particularly in the case of the major handicraft exports – gems and jewellery, carpets, art metalware and handprinting – the bulk of which are produced by Muslims in northern India, lies in the change in the organisation of production required to meet the increase in exports. A consequence of the transition from family units to these more commercialised forms of craft production has been a decline in the participation of women as artisans. In some cases this may be because they are predominantly Muslim and required to stay in purdah. For example, in the Farrukhabad handprinting industry, only twenty women were employed in the seventy-five units studied, out of a total workforce of 1307 – the increasing use of (male) hired labour over the 1970s was associated with a decline in the use of (female) family labour (GIDS, 1980, p. 26). In Coimbatore, Tamil Nadu, Baud (1982) also found that the use of female labour in the handloom sector fell with the size of unit (as measured by the amount of working capital); the fall was particularly marked for wage labour. But this was partly offset by an increase in female family labour, so that on average women still accounted for 46 per cent of the work force.

More important, perhaps, for many women are the substantial difficulties of combining work outside the home with domestic and other responsibilities. Thus their participation in handicrafts has been reduced by the shift in location of production to non-household areas.[2] In handprinting this has been particularly marked. The incentive to move away from households lies in the technical economies obtainable from screenprinting, which requires more space than available in the average household units; it is the medium and larger units (those with more than six printing tables) which account for most of the screenprinting, whereas the units with two tables or less concentrate on block printing (Ashraf, 1980, p. 16). Similar displacement of Chippa women, who traditionally blockprinted cloth in their homes on low padded tables, by men (often their husbands, brothers and sons) using screenprinting techniques, and operating in worksheds, has been noted in Ahmedabad, another major handprinting centre (Groenou, 1977; SEWA, 1980). Some handprinted cloth is still competitive (for example, when complicated designs or a small print run are required, and in the processing of coarse cloth for rural markets) but increasingly blockprinters' wages are being depressed by the higher productivity of screenprinting.

Other changes in the technology of crafts production, have also displaced products and processes typically performed by women – such as the increased use of machine-plyed semi-worsted wool for carpets (IDS, 1983/2), the changeover from hand wax polishing of wooden products to spray-on polyurethane varnishing, and the introduction of improved fly shuttle handlooms in Kashmir, using mill-spun yarn and machine-prepared warps instead of handspun yarn and warps prepared by women (ISS, 1979).

Another explanation for the low proportion of women could be the use of migrant labour. Typically, it is argued, men migrate to centres of handicraft production, leaving their families behind to tend to their land (though there are instances of whole families migrating in which case women may work alongside their husbands, for example, plying the yarn and preparing it for weaving). In the case of carpets, levels of migration are not very high – in the Bhadohi-Mirzapur carpet belt it is estimated (IDS, 1983/2) that only about 5 per cent of weavers are migrants from the surrounding areas of UP or Bihar, and 10–15 per cent of those employed in finishing activities. This contrasts sharply with the garment industry in Madras (Kalpagam, 1981), where nearly half of the women in the non-factory sector were migrants (though for men the proportion was still higher, with 63 per cent) and a third of all workers in the factory sector. Unfortunately the data are not available for testing the effects of migration on female participation in craft production even in a general way.

To sum up, women are primarily involved in two different types of crafts production. First, they take part in independent craft production, where the unit is the family. Typically this sort of unit produces goods for the local market; production for export is rare as a result of marketing constraints and an inability to compete with more organised forms of production. Secondly, they take part in domestic production organised as part of a putting-out system, performing skilled or, more usually, ancillary tasks. Participation in workshop or factory production, however, is low (and lower than in the handloom industries), and as the expansion of exports has strengthened the shift away from household to workshop production, the role of women has diminished.

Two questions arising are whether this trend can be reversed and whether the lot of women artisans can be improved. There are various ways of increasing women's participation, such as the carpet training schemes operated in parts of UP for young girls, often non-Muslim, or very poor Muslim, families. But to be effective these require Government assistance with the provision of looms, as it has been found that unless the girls marry into weaving families they usually do not continue the craft. Another way would be the establishment of entirely women-run workshops. Some such ventures have been set up with the help of voluntary agencies and the co-operative movement, although their scope is restricted by a shortage of trained women willing to act as managers.

These measures will not necessarily strengthen the participation of women with binding domestic and other responsibilities, however. For them other forms of support appear to be required, both in terms of marketing – from the alternative marketing network (co-operatives, Government buying offices, and voluntary agencies) which could help to reduce their dependence on private subcontractors or middlemen – and in terms of technology – with improvements needed in productivity to keep domestic workers competitive with non-household producers.

As long as the alternative marketing network remains small, it may be difficult to improve the lot of the artisan. Attempts to enforce minimum wages and factory legislation have generally failed, as have measures to protect some handicrafts (handprinting, handloom weaving) from mechanised production (some forms of screenprinting, powerloom weaving). Another strategy would be to impose a system of quality controls on exports, in an attempt to raise the value of the final product, and so put an end to the squeeze by middlemen on wages. (This may be necessary even to sustain present wage levels as the low quality of many products is said to be damaging the international demand for Indian handicrafts). Finally, promotion of Indian products in new international markets, as well as within the national market should help to raise the demand for artisans.

Notes

1. This paper was written in the course of a project carried out by the author with Dr Vincent Cable at the Overseas Development Institute (ODI), London, together with L. C. Jain, Sanyay Sinha, Rita Kapadia, and R. N. Arya, of Industrial Development Services, New Delhi, with funding from the UK's Overseas Development Administration and the Ford Foundation. The results were due to be published in India in late 1985 under the title *The Commence of Culture: The Experience of Indian*

Handicrafts. As the project concentrated primarily on the contribution of handicrafts and handloom exports to the Indian economy, rather than focusing on women in particular, this paper draws heavily on other research in the field, much of it unpublished or at least not available outside India.

2. Both explanations are borne out by Akhtar (1981) who found a significant negative relationship in twelve Indian States between female labour force participation rates on the one hand, and the proportion of Muslims, and workers engaged in non-household industry on the other. The Muslim factor was more important in rural areas than in urban areas, whereas for the proportion of non-household industry the reverse was true.

References

Akhtar, S., *Regional Analysis of Indian Female Labour Force Participation*, Social Science Working Paper no. 43, Paisley College of Technology, November 1981

Allal, M. and E. Chuta, *Cottage Industries and Handicrafts. Some Guidelines for Employment Promotion*, (Geneva: ILO, 1982)

Ashraf, M. S., *Economics of Cloth Printing in the Decentralised Sector*, Giri Institute of Development Studies (1980 (mimeo))

Aziz, A., 'Rural Artisan Development Strategies and Employment Generation', paper presented at the Indian Economics Association Conference, Pune, March 1980

Baud, I., Production Organisation and Women's Employment in the Textile Industry in Coimbatore'. Madras Development Seminar Series, *Bulletin*, July 1982

Dhamija, J., 'Handicrafts: a source of employment for women in developing rural economies', *International Labour Review*, December 1975

——— 'Women and Handicrafts: Myth and Reality', *Seeds*, no. 4, 1981

Groenou, W. V., 'Muslim Artisans in Ahmedabad – an exploration of the change from blockprinting to screenprinting', *Bulletin of the Institute of Traditional Cultures*, Madras, 1977

Herman, T., 'The role of cottage and small-scale industries in Asian economic development', *Economic Development and Cultural Change* (1955/6)

Ho. Y. and Huddle, D., 'Traditional and smallscale cultural goods in international trade and employment', *Journal of Development Studies*, January 1976

Indian Co-operative Union (ICU), *Women's Employment in the Handicraft Industry* (1973 (mimeo))

Industrial Development Services (IDS), Contribution of Handicrafts and Handlooms to Indian Development, Product Review Papers: 1. *Handlooms*; 2. *Carpets*; 3. *Handprinting*; 4. *Art metalware* (Delhi 1983 (mimeo))

Institute of Social Studies (ISS), *A Case Study on the mechanisation of the traditional handloom weaving industry in the Kashmir valley* (Delhi 1979 (mimeo))

Kalpagam, U., *Female Labour in small industry – the case of export gar-*

ments, Madras Institute of Development Studies, Working Paper no. 18, June 1981

Little, A. Inc, *The World Market for Handicrafts* (1974 (mimeo))

Littlefield, A., 'The Expansion of Capitalist Relations of Production in Mexican Crafts', *Journal of Peasant Studies*, vol. 6, no. 4, July 1979

Mathur, R. S., *Report on Chikan Handicraft*, Giri Institute of Development Studies, Technical Report no. 2 (1975 (mimeo))

Mies, M., *Housewives Produce for the World Market. The Lace Makers of Narsapur*, ILO WEP Research Working Paper (1980)

Minkes, A., 'A Note on Handicrafts in Underdeveloped Areas', *Economic Development and Cultural Change*, 1952/3

Rodgers, B., *The Domestication of Women* (London: Kogan Page, 1981)

Self-Employed Women's Association (SEWA), Socioeconomic survey of Chhipa women, Ahemdabad, 1980 (mimeo)

Taimni, K., 'Employment generation through handicraft cooperatives: the Indian experience', *International Labour Review*, July–August 1979

10 Front and Rear: the Sexual Division of Labour in the Israeli Army[1]

Nira Yuval-Davis

In recent years the role of women in the military has been widely debated. While some feminists are opposed to women's participation in military activity of any kind, others favour the integration of women into the 'male domain' of the armed forces. The largest feminist organisation in the United States, the National Organization for Women, for example, argues that if men are drafted into military service, women should be as well. In NOW's view, women's equality means an equal share in both the 'rights' and the 'duties' of society.[2]

This issue is generally debated at a moral or philosophical level. This paper explores it more concretely, by examining the historical experience of women in the Israeli army, the first army to recruit women by national law. The Israeli case suggests that the incorporation of women into the military may change the nature of, rather than eliminate, their subordination. Being formally a part of the military does not guarantee equality, either in terms of the actual tasks fulfilled by women or in terms of the power they exercise. On the contrary, in the extremely hierarchical and bureaucratic modern army machinery, gender differentiation can be even more formal and extreme than in the civilian labour market, as the Israeli case illustrates well.

Traditionally, the military has been considered an exclusive male domain. This was, however, never absolutely true. For example, in the siege of Jerusalem 2000 years ago, women helped to pour boiling oil on the attacking Romans. Women were also part of the attacking army, accompanying the Roman battalions, not only to fulfil the sexual needs of the soldiers, but also to provide general servicing and maintenance for the army. In a sense, very little has changed since then. However, only since the First World War, and then only in a temporary and marginal way, have women come to constitute a *formal* part of the military. Even today, there are very few States in which women are conscripted into the armed forces (except in times of emergency) by law.

Yet women do constitute an integral part of most armies throughout the world, even if the exact extent of this participation is difficult to determine. For administrative or historical reasons, women performing identical jobs (like clerical work or nursing) in different countries may be considered formally military personnel in one case and strictly civilian employees in another. But if women's work is important in all contemporary armies, in none – be it liberation army, national army, or professional army – are women represented to an extent approaching that of men. In most cases, women constitute no more than 5 to 7 per cent of military personnel, often much less. Furthermore, in no army do women have *de facto* (and almost never *de jure*) equal access to military roles. There are almost always some military professions closed to women and some in which they are heavily concentrated. The allocation of military roles is, then, virtually always sexually ascriptive. This does not necessarily mean that all military professions are exclusively male or female, or that there is no fluctuation in the accessibility of certain jobs to men and women. But it does mean that a vital aspect of each military role is its definition as open to men and/or women.

FRONT AND REAR

Front and rear are terms which are used regularly in military discourse. Generally speaking, this dichotomy reflects the actual continuum of geographical and functional areas involved in a military confrontation. The front is where the territory under control of the fighting collectivity ends and the confrontation with the enemy takes place. The rear is where most of the members of the collectivity stay in relative security defended by the fighters, who are prepared to die for the sake of the collectivity – to defend the lives of its members, its territory, or in some cases to expand and glorify it further. The rear, on the other hand, provides for all the needs of the fighters at the front.

Rear and front are not static structures. Once the front expands, the rear follows, and certain areas of the former front become part of the new rear. What is crucial though, is that certain functions of the rear, those of service and administration, are always part of the rear, while face-to-face fighting always takes place in the front.

Traditionally, the territorial front/rear and combatant/non-combatant dichotomies overlapped considerably. Although there were always people who fulfilled non-combatant roles at the front zone – essential medical, communication, and other services – most of the people at the front were engaged in actual fighting. Until relatively recently, no combat roles were actually possible away from the front, although combat-type activities in training and drilling often constituted a significant part of the military rear activities.

The development of modern warfare has drastically changed both the ratio of combatant to non-combatant military forces, and the relationship between front and rear positions. It is estimated that approximately twenty non-combatant personnel are needed for every one combat role in a modern army. Many more auxiliary positions are required (in such areas as technology, communications, and administration) in addition to the traditional service and maintenance ones. At the same time, physical proximity is no longer necessary, in a growing number of cases, in order to hit the enemy. The 'functional' front, then, does not always overlap, the 'territorial' one, nor does the relatively higher safety of being in the rear always exist anymore. The most consistent characteristic of the front which has survived into the era of modern warfare is that it is where the fighting activities considered to be most important for the success of the military operation are located – even if they only involve pressing a button.

Men and women are not equally represented at the front and the rear. In most armies, even where women are present, they are formally barred from the front zone and/or combatant roles (the functional front). The sexual division of labour in the military, as in society as a whole, is based on ongoing traditions concerning the 'proper' areas of labour for males and females.

There is a nearly universal ideological tradition of sexual difference which focuses on the image of men as fighters. In modern patriarchal society this tradition dictates that in the military, even more than in civilian life, men take up the heaviest and most risky jobs. Women, on the other hand, are expected both to reproduce future 'manpower' in their capacity as mothers, as well as to serve the men, to raise their morale, and, when front demands expand, to perform the tasks men cannot fulfil, in their capacity as 'men's helpmates'.

The dynamic nature of the front/rear division means that what determines the roles of women in the military is the extent to which the men are needed at the front. In other words, it may not be the specific military task which determines it as a 'woman's job' in the army, but rather its relation to the demands of the front and the pressure on 'manpower' resources. Women's engagement in occupational roles formerly filled only by men does not necessarily mean, then, a weakening in the sexual division of labour. It often represents simply an expansion of the military and/or economic front with women 'filling in' for men – a situation which is easily reversed when the front regresses. As long as non-differential gender roles are a product of emergencies, such as revolution or war, the sexual division of labour will reassert itself along traditional lines once the crisis has passed.

I propose the front/rear model as a convenient framework of description of the shifting sexual division of labour, not only because of its dynamic nature, but also because it focuses attention on how national ideologies and mobilisations, mediated by States or political movements, can affect the sexual division of labour. This is true despite the fact that these national ideologies often focus on the perceived necessary role of men, rather than of women, in the military. I do not contend that even within the military the front/rear dynamic is the only dynamic of the sexual division of labour. Moreover, in each concrete historical situation, there is no unitary category of 'women' and 'man' in the labour market; ethnicity, class, age or place in the life cycle all affect the specific position of various categories of men and women in the military, as in the civilian labour market. Political and economic forces, from the feminist movement to the multinationals, can affect the front/rear dynamic as well.

These issues, however, cannot be discussed only in the abstract. Let us turn now to the case of the Israeli military and explore the dynamics of the sexual division of labour in its pre-State and post-State history.

HISTORICAL BACKGROUND OF THE ISRAELI CASE

Cynthia Enloe[3] remarks that the integration of women into the army is usually defined as part of the *national* security policy, while in reality it is an expression of the *State* security policy. This is an important differentiation in every case, but especially in the case of

Israel, where women's participation in the military started in the pre-State period, and continued after the State was established. Israel defines itself as a Jewish State, recruiting initially only Jewish people, including women, to its military. Many of its citizens however, and even more so those under its control, are not part of the Jewish national collectivity. The relationship between 'the nation' and 'the State' is, therefore, of prime importance when examining the sexual division of labour in the Israeli army.

The Zionist immigration, which started in 1882 with the first *Aliya* (wave of immigration) from Russia, was the first to conceive of immigration to Palestine as an act of a national movement.[4] Almost from the beginning of the Zionist settlement, the Zionists wanted to establish a Jewish society and State in Palestine. Using socialist ideologies, they wanted to exclude the native Palestinians from the new society they were creating – in other words, to dispossess rather than to exploit them.

This strategy had two natural results which affected the involvement of women in the military: (a) almost from the beginning it created confrontations with the Palestinians, who resented the new phenomenon and, felt more and more threatened. The Palestinians attempted in various ways to struggle against the 'invaders'. This confrontation started on local levels, and gradually grew to a national movement: on a Palestinian level, it reached its peak in the 're- bellion' of 1936–9, and on a national Arab scale, in the war of 1948, with the invasion by Arab armies into Palestine. Thus all through the history of the Zionist settlement and the State of Israel, military occupation had a central place in the life of the settlers. In this sense, Israeli society was from the outset a 'war society' needing loyal and trained human power to help with the military effort.

The other result of this 'socialist strategy' of colonisation was that women were considered (ideologically although not practically) to be equal members of the new society. From the beginning, this enabled women to be potentially part of the human power pool, which would be used in the pursuit of militarisation.

Until the establishment of the State only volunteer women (and men) served in the military. There were circles in the *Yishuv* (the pre-State Jewish settlement in Palestine) like the religious sector, from which hardly any women participated at all. Those who did participate, were involved, on the one hand in the military organis- ation of the *Yishuv* (like the *Hashomer*,[5] *Hagana*,[6] *Palmach*,[7] *Ezel*, and *Lehi*[8]) and on the other hand in the ATS[9] of the British army.

The sexual division of labour in the *Yishuv* military organisations, was much less formal than that of the ATS, where women were in separate units and performed very specific 'women's' tasks. In the *Yishuv* organisations, the sexual division of labour was dependent to a great extent on the specific state of the conflict. The expansion of the territory controlled by the *Yishuv*, and the growing centralisation of the military organisations made the sexual division of labour more and more distinct, although all along women were a minority in the military forces and even when they were in the front, they fulfilled mainly auxilliary roles of communication and nursing.

With the establishment of the State significant changes were brought to the nature of women's participation in the Israeli military. Unlike in the time of the *Yishuv*, the military State policy has had to relate to all sectors of the State population, and not just the volunteers, although not necessarily in the same way.

Also, in the pre-State period there was ambivalence, inconsistency and vagueness in relation to the nature of women's participation in the military, and in many cases, it was a result of ad-hoc decisions, rather than a planned policy. In addition there were at least three opposing ideologies (represented most clearly by the *Palmach*, ATS and the religious sectors) concerning the desired nature of women's participation. These ideologies could continue to co-exist as parallel and separate *ideologies* after the establishment of the State, but a coherent, unified (although not necessarily homogeneous) State *policy* had to be crystallised.

ZAHAL (ISRAEL DEFENCE ARMY)

'*Zahal* is the army of Israel to which the guardianship of its sovereignty and security is commanded. It also fulfils an important role in absorption of immigration, integration of various ethnic groups, education of national consciousness and learning.'[10] It was formally established on 31 May 1948, and consists of a small professional core, a large number of conscripts and a reserve army.

According to Shif and Haber,[11] its structure and basic strategy is to keep maximum mobility; to transfer the war to the enemy territory and to develop preventive wars. This is based on the assumption that Israel will always be quantitatively inferior, of small strategic importance and surrounded by enemy countries.

CHEN (CHARM; WOMEN CORPS)

Chen is defined as one of the goal-orientated command units of *Zahal*.[12] Its structure and character emerged from the debate between those who wanted to adopt the model of the British Army and those who wanted to adopt the model of the *Hagana-Palmach*. One of the basic disagreements concerned the extent to which women should be kept in separate corps, as in the British army, or in mixed ones, as in the *Hagana-Palmach*. The solution which was accepted was some kind of compromise. It is not incidental, however, that from the establishment of *Chen* in 1948 until 1970, all the commanding officers were ex-ATS officers. The name of the command unit was also a result of a compromise. It was first suggested that it should be called Auxiliary Women Corps, but the name Women Corps was finally adopted, both because its initials in Hebrew then meant 'charm' (a feminine characteristic emphasised in the corps) and because it has more egalitarian connotations.

All the women in *Zahal* formally belong to *Chen*, but their membership in the corps is more partial than the membership of the men in their units. This is because most of the women in the army are under the day-to-day authority of male officers from the other units. They are sent to fulfil their various jobs in the army, not as a result of the decision of *Chen*, but as a result of manpower decisions taken by the General Headquarters and the different command units which are all staffed by men. The senior officers of *Chen* only have advisory capacities in the General Headquarters and in the different branches and command units of the army. As Shif and Haber sum up the situation 'The synthesis was crystallised (in the 50s) between senior officers (in *Chen*) as consultants, and junior officers as commanders'.[13]

The commanding power of the junior officers of *Chen* relates to the two areas which are exclusively under *Chen* authority – basic training and juridical authority. Every woman who is recruited to the army undergoes a course of basic training, which usually takes about three weeks. In this course she is trained in physical fitness and use of personal arms, given lectures on various topics from Zionism to cosmetics, and most of all, is adjusted to military discipline. Exclusive juridical authority over the women soldiers rests with *Chen* officers, who alone can judge women accused of any military offence (although most complaints come from the males under whom they are working). In addition, *Chen* officers in big army bases are usually responsible for the separate living quarters of the women soldiers (woman in *Zahal* are not allowed to live in places where separate showers and minimal facilities are not available) and for the guard duties of female soldiers.

The length of service of women in *Zahal* has usually been 18–24 months, which is 4–6 shorter than that of the men. They are then obliged to serve in the reserve army until they are pregnant, mothers, or reach the age of 24 (previously 26); in specific desirable professional roles they might be asked to serve in the reserve army until the age of 34. Some women do continue to serve in the professional army, but they constitute less than 10 per cent of its composition and are usually concentrated in the lower ranks.[14] The salaries of female soldiers are identical to those of men at the same rank, as are their welfare benefits (although until a few years ago, there was some discrimination in favour of male soldiers concerning the latter).

THE MILITARY ROLES OF WOMEN IN ZAHAL

> The aim of the female soldier's service in *Zahal*: Strengthening the fighting force by fulfilling administrative, professional and auxilliary roles, in order to release male soldiers to combat roles; training women to defend themselves and their homes and integrating them in the security effort of Israel, even after the termination of their active military service. The female soldiers also help in the educational activity of *Zahal* – in the educational system as teachers, and in *Zahal* as a whole, in the areas of crystallising the morale of the units and taking care of the soldiers of the units.[15]

Out of 850 military professions recognised by *Zahal* in 1980, women were engaged in only 270.[16] About 50 per cent of the professions open to women were clerical, a percentage more or less identical to the combat roles which were closed to women. According to Ann Bloom, the actual percentage of women soldiers who were engaged in clerical occupations was 65 per cent while the other 35 per cent were engaged in technical, mechanical and operational duties.[17]

The exact professions in which women are engaged in the army are not static – they change according to *Zahal*'s manpower needs. The 1952 law concerning the roles of women in regular army gives a list of 25 such roles, but also declares that a woman can fulfil any other military roles if she agrees to it in writing.

There are several occupations from which women have been

excluded over the years, e.g. hand-grenade throwing, heavy artillery and driving (the latter role was renewed in the 1970s). A significant number of the 35 per cent who are not engaged in clerical work were engaged in welfare and teaching duties for soldiers from lower social strata who need 'cultivating'.[18] In addition to serving in the army, women are 'lent' to fulfil other nationally important teaching and welfare roles outside the army, as well as strengthening the politics, especially the border police, in special units.

A major category of women's work in the army, as in the civilian labour market, is that of office work. In that type of work, women are found in positions which are in principle inferior to those of men. As late as February 1981, the military attorney issued a judgement that coffee-making and floor washing cannot be seen as outside the legitimate duties of military secretaries.[19] The power relations between the boss and his clerk is intensified by the added power of the boss's military authority. Although women can be judged only before *Chen* officers – and they can be used as a brake on the boss's power, – the complaints about the soldier and her breaking of military discipline come from the boss. Unlike in the civilian market, resignations are not accepted here.

Another aspect of the work of women soldiers in the offices of the different units is reflected in the name of the women's corps – 'charm'.

The subject of explicit sexual relations between women and men in the Israeli military is *formally* ignored (except when a soldier becomes pregnant and it becomes known to the military auhorities. In this case, her service used to be hastily terminated, but now she is allowed two free abortions first. *Zahal* officially encourages, however, emphasising sexual differences between male and female soldiers. A central demand from the women in the army is that they 'raise the morale' of the male soldiers and to make the army 'a home away from home'. Already, during the basic training of the women, they are coached to emphasise their feminine characteristics and their neat appearance, and they receive cosmetic guidance to help them in this respect. In the words of the *Zahal* spokesman: '*Chen* adds to *Zahal* the grace and charm which makes it also a medium for humanitarian and social activities'.[20]

The emphasis on the feminine essence of women soldiers puts them in a position of inferiority to that of the male soldiers, that is, as being there for their sake, to make them happier and humanise military service. However, especially when they fulfil jobs in the areas of education and welfare, it also gives them certain powers. Here their femininity is basically an extrapolation of the feminine mother role, and not that of the wife or mistress. This power, however, usually has a class bias. The objects of the work of the women soldiers as teachers and welfare-officers are usually men from lower class origins than that of the women themselves (while in the offices very often the men and women come from the same class background).

The pressure on manpower resources in *Zahal* led in 1976 to a conscious policy to widen the range of occupations for women in the army. The new openings have been mainly in two directions: (a) military combat occupations which are fulfilled by women in non-combat conditions (for example, learning to drive tanks in order to become trainers and release experienced men to roles at the front); (b) maintenance and electrical roles which are related to the new technology involved in sophisticated armaments, in the Ammunition and Air Force command units.

Such new roles opening to women have created problems concerning the length of service for women in the regular army. This is a 'Catch 22' situation: the relatively unskilled character of women's roles enable the army to release them earlier than the men, yet the short length of their service becomes an obstacle in allocating them to professional jobs, which involve a long period of training. The ad-hoc solution found was that women who agree to be involved in these types of occupations have to commit themselves to serve one additional year in the professional army after their regular military service is over. In addition, the army attempted to develop, in co-operation with the Ministry of Labour, pre-army training courses, which would enable the army to use their women graduates in relevant professional jobs and would also enable the women to work in the parallel occupations in the industry after their release.[21] Some of the women involved in the courses have been women whom the army would not otherwise have recruited for 'qualitative' educational reasons. However, the new higher status openings for women in the army are only a negligible percentage, in comparison with total number of women in it. Nevertheless, for almost the first time, women are occupying professional jobs in the army and this might affect not only their length of service, but also their dispensability in times of emergency at the front.

Over the years, with the acquisition of new kinds of military techniques and changes, there has been a corresponding change in the relative degree of overlap between female and male roles. The crucial factor which determines the sexually ascriptive nature of the military is that each task at each point in time is defined as open either to men and/or women as a vital characteristic of the job description. In spite of the change of the actual roles open to men and women in the army with time, the ascriptive sexual division is not random and is directly related to the division between front and rear.

Since the 1948 war, women have not been allowed to remain in the front once an emergency is declared, and the front actually starts to function as such. It was emphatically stressed by the authorities that the three women soldiers who were killed during the 1973 war met their death by staying at the front illegitimately and disobeying explicit orders. Even in the report of the Government committee on the position of women in Israel, which aspires to egalitarianism, the recommendation is to open all the roles, with the exception of the fighting roles at the front, to women's service.

The demand for human resources pressuring the Israeli army during the last few years has opened to women more participation in combat roles, but this has not diminished the basic principle of the front/rear sexual division of labour in the army.

The sexual division of labour in the Israeli military bears some similarity to its civilian one. Although the civilian labour market is less rigid than that of the military, 54.8 per cent of women participating in the civilian labour markets are engaged in clerical and administrative jobs, and 52.3 per cent of them are engaged in the areas of public and community service. Similarly, women have started to penetrate into the areas of new mechanical and electronic industry. Because an overwhelmingly major part of the electronic industry is connected to the security and armaments industry, Palestinian men and women are not considered as a suitable 'rear' human power source in this context.

The exclusion of Palestinians from 'security' positions in the civil labour market and from all military positions, raises the question of the relationship between the sexual divisions in the Israeli military and in Israeli society as a whole. We can explore this relationship by finding out not only what positions are filled by women rather than men in the army, but also which *categories* of Israeli women fulfil these roles and which categories of women are excluded, or are not properly represented, in the military.

CATEGORIES OF WOMEN

As with many other seemingly universal laws, which in practice are not so, the law of national security service which recruits Israeli men and women to the army is misleading. The law of 1969 states that every Israeli citizen or permanent resident has to enter the regular army; a man between the ages of 18 and 29, and a woman between 18 and 26, unless they are medical doctors or dentists, in which case they can be called up until the age of 38. Nevertheless, in the year 1976–7, only 51.5 per cent of the Jewish women (and none of the non-Jewish women) in that age group were recruited, and it seems that the percentage has been even smaller since, after legal changes in the procedure for releasing religious women from the service were passed by the Begin government. The 48.5 per cent who were not called to serve in the army included: 2 per cent who were released for medical reasons; 0.5 per cent who were released for administrative reasons, 18.5 per cent for religious and conscientious objection; 8 per cent married before recruitment age; 0.5 per cent were dead or otherwise unavailable; 19 per cent were unsuitable for personality reasons or education. It must be noted however, that most non-Jewish men as well as all non-Jewish women (who constitute about 15 per cent of the female population in Israel proper within the pre-1967 borders) are not called to serve in the army. Within the Jewish population, it is religious-conservative homes and insufficient education which leave about two-fifths of women outside the 'universal' recruitment of women to the army.

A large category of women who are released from serving in the army are those the army decides are 'qualitatively' unsuitable. The qualities required include a knowledge of Hebrew, a minimum level of education and a certain level of performance in psychotechnic tests. Those with a criminal record are also not recruited to the army. The release of soldiers on qualitative grounds is much higher among women than men.[22] One-fifth of those women who are recruited are classified as 'officer' quality, in contrast with only one-tenth of male recruits.

This differentiation in the class origin of men and women in the Israeli military strengthens a tendency which is found in most labour markets, including Israel, in which the class positions of men in the labour market are much more heterogenous than those of women who are mostly concentrated in the lower-middle class positions.[23] This strengthens my earlier observation that, although in general women are subordinate in the military, their power relations are very different *vis-à-vis* middle-class men (of similar origin to the majority of women who serve in the army) and *vis-à-vis* working class men (who are often their 'clients' as pupils or as welfare cases).

The second category are women released on religious grounds. In 1977 it was agreed that a 'genuine declaration' of 'religiosity' would be legitimate grounds for women not to serve in the army. The release of women on these grounds was a concession to the religious parties who had objected initially to any women in the army, for fear of their 'moral corruption'. Women released from service were originally supposed to work in alternative civil service, but the law was never enforced and only a negligible number volunteer to do so, mainly in hospitals.

The third category of women released from regular military service are those who have already started to fulfil their reproductive role: married women, pregnant women, or women with children are released even if they are in the middle of their service, and are not called in to the reserve army. Only women in the small professional army are allowed to serve when they have families.

The high percentage of women who are excluded from the military has direct implications for their involvement in the intensive process of social and national integration that takes place in *Zahal*. Constant military confrontation and the relatively small size of the Israeli-Jewish nation created a need for maximum mobility of the people in and out of the army under the slogan of 'There is no alternative'. This meant creating a strong symbolic identification between the people and the State, with the army as a major mediating mechanism for solidifying the 'national consensus', despite the class and ethnic distinctions reflected within the internal stratification of the army.

The exclusion of women from this national integration process, applies to almost *all* Israeli Jewish women; few serve in the army after their early twenties (apart from the few who serve in the professional army). The Israeli men, however, serve in it until they are 50 years old, at least one month a year. Israeli Jewish national cohesiveness is, then, a major product of the patriarchal male bond of the military. Correlatively, the role of the Israeli men as soldiers is their most important national role and has a high symbolic as well as practical significance. (Only in this context can we understand the far-reaching implications that the growing movement of draft resisters in the Israeli army around the Lebanon war has had on the Israeli society.)

The most important national role of Israeli Jewish women also relates to the army, namely as reproducers. It used to be common in Israel (before the national mood had changed in the 1980s) to say to a pregnant woman, 'Congratulations! I see you are soon going to bring a small soldier into the world!' . . . Motherhood – and of boys in particular – is definitely a military role, and the most important national role of Israeli Jewish women.[24]

As Geula Chohen, an MP and ex-member of the dissenting organisation Lehi, put it:

> The Israeli women is an organic part of the family of Jewish people and the female constitutes a practical symbol of that. But she is a wife and a mother of Israel, and therefore it is of her nature to be a soldier, a wife of a soldier, a sister of a soldier, a grandmother of a soldier – this is her reserve service. She is continually in military service.[25]

Likewise, David Ben-Gurion expressed the hegemonic ideology in Israel concerning woman's military role, adding that second factor must be remembered: 'The woman is not only a woman, but a personality in her own right in the same way as a man. As such, she should enjoy the same rights and responsibilities as the man, except where motherhood is concerned.'[26] Women, therefore, can participate as 'honorary' men in the army, until they start (and some strata of women are encouraged, by being excluded from the army, to start even earlier) to be mothers.

It is not incidental that the attitude of the State of Israel to widows, parents and orphans of war is very different from that of any other state. Israeli society perceives in their loss an active national contribution on their part, and seeks to reward them through the Ministry of Security, by attempting to replace their dead relative, symbolically and practically. The war widow has a high salary from the State and other privileges which do not bear any relation to the income of her husband before death.[27]

During the Lebanon war, however, for the first time, 'human sacrifice' was not accepted as a legitimate, if heart-breaking aspect of membership in the Israeli-Jewish national collectivity. One of the reasons, it is rumoured, for Begin's nervous breakdown was the impact of bereaved parents, mainly mothers, who continuously demonstrated in front of his house, accusing him of the death of their sons and refusing to be consoled by paeans to maternal sacrifice.

CONCLUSION

The military cannot be seen as totally separate from other spheres in Israeli society. The sexual division of labour in the Israeli army constitutes both a part and an extension of the sexual division of labour in the civilian labour market. The main difference is that of military uniform and discipline. The only major women's occupations in the civilian sphere which are not represented in the military are those connected with the bearing and rearing of children. This reflects the basic nature of women's participation in the military, which unlike men's, is only a temporary phase in their lives, before marriage and motherhood. It also reflects the fact that the categories of women in Israeli-Jewish society who bear the main responsibility for 'child production': that is, Oriental, poor, and religious women – are under-represented in the army population.

Since the time of the *Yishuv*, a consistent pattern has defined the sexual division of labour in the Israeli military, that of the front/rear. Once the front and the rear are defined as two separate functional/ geographical areas, if only by the first being the fields of the settlement and the latter its buildings – men will usually go to the front and women will be left in the rear. It is interesting to note, however, that during the pre-State period, when the rear and the front were less differentiated geographically, the most important emphasis was on functional differentiation – allocating women, with some exceptions, to auxiliary non-combatant roles in the front, as well as in the rear area. Later, after the State and its army were established, the emphasis changed to the contextual-geographical (the front during times of war) in addition to, but even more important than, the functional differentiation.

Several explanations are possible for this change. It is due in part to the State's ideology concerning the nature of the military. In the *Hagana* and *Palmach*, a more 'socialist' or 'liberationist' ideology prevailed, which was both informal and flexible in its nature. In *Zahal*, the ideological inspiration has come to a great extent from other Western State armies, particularly the British, which have a much more conservative approach to sexual divisions in the military. Another explanation, however, could be that with the transformation of the Israeli military from a voluntary to a regular-recruited army, enough men became available to fulfil the non-combatant functions in the front itself. These men were most probably part of the post-1948 mass migration of Oriental Jews and refugees to Israel.

In different categories of military labour, then, the dynamics of front and rear are determined by different patterns in which various categories of men and women drawn from Israeli society are differently located. Ethnic and class divisions, which transcend the boundaries of the military and operate in Israeli society as a whole, intermesh with the sexual division of labour.

Beyond the conditions of labour power availability, according to different gender and social categories, or even the 'objective' threat of Palestinian and Arab military attacks, a crucial dimension determining the dynamics of the front/rear pattern in the Israeli military has been its national/political/strategic goals. The most important exclusionary boundary specifying the categories of Israeli people who participate in the military has been the national one. Hence 100 per cent of the women and the overwhelming majority of the men who participate in the Israeli military are Jewish. In the 1970s, pressure on 'manpower' in the army intensified, not so much because the mass migration to Israel stopped, as because of Israel's determination to keep the occupied territories. We have seen how national strategies and goals play a central role in determining the sexual division of labour within and in relation to the military. They determine to an extent the role of women as mothers – suppliers of future soldiers, they determine the role of women inside the army – as educators, integrators, and morale-boosters of male soldiers, as well as affecting the degree to which, as men's 'helpmates', they will be needed to fill in the former male posts, in times of expansion of the front.

Analysis of the 'military labour market' also reveals how the State treats different groups of women differently for national purposes. Whatever is defined as the 'national interest', however, is of course not homogenous, and contradictions and conflicts often emerge even within one hegemonic ideological trend. For instance, the Israeli military use of mainly educated Jewish women, has been one of the reasons that poor and religious (mainly Oriental) women have been the major reproducers of human power in Israel. However, the resulting long-term change in the nature of the 'human material' in the army in terms of ethnic and class origin, is portrayed as one of the major causes of its deterioration.[28]

This complexity of factors is often missing from the various approaches used to analyse women's labour market situation. Sex difference is by no means the only relevant signifier in allocating positions within the labour processes. Class, ethnic origin and religious beliefs have been operating all along and have to be considered in order to understand the division of labour, both within the military and outside it. Moreover, to understand women's position in the labour market at a specific historical situation, national ideologies and policies concerning the role of the military in general and men's roles within it in particular, are no less important, and sometimes even more so than understanding the specific ideologies concerning women's position. Therefore, the conventional framework of analysing the labour market has to be expanded and included in it in addition to paid employment, not only domestic labour and voluntary work (as has been pointed out by V. Beechey)[29] but also the categories of work which constitute 'national service', military or civil.

Notes and References

1. The first draft of this paper was presented at the conference on Women in Militaries at the Transnational Institute in Amsterdam, out of which came the book *Loaded Questions* edited by Wendy Chapkis. I would like to thank the participants in this conference, especially Cynthia Enloe, for their useful comments. The same goes to all others who gave their time to read and respond to the paper – Prof. Ben-Yoseph and Prof. Lisak of the Hebrew University, Daphne Izraeli from Tel-Aviv University, Floya Anthias and Nance Goldstein from Thames Polytechnic and the members of the *Feminist Studies* collective, especially Ruth Milkman. I thank you all but hold only myself responsible for what has eventually emerged. A more expanded version of this is being published by *Feminist Studies*, Fall 1985, vol. 11, no. 3, pp. 649–76.
2. A discussion on that question, among others, can be found in C. Enloe's book, *Does Kahaki Become You* (Pluto Press, 1983).
3. C. Enloe, 'Women – the Reserve Army of Army Labour', *Review of Radical Political Economics*, 12, 1980.
4. A historical review of the participation of women in the pre-State period can be found in the *Feminist Studies* version of this paper. Other more detailed historical reviews can be found in two papers which were presented at the Inter-University seminar on Armed Forces and Society National Conference at the University of Chicago, October 1980 – A. R. Bloom, 'The Women in Israel's Military Forces', and N. L. Goldman and V. L. Wiegand, 'The Utilization of Women in Combat: the Case of Israel'.

   For more detailed general historical reviews of this period some of which differ in perspective from that given here, see, for example, the following: A. Bober (ed.), *The Other Israel* (New York: Doubleday Anchor, 1972); U. Davis, A. Mack and N. Yuval-Davis (eds), *Israel and the Palestinians* (London: Ithaca Press, 1975); S. N. Eisenstadt, *The Israeli Society* (Tel-Aviv: Magnes Publishing House, 1967); M. Lisak and D. Horowitz, *From Yishuv to the State* (Hebrew) (Am Oved, 1977); M. Rodinson, *Israel, a Colonial Settler State?* (New York: Pathfinder, 1973); N. Weinstock, *Zionism, False Messiah* (London: Ink Press, 1981).

5. *Hashomer* – the first organisation of full-time guards which was established at the beginning of the century to defend Zionist settlements.
6. *Hagana – The Defence*, the largest national military organisation dominated by the labour Zionist movement.
7. *Palmach* – the commando battalions of the *Hagana* in the pre-State period.
8. *Ezel, Lehi* – the 'Dissenting organisations' which had an extreme policy of military confrontation with the Palestinians and the British.
9. ATS – Auxiliary Territorial Service: Women's Corps in the British Army, where women from Palestine served in the Second World War.
10. Z. Shif and E. Haber, *Lexicon of the Security of Israel* (Hebrew) (Tel-Aviv: Zmora Bitan, 1976) p. 439.
11. Ibid., p. 440.
12. Ibid., pp. 216-18.
13. Ibid., p. 218.
14. The Government Report of the Committee on the Position of Women, The Prime Minister's Office, *Discussion and Facts* (Jerusalem 1978) p. 103.
15. Ibid., p. 89.
16. Ibid., p. 97.
17. A. R. Bloom,'The Women in Israel's Military Forces', p. 46. She quotes the figure from a high ranking officer in 1980.
18. Shif and Haber, *Lexicon of the Security of Israel*.
19. Report in *Ha'aretz* newspaper, Feb. 1981 (Heb.).
20. 'Chen' – The Women's Corps', Spokesman, Israel Defence Forces, 30 May 1972.
21. The Government Report of the Committee on the Position of Women.
22. Ibid.
23. D. Israeli and K. Gaier, 'Sex and inter-occupational Wage differences in Israel' in *Sociology of Work and Occupations*, November 1979, pp. 404–29.
24. For more detailed analysis of the Israeli-Jewish women's role of national reproduction see my forthcoming paper on this topic in the book *Women, Nation, State*, edited by Nira Yuval-Davis and F. Anthias (Verso 1986); see also my booklet, *Israeli Women and Men: divisions behind the unity* (Change Publications, 1982).
25. L. Hazelton, *Israeli Women - the reality behind the myth* (Hebrew) (Idanim, 1978).
26. David Ben-Gurion, *Israel, a personal history* (American Israel Pub., 1972) pp. 323–4.
27. L. Shamgar, *War Widows in Israeli Society*, Ph.D. thesis (Hebrew) Hebrew University, 1979. Since the economic crisis, however, the economic position of many of the widows has severely deteriorated, and

lately a protest movement of war widows has arisen which receives a wide popular support for their demands.

28. See, for example, the series of articles which appeared in April/May 1985 in *Ha'aretz*.

29. V. Beechey, 'Women's Employment in Contemporary Britain', paper presented at the British Sociological Association Conference, 1984, p. 46.

11 Controlling Women's Access to Political Power: a Case Study in Andhra Pradesh, India

Carol Wolkowitz

This article is concerned with one aspect of women's relation to State power, their access to positions in public office.[1] Of course we no longer expect that having more women in public office will necessarily work to the advantage of women in the wider population. So far as policy decisions are concerned, the gender of individual office-holders, like their class membership, is not likely to make very much difference. Significant shifts in policy are not produced simply through the selection of different individuals to office, and have to be analysed at a different level. Research interest in women and the political process has therefore shifted from a concern with women in office to women's struggles in other arenas, and the relevance of women's office-holding to the problem of women and State power has received comparatively little theoretical attention.[2]

None the less, many feminists would retain the notion that women's presence in public office is important. One way to begin thinking through some of its implications is in relation to the potential ideological impact of women's office-holding. One feels intuitively that were a considerable number of women to hold public office, and were they seen to wield power, this would be highly disruptive of conventional definitions of the relative status of men and women.

The fact that women's office-holding does not have this effect is partly because there are so few women in office anywhere. But it is also due to social constructions of women's office-holding which curtail its potential ideological impact. The existence of ideologies which distort the meaning of women's participation in the paid labour force, the notion that married women work only for 'pin money', for instance, is familiar to us. Women's participation in public office is similarly bounded by what can be termed 'accommodating ideol-ogies', representations of women office-holders which accommodate their political activity within acceptable, conventionally-defined roles as wives and mothers.[3] Because these representations can distort the meaning of women's office-holding, they need to be scrutinised critically, and when necessary distinguished from the actual processes whereby women obtain or are given access to public office.

This article looks critically at one interpretation of the position of women office-holders, the notion that it is 'through the family' that women have most easily acquired power and position in the public domain. Because this construction of women's office-holding presents women's domestic identities as a source of political power, and conversely, sees their office-holding as derived from positions in the family, it poses little threat to marriage relations as conventionally defined. An example is the term 'male equivalence', which Currell used to describe the situation of women office-holders whose position in public office derives from their relation to male kin.[4] Although she used the term in the context of a narrowly-focused discussion of women's office-holding, it has since been picked up by other researchers, who have used it to support a particular theoretical perspective on women's power.[5] It is partly for this reason that I think the term 'male equivalence' deserves more rigorous investigation than it has so far received.

The theory is that the family is not always a site of oppression for women, for in many societies women's position in the family gives them access to political power. The example usually cited is the situation in many traditional political systems, in which the widow or daughter of a king can inherit the throne as a 'male equivalent'. In these societies, it is argued, in which the family is the critical unit of political and economic life, women's confinement to domestic roles does not prevent them from exercising power. Rather, it is in modern societies, in which access to political office is gained not through the family but through participation in specialised political institutions, and in which competition for political office is perceived to take place between individuals, that women lose out.

These commentators also point out, however, that access to political power through the family is not wholly confined to traditional political systems. Many women legislators in modern parliamentary systems have been elected or appointed to public offices vacated by male relatives. Their situation suggests that in women's access to political office 'private' power, based in the family, remains important and that women are advantaged by this. While some women legislators in this situation serve only as proxies for men relatives, others go on to wield real political power. Thus the fact that some women still gain access to public office through the family is seen as welcome evidence of women's private power, and of the possibility that they can translate it into power in the public domain. What is conveyed by this argument is also, by implication, that in these cases women have successfully looked to their families for political support, or at least that their families believe themselves to have common interests in office-holding which can be equally well served by women family members.

The main purpose of this article is to question the adequacy, theoretically and empirically, of this interpretation of the position of women office-holders who have followed male relatives into office. In the first place, to direct attention to recruitment 'through the family' tends to push decisions and processes located in the public domain to the background. I would argue that this emphasis is misplaced. As Harris has pointed out, so-called 'private power' is ultimately derived from the public sphere.[6] A man who wields power in the family as 'head of household', for example, does not derive his power from his position *in the family*, but from the prerogatives allocated by the State to those its legal system defines as heads of household. His 'private power' cannot be maintained unless it is supported in the public domain. Similarly, in societies in which women can wield power as heads of household, as widows for instance, this is by virtue of the legal system.

In the case of women office-holders, this shift in perspective directs attention towards the conditions under which women can succeed male relatives in office. This makes it apparent that power is acquired through the public domain. The queen who inherits her rule, for instance, in one sense can be said to acquire her position 'through the family', but we can with perhaps greater accuracy say that she reaches the throne through rules of genealogical succession formulated and enforced in the public domain. Similarly, when women in a modern political system fill places vacated by male relatives, this depends on the willingness of political parties and their leaders to accept a woman as the appropriate successor to her male relation. Indira Gandhi, for instance, 'inherited' her position as Prime Minister of India from her father, but only because leading politicians at the time thought that this would work to their own advantage. When Indira Gandhi's daughter-in-law Maneka, Sanjay Gandhi's widow, tried to take her husband's place as his mother's successor, her claim was rejected by Mrs Gandhi and other political leaders in favour of

Sanjay's brother, Rajiv.[7] Whether or not a woman succeeds in using 'male equivalence' to reach a position of power is decided in the public domain.

Moreover, to describe a woman politician as a 'male equivalent' in many cases may not even be accurate empirically, but simply an ideological representation of women office-holders as powerless prox- ies. It is quite possible for a woman office-holder to have been nominated in her own right, or as the client of an unrelated patron, but still to be described as a 'male equivalent' by those who wish to devalue women's office-holding. Struggles for the definition of partic- ular women office-holders, or of women office-holders as a category, take place in and around the State, among politicians and State officials, in the press, and in campaigns directed at the electorate. Whether or not women acquire the full prestige and authority office- holding confers depends partly on their outcome.

Indian politics provides many opportunities for exploring what is actually 'going on' when women succeed male relatives in public office. My evidence is drawn from electoral politics in the South Indian State of Andhra Pradesh, where a large proportion of women legislators have male relatives who preceded them in political office or in whose name they are said to hold office. These women legis- lators therefore appear to be dependent on their male kin for their position. However, close examination of their political careers sug- gests that actually these women legislators cannot depend on their families for political support, and do not derive their position in politics from them. In their case the notion that some women obtain office 'through the family' clearly mislocated the crucial processes involved. At least in Andhra Pradesh, the depiction of women politicians as dependent for their success on their male kin is a very partial picture of their position, one which confirms rather than challenges the notion that women should be defined and accorded political identity in relation to their husbands, as wives.

My data is based on the political careers of all women who were Members of the Legislative Assembly (MLAs) of Andhra Pradesh from 1952 to 1976. Fieldwork, including interviews with most of these women, was conducted in 1975–6, and later updated through press reports. Thirty-seven of the fifty-five women MLAs had a 'kinship connection' to a male politician, in most cases their husband. These husbands had either previously held office in the state legislature, or the woman MLA was said by the politically informed to have stood for the Assembly on her husband's name. The term 'kinship connection' or 'kinship link' is less evaluative than 'male equivalence' and allows more scope for discovering, empirically, its meaning in individual cases.

STATE-LEVEL POLITICS IN ANDHRA PRADESH

As in the other states of India, the State legislature of Andhra Pradesh is composed of a popularly-elected lower house, the Legislative Assembly, and an indirectly-elected upper house, the Legislative Council. Under the Indian Constitution powers of legislation, taxation, and maintaining law and order are shared between the State legislatures and the central Parliament. The head of the State government, the Chief Minister, is elected by the majority party in the Assembly from among the members of the legislature, and he or she then chooses other members for the State cabinet. In Andhra Pradesh the Congress Party was in power from the first elections following Independence until the elections of 1983, that is, throughout the period with which this article is concerned.[8]

Women Members of the Legislative Assembly (MLAs) or Andhra Pradesh are participants in a historically and institutionally-specific political system and their political careers are highly coloured by its character. While this is true of politicians everywhere, the political careers of women MLAs, as is shown below, are almost entirely dependent on the nature of the political system, and it plays a more important role than the resources which women can bring to bear from outside it. There are a number of reasons why this is the case.

In the first place, few women in Andhra Pradesh have direct access to the kinds of resources which men use to launch and sustain political careers. The resources required for a successful political career are held by families, especially landed wealth and political patronage, the latter accumulated by other family members through holding political office at central, state, or local level. Most male MLAs are rural landlords, although they sometimes have legal training and reside in urban areas, and they usually belong to families in which one or more other members also hold office.[9] Kinship links are typical of most MLAs, men as well as women.

Which family members are to represent a landed family's interests by seeking political office is normally decided by the household head. If he does not want office for himself, he normally chooses one of his sons. This son plays such a critical role in preserving the family's fortunes, mediating between his family and State officials of various kinds, that he can expect to play a central role in family decision-making. In exceptional cases a widow is the head of household, and can decide to seek office herself. But in most circumstances women require the permission of the head of household, either their husband or his father. This permission is not readily granted. Men are willing to have their womenfolk nominated to the seats in local government reserved for women because otherwise these seats would be taken by the women kin of their political opponents. As I demonstrate below, however, when it comes to State-level office, men are unlikely to permit their wives to stand unless constrained to do so by more senior political leaders. In other words, for most women access to political resources controlled by (male members of) the family depends on either the legal provision of reserved seats or the support of politicians from outside the family.

That women are able to obtain support from politicians outside the family who can constrain the actions of male politicians in their families, is largely because the selection of candidates in the political parties is highly centralised. This is particularly the case in the Congress Party, to which forty-nine out of the fifty-five women MLAs belong. Congress leaders, especially ministers in the central and State cabinets, play a large role in the selection of Congress candidates for the Assembly and Parliament.[10] Before Parliamentary and Legislative Assembly elections the Pradesh (or state-level) Congress Committee (PCC) compiles a list of aspiring applicants for the Congress nominations, winnows it down, and then sends it to Delhi where the final selection is made. Similarly, Congress men or women who seek election to the State upper house, the Legislative Council, need to be chosen by the Chief Minister from among the many aspirants seeking inclusion in the official slate of Congress candidates.

The reason for the persistent involvement of central and State ministers in the nomination of Congress candidates is related to the existence of competing factions within the Congress.[11] Ministers depend for their own positions as leaders of factions on retaining the loyalty of the MPs and MLAs who comprise part of their 'following'. The nomination process is crucial to forming and cementing the ties which link the minister, as patron, with his or her clients in the legislatures. In fact, personal control of the nomination of Congress candidates, including the re-nomination of sitting members, was a key feature of Mrs Gandhi's rule. She used the nomination process to bring in her own supporters, and to oust sitting members who were or might become disloyal. It is within this context that women acquire the Congress nomination, as sitting members of the Assembly obtain re-nomination, or are elected to the Legislative Council.

KINSHIP CONNECTIONS AND THE NOMINATION PROCESS

Close examination of the nomination process in Andhra Pradesh shows that many male politicians resist giving their women kin the opportunity of standing for office. Although six of the thirty-seven women MLAs who are related to male politicians are widows who succeeded a husband in office, the single most frequent situation is when a woman obtains the nomination *instead of* a living husband. These husbands are very reluctant to see their wives as their equivalent, and have to be forced to do so by Congress leaders. Thus despite the importance of family membership to becoming an MLA, women are almost entirely dependent for their nominations on political leaders outside the family. The circumstances under which women replace their husbands as the Congress candidate are varied. The most interesting occurred in the Legislative Assembly elections in 1972. The nomination of women by the Congress Party (including the nomination of Congress women candidates without kin links) reflected the nomination strategy adopted by Indira Gandhi in 1972. One-third of sitting Congress MLAs were 'retired', that is refused the Congress nomination, and replaced by previously under-represented categories: lower castes, minorities, labour, intellectuals and women. Although the Congress Party has long given superficial support to a 15-per-cent quota of women candidates for Parliament and the State legislatures, 1972 was the first time it was actually enforced. Indira Gandhi used the recruitment of women and other categories to justify the ousting of established politicians who owed their primary loyalty to State party bosses rather than herself.[12] Two illustrative examples are examined below.

Temina Devi[13] first obtained the Congress nomination in 1972 and was elected to the Assembly. She saw herself as her husband's equivalent ('In my husband's name only I am MLA', she said). She said that: 'Some state leaders took my husband's side, and asked the Prime Minister to give his wife the seat, and so Indira Gandhi made it into a "ladies' seat" [that is, part of the 15 per cent quota of nominations to be awarded to women].' But although this woman MLA said that her husband was instrumental in her selection, in fact she was nominated in order to prevent him from standing. Her husband, a sitting MLA, was then faced with either accepting and supporting her candidature, or competing as an Independent against an unrelated Congress candidate. According to another woman politician, a member of the State Congress leadership at the time, Temina Devi's husband headed a district-level faction which threatened the Chief Minister's control of the State Congress. This woman leader went on to say, 'It is like a game, by choosing a lady we can defeat a rival. We thought she will be more loyal to our group than her husband, which she was until the leader of our group was replaced as Chief Minister [by Indira Gandhi].' The reason Temina Devi was thought more likely to remain loyal to the Chief Minister's group was because as MLA she had no followers in the Assembly and owed her nomination to the party leadership. In other words, although the MLA presented herself as her husband's equivalent, had she been considered as fully the equivalent of her husband, she would not have been nominated. Her husband was forced to support her nomination, and accepted it only at a late stage in the nomination process.

Another woman MLA first elected in 1972, in full-time professional employment, also told me that her nomination by the Congress was intended to help her husband, a municipal councillor, and had been suggested by him. She described him as 'the main representative of our community in our district'. In a first interview she said that her standing for office resulted from their joint decision. Published electoral records indicate that her husband had in fact submitted and later withdrawn his own name, so I queried this account, but the MLA insisted that her husband had never applied: 'We knew the situation earlier'. But in a second interview (perhaps after talking to her husband) she said,

> My husband and I were approached jointly to run, we were told that we are the only people from the Muslim community who are educated, I was the only woman not observing *purdah*, who goes out to public functions. *But in spite of that only my husband applied*, and when the PCC was deciding only his name was there. The applications were processed and sent to Delhi. In *Delhi* they were in favour of giving seats to ladies and minorities. They said –

if it is going to be Ahmed, we suggest his wife put in her name, because then there will be no competition [because she could take advantage of the effort to bring in both women and Muslims]. Two Union ministers from this area said that instead of taking both their names, just put hers in now. If we choose the wife, we can choose without even showing the names of the other contestants to the Prime Minister and make the decision now. *So I got instructions from Delhi through the PCC saying that my nomination papers were wanted.* [author's italics]

This case differs from Temina Devi's in several respects. In the first, party leaders did not see the male politician's wife as his equivalent, while the second they did. A wife's nomination was in one case used to oust a husband who was becoming too powerful, in the other to help 'his' chances. But from a theoretical point of view what is significant about both cases is that neither woman had the support of her husband. Both owed their positions to the overwhelming importance of the role of extra-familial political leaders in political negotiations outside the domestic domain. It is these leaders who determine whether or not a kin-linked recruitment takes place, and therefore whether or not women obtain access to the political resources and reputation of their husbands or his family. Neither woman commanded private power.

The nominations of kin-linked women in earlier years were not part of a systematic strategy of the kind adopted by the Congress in 1972. In earlier years most husbands had been denied the Congress nomination because they had previously contested on the ticket of an opposition party, or as an Independent. In a few cases, the nomination of a woman stemmed from her membership of a powerful political family (but see below). But although the 1972 elections are exceptional, they highlight the processes of political bargaining and compromise through which women had obtained the nomination in earlier years as well. In their cases also the role of extra-familial party leaders was paramount.

The role of political leaders can be equally important in the nomination of a male politician's widow. One such case appears at first sight a simple case of 'widow succession'. This woman MLA was the widow of an opposition party candidate who died just before nominations closed, in what was reputed to be a political murder. She preferred to be 'in the home only' and was persuaded to stand against her own wishes. Her nomination was also opposed by her mother-in-law, a municipal councillor who 'did more public service even than my husband, and was conversant with politics'. The mother-in-law was 'keen to contest' in her son's place. However, the party leaders believed that the murdered candidate's young widow would be more likely than his mother to capture a 'sympathy vote', and insisted the widow should stand. Only then did her mother-in-law 'compel' her to do so. The mother-in-law had far more interest in and experience of political life, and as head of their household could compel her daughter-in-law to stand. But as far as obtaining a nomination for herself was concerned, her position carried little weight. What determined the nomination outcome was the way in which the political leaders defined their party's interests.

Examples of the nomination of women with kinship connections, like those above, demonstrate that when nomination for political office is seen as a process rather than a single event, this reveals tensions and disagreements which would otherwise remain obscured. They also suggest that this process may be seen quite differently by the different actors involved in it. The woman MLA who is married to a male politician usually proffers a version of events which replicates or colludes with ideologies of conjugal loyalty and common interest. Like the notion of 'male equivalence', this obscures the fact that family members are actually competitors for political office and for the central role in the family it potentially offers. Only in the third of these cases, where a conflict took place between two women in the family, was the woman MLA willing to acknowledge the conflict publicly.

Moreover, at least for my informants in Andhra Pradesh, whether or not the kin-linked woman MLA is seen to obtain the nomination primarily through her husband is closely associated with the evaluation of her political talents. For instance, the woman who said that the party leadership was responsible for Temina Devi's nomination, not her husband, also said that although Temina Devi had been a housewife prior to becoming an MLA, she had rapidly developed into a 'shrewd politician'. Several other informants, however, said that Temina Devi was so 'uneducated' that 'her husband must be doing the work'. Similarly, whereas one journalist saw the Muslim woman MLA as dependent on her husband, 'who has some standing as a businessman in that area', another informant said that 'as a Muslim woman and school headmistress' she had been an 'attractive candidate'. Because reputation is itself a political resource, attempts to promote or demean the status of any particular woman politician in this way have serious repercussions for her political career. They also reflect and contribute to the status of women as a category of political actors.

KINSHIP CONNECTIONS AND THE POLITICAL CAREER

In considering woman's kinship connections to other politicians, it is important to look beyond women's initial entry to political office. Account also has to be taken of other, longer-term measures, of access to political power.

In Andhra Pradesh, a single term in the Assembly is not sufficient to establish a politician's reputation or for him or her to build up a 'following', that is, supporters who he or she can claim in competing for a position in the Cabinet. Politicians who have some 'say' have served in office for several terms. Remaining in office is necessary to the acquisition of political power and is at the same time a demonstration of it.

For this reason it is useful to know what proportion of women *length* MLAs have been able to sustain political careers in legislative office. *awoke* Of the thirty-seven women MLAs whose careers could be categorised according to their length, thirteen served for only a single term. Some were defeated when they stood for a second term, and others stood only once. In contrast, seventeen women MLAs were legislators for three or more terms in office. Some were re-elected to the Assembly. In other cases the MLA continued her political career in *not good.* the State upper house, the Legislative Council, or went on to Parliament, but obviously they should be included as having long political careers. A residual category of 'middling careers', falling between those two stools, are the seven women MLAs who served two terms as legislators.[14]

Several different explanations of the failure of many women MLAs to sustain political careers could be suggested. The most obvious is that they did not want to stay in office beyond a single term, or that in comparison with women with long political careers they were less highly motivated, or more easily discouraged by electoral defeat. While this explanation has the merits of common sense, it is not very helpful, I think, to adopt such a voluntarist conception of the factors which make for political success. In a political environment which is generally hostile to women's participation in public office, it is important to consider the structural variables which are associated with women's remaining in or continuing to contest for office.

Whether or not women MLAs had kinship connections with male

politicians clearly differentiates between long and short careers in legislative office.[15] Twelve out of the thirteen 'short careers' had male relatives who were politically active or former office-holders, and so did four out of the seven middling careers, as categorised above. In contrast, less than half of the women MLAs who sustained long political careers 'seven out of seventeen' had kinship connections to male politicians. Although having family political connections may, with the support of outside political leaders, have helped in or been necessary to obtaining political office, the presence of the kinship connection actually seems to be a disadvantage in the long term.

Why is this the case? Women MLAs with kinship connections are fairly rapidly replaced in office by their husbands or another male relative. When they first obtained the Congress nomination, they had the support of leading Congress politicians. But this support was not given primarily out of support of women as such, or in many cases, for particular women as individuals, but for short-term political advantage. Once the original political considerations lose their force (or once those who 'brought in' the woman MLA lose their own positions) the husband can call upon his political allies to support his return to office. The woman MLA who wants or needs to maintain good relations with her husband is then forced to retire from seeking major office, for her participation can no longer be accommodated as 'necessary' to family interests.[16]

A good example is the career of MLA Susheela Devi. She was defeated when she contested for a second term, but afterwards continued to play an active role in public life. When it came to legislative office, however, her husband took over the political career at the first opportunity. As soon as a distant cousin of his became Chief Minister, the husband asked the Chief Minister to include him in the official Congress slate of candidates for the Legislative Council, and he was subsequently elected to it. According to Susheela Devi, in her husband's appeal to the Chief Minister he cited his need to 'provide for his family', and 'because the Chief Minister likes my husband very much' obtained his support. In other words the husband replaced his wife as the 'main' politician in the family, in part because he was able to obtain the support of male political allies, using an argument which makes direct reference to a man's appropriate gender role. She then confined her activities to less overtly political voluntary organisations.

In another, very intriguing case, the positing of male prerogatives also occurred, but this time claimed within the electoral process rather than informal political negotiations. When Sarala Reddi stood for a second term, she was opposed by her brother-in-law. He had been given the nomination by a different political party in order to divide the votes commanded by the powerful landed family to which Sarala Reddi's husband and his brother belonged. According to Sarala Reddi, her brother-in-law fought his campaign in terms of his rights to family property which he argued had been denied him by his brothers. In speeches throughout the constituency he called on voters to restore his 'rights', not simply his property but his status as a full member of his family and as the most appropriate representative of it in the Assembly. There was a strong implication that this was more appropriate for a male member of the family, for he was always accompanied in his campaign by his four-year-old son, who sat on his shoulders during his speeches. He would point to his son and say 'Do you want me and this young boy to be denied our rights?' He made the gender of the candidates into an issue. Ideas regarding the connection between landed property and political rule, both traditionally monopolised by male members of families of this kind, were mobilised. Once Sarala Reddi was opposed by a male member of her family, her claims to represent it were rejected by the electorate.

Cases like these seem to indicate that the initial selection and election of a woman as an MLA does not in itself infringe the expectation that men are the 'real' politicians, for women can be portrayed as only temporary proxies for their menfolk. Arguably, however, one can go somewhat further and say that the selection of a woman for office is not 'allowed' to challenge women's status as only proxies, for they are prevented from sustaining a political career long enough to threaten this image. Men come back into office and so restore their positions as the key mediators between family and State. In most cases they benefit from the co-operation of male political allies in doing so.

KINSHIP CONNECTIONS IN LONG POLITICAL CAREERS

As already noted, however, a proportion of women MLAs in Andhra Pradesh have been able to sustain long careers despite their kinship connections with male politicians. These exceptions indicate that women's kinship connections with politicians are treated by political leaders differently, depending upon the particular type of kinship link and upon the social status of the women concerned.

In the first place, it appears that the daughters of male politicians stand a better chance of sustaining political careers than their wives or widows. Three women MLAs were the daughters of male office-holders. One died during her first term in office, but the other two were among very few women MLAs who held onto their seats in the 1978 elections.[17] If we see both women as launched into long careers, it appears that there is a real difference between natal and conjugal ties in sustaining political careers.

If we consider only the case of daughters, it does appear as if family connections work to women's advantage in seeking and rataining office. But two important caveats have to be noted. In the first place, none of the women MLAs who were the daughters of politicians had brothers, and there was thus no individual who could prevail upon other politicians to accord him status as the proper inheritor of the father's seat. Another factor to consider is that these women did not follow tradition in making their marital home with the husband's parents. They remained full members of their natal family, and therefore retained rights to its resources.

In contrast, most women in Andhra Pradesh lose rights in their natal families when they marry, and are conceptualised as members of the husband's family.[18] Patrilocal marriage tends to marginalise women from access to the resources of their natal families, but they never acquire the same rights as their husbands in his. The unusual position of these women MLAs suggests that, although some few women may benefit from family connections, when crucial political resources are shared among kin this largely benefits men and not women.

The second set of women MLAs who were able to sustain political careers despite their kinship connections are the women MLAs who are *Harijans* or 'Untouchables'. All the *Harijan* women who were first elected in or before 1967 served for three or more terms, and the proportion who became ministers in much higher than for the upper-caste women. In fact, ten out of the seventeen professional women politicians, that is, those with long political careers, are *Harijans*, or from lower castes which rank above Untouchables in the caste hierarchy, or from religious minority groups. Only a few belong to the rich peasant castes which dominate the Andhra Pradesh political economy.

The predominance of *Harijan* and lower-caste women among successful women MLAs in Andhra Pradesh is surprising, for it means that women MLAs from the most humble social origins (in economic standing as well as social status) have been more successful than the better advantaged. The presence of many women of working-class or lower middle-class origins in State legislatures in India has even led one observer to argue that 'class' is not a factor in what she argues to be women's successful entry into politics in India.[19]

This interpretation misses the point. The most important reason for the presence of so many persons of lower-class social background in the Assembly is that a certain proportion of seats in the State legislatures and in Parliament are constitutionally set aside or 'reserved' for *Harijans*, in what are called Scheduled Caste seats. However, this does not explain why there are so many *women* holding Scheduled Caste seats, or why they sustain long careers in office.[20] One explanation would be that husband – wife relations in 'Untouchable' families are more egalitarian than in caste Hindu families,[21] and that this is reflected in the political careers of Scheduled Caste women. However, just as is the case for the short careers of upper-caste women, we have to again consider the possible role of extrafamilial political leaders in allocating nominations between family members. I was told that Congress Party leaders are happy to nominate women to Scheduled Caste seats, for this enables them to give superficial support to the informal quota of women candidates while at the same time saving seats for the political actors who really matter to them – upper-caste men. The presence of Scheduled Caste women in the legislature is at least partly due to a policy of killing two birds with one stone.

However, there may be additional reasons behind the long careers of Scheduled Caste women MLAs, reasons which relate directly to the theme of this paper, that is, the real effects of kinship connections on women's access to political power. One is that, at least until the early 1970s, Scheduled Caste MLAs, male or female, rarely had relatives who were office-holders.[22] Most of the Scheduled Caste MLAs joined the legislature soon after Independence, as young men and women, and were the first members of their families to hold public office. Because so few of the Scheduled Caste women MLAs' husbands are politicians, they have been less vulnerable to displacement by them.

Interestingly enough, however, even the two Scheduled Caste

women MLAs whose husbands were also office-holders have been able to sustain political careers. In one case, for instance, the woman MLA, her husband and her brother-in-law, an MP, were all defeated in electoral contests, but it was the woman MLA who was slated by the Congress leadership for inclusion in the upper house.

This example is partly an instance of Congress leaders killing two birds with one stone. But it is also possible that Scheduled Caste male politicians are unable to prevail upon upper-caste men politicians to mark them out as the 'real' politician in the family. Upper-caste party leaders do not appear to be so concerned about the relative status of men and women in Untouchable families, and do not intervene to establish or re-establish men's prerogatives as regards office holding. This accords with more general aspects of Indian social structure. The capacity to subordinate women by confining them to the home is traditionally the prerogative of the upper castes. Indeed, the capacity of the upper castes to privatise their women is, in the ideology of caste, a justification of their superior social status.[23] While the difference between the long careers of Scheduled Caste women and the short careers of upper-caste women does not stem directly from this aspect of social structure, it does confirm and reproduce the more general relation between caste standing and women's subordination to male kin.

CONCLUSIONS

To write of a man or a woman as being the 'real' politician in a family goes against common sense – one surely is a 'real' politician or one is not. In fact this is not the case: being a politician is defined partly by the political activities one undertakes, but it is also a social status, one which can be withheld from certain office-holders for ideological reasons. Such persons are defined as proxies for the 'real' political actor in their family, usually a husband.

Feminists looking at the position of women politicians with kinship connections should I think be wary of perpetuating this view by adopting a label like 'male equivalence', and should be more concerned with identifying the processes and negotiations which reproduce it. What is particularly interesting about the situation in Andhra Pradesh, as described above, is that although the definition of women as short-term proxies ultimately derives from women's position in the wider society, conventional political processes are of considerable importance in replicating women's social status in the sphere of State politics. In Andhra Pradesh, both men and women *upper* *caste* hold public office, and most undertake the political activities required of MLAs. But the opportunities for upper-caste Hindu women to sustain careers in politics, and thereby gain the political power, social prestige and financial rewards which office holding potentially carries are restricted in part by the unwillingness of party leaders to encourage them in the long term. Upper-caste women MLAs married to male politicians are 'permitted' to remain in office for only a short period, and thus their status as only 'proxies' is maintained rather than challenged. In this way the State, through the actions of the ruling political party, helps to maintain, ideologically, the relative powerlessness of upper-caste women as wives.

Why devote so much attention to the ideologies which accommodate women's temporary presence in legislative office, or to the length of women's political careers? In the case of Andhra Pradesh, the recruitment of women with kinship connections does not greatly affect the policies towards women which are embodied in legislation. However, the meaning of holding political office in Andhra Pradesh extends beyond the possibility of effecting policy shifts. Membership in the State legislature is associated with other dimensions of power which make the existence of informal restrictions on women's officeholding of considerable interest. Unfortunately the space is lacking to discuss these in any detail. But it is important to the argument of this article to mention that many male politicians believe that women's membership in the Assembly threatens conventionally-defined marriage relations. Membership in the Assembly potentially gives access to financial rewards (bribes) and therefore economic independence. Women MLAs who are presumed to be 'proxies' for their husbands do not have direct access to these financial rewards, because their relations with constituents are mediated through the husband. In contrast, women who are not seen as under male protection have direct access to these rewards. Moreover, a successful political career for women is believed to be associated with sexual independence, and marital breakdown or estrangement, and to a certain extent may be so in fact. One male informant even told me that there are two 'types' of women in politics in Andhra Pradesh, those who simply 'follow their husbands' and those who once they are successful 'throw their husbands away like collar studs'. My informant's two mutually exclusive but for him exhaustive types of women politicians suggest that he and others believe that many women politicians would dispense with their husbands if they were able to do so. In these circumstances it is not surprising that the possibility of a woman MLA keeping the support of political leaders outside the family, and thereby establishing a political career instead of her husband, is feared. The sexual freedom associated with State political office also makes husbands' unwillingness to allow their wive's access to family resources, unless constrained to do so by outsiders, more intelligible. Although members of a family can share some of the benefits of office-holding, other perquisites of holding office are clearly felt to be divisive.

My informant's comments are an example of what women in India call 'character assassination' or 'mud-slinging', that is, the attempt by men to inhibit women from standing for office by maligning the sexual reputations of women politicians.[24] But the 'concern' expressed for women politicians' sexual behaviour also suggests that office-holding is felt to have considerable ramifications for a range of aspects of women's subordination. In this situation the curtailment of so many women MLAs' political careers to a short term in office, and their depiction as only temporary proxies for their husbands are readily recognised as sexual politics. What is perhaps surprising is how overtly sexual politics permeates conventional political processes, and is in turn constrained by them.

Notes and References

1. This article is based on a dissertation which examines a range of issues regarding women and the political process in India (Carol Wolkowitz *Gender as a Variable in the Political Process: A Case Study of Women's Participation in State-level Electoral Politics in Andhra Pradesh, India* University of Sussex unpublished D. Phil. dissertation, 1985). I wish to express my thanks to Ann Whitehead, who as thesis supervisor commented on successive drafts, and to the many women and men in Andhra Pradesh and Delhi who contributed to the research in various ways.
2. The Marxist arguments for giving little importance to office-holders as individuals were developed by Nicos Poulantzas, *Political Power and Social Classes* (London: Verso 1973) and 'The Problem of the Capitalist State', *New Left Review*, 58. Women as office-holders has never been a popular topic among feminist scholars guided by Marxist theories of the State. For a brief discussion see Michele Barratt, *Women's Oppression Today* (London: Verso, 1980).
3. Wolkowitz, *Gender as a Variable*. See also Sylvia Rodgers, 'Women's Space in a Men's House: The British House of Commons' in Shirley

Ardener (ed.), *Women and Space: Ground Rules and Social Maps* (London: Croom Helm, 1981).
4. Merville Currell, *Political Women* (London: Croom Helm, 1974).
5. V. Randall *Women and Politics* (London: Macmillan, 1982); Margherita Rendel (ed.), *Women, Power and Political Systems* (London: Croom Helm, 1981); Margaret Stacey and Marion Price, *Women, Power and Politics* (London: Tavistock, 1981); Jane Jacquette, 'Political Participation in Latin America', in June Nash and Helen Safa (eds), *Sex and Class in Latin America* (Brooklyn, New York: J. F. Bergin, 1980). Ardener, *Women and Space*. includes 'male equivalents' in the larger category she terms 'fictive men'. Most of this work draws indirectly on the interpretation of the division between private and public spheres developed by Michele Rosaldo and Louise Lamphere (eds), *Women, Culture and Society* (California: Stanford University Press, 1974).
6. Olivia Harris, 'Households as Natural Units', in Kate Young, Ros McCullagh and Carol Wolkowitz (eds), *Of Marriage and the Market: Women's Subordination in International Perspective* (London:CSE Books, 1981).
7. See, among others, Tariq Ali, *The Making of the Nehrus and the Gandhis: An Indian Dynasty* (London: Picador, 1985).
8. By Congress Party, I refer firstly to the undivided Congress and, after successive splits in the party, to the Congress Party (I) headed by Indira Gandhi. Members of the Legislative Assembly are elected from single-member constituencies. Members of the Legislative Council are elected from variously-defined constituencies, including the Legislative Assembly itself, Teachers' and Graduates' Constituency, and so on. A few members are appointed by the State Governor on the advice of the Chief Ministers.
9. M. Kistaiah, 'Social Background to the Members of the Andhra Pradesh Legislative Assembly, 1969–1972', *Journal of Constitutional and Parliamentary Studies*, vol VI no 2; Hugh Gray, 'The Landed Gentry of Telengana, Andhra Pradesh', in E. Leach and S. N. Mukherjee (eds), *Elites in South Asia* (Cambridge University Press, 1970).
10. Stanley Kochanek, 'Mrs Gandhi's Pyramid: The New Congress', in Henry Hart (ed.), *Indira Gandhi's India* (Boulder, Colorado: Westview Press, 1976); K. Seshadri, *Political Linkages and Rural Development* (Delhi: National Book Agency, 1976); Dagmar Bernstorff, 'Eclipse of Reddy Raj? The Attempted Restructuring of the Congress Party Leadership in Andhra Pradesh', *Asian Survey*, vol. XIII, no. 10 (1973); Norman Palmer 'Elections and Political Systems in India: The 1972 Elections and After', *Pacific Affairs*, vol IV. no. 4 (1972).
11. Kochanek, 'Mrs Gandhi's Pyramid'; Seshadri, *Political Linkages*; Bernstorff, 'Eclipse of Reddy Raj?'; Palmer, Elections and Political Systems'.
12. Kochanek, 'Mrs Gandhi's Pyramid'; Bernstroff, *Political Linkages*; Palmer, 'Elections and Political Systems'.
13. All names of women MLAs are fictitious. Identifying details have also been altered.
14. Short, long and middling careers total 37, less than the full sample of 55 women MLAs. This is because when the thesis on which this article is

based was completed in 1982, the last cohort of women MLAs who could have been elected for three or more terms first joined the Assembly in 1967 (and were re-elected in 1972 and 1978). However, women MLAs who were first elected in 1972 but did not stand again in 1978 were included as 'short careers' since it could be assumed that their legislative careers had finished. In the 1978 elections most sitting women MLAs lost their seats, and by 1983 practically none of the original sample were still in legislative office.

15. Other variables which distinguish between long and short careers, and the social and political processes which make them important, are discussed in Wolkowitz, *Gender as a Variable*. Like the kin link variable, they apply only before 1978, during the period when the Congress Party dominated Andhra Pradesh State-level electoral politics. From the 1978 elections the overall success of the party to which any individual woman MLA belonged was the more important element in her career.

16. The notion that a woman's participation in Indian politics is frequently accommodated because it is perceived as 'necessary' is mentioned by Ursula Sharma, 'Segregation and its Consequences in India', in Pat Caplan and Janet Bujra (eds), *Women United, Women Divided* (London: Tavistock, 1978).

17. One of these two MLAs was first elected in 1967 elections and is included among the 'long careers'. As the other only joined the Assembly in 1972, as explained in note 14, she is not actually included among the long careers.

18. This is a highly simplified description of complex arrangements which are by no means uniform among the different regions, castes and communities in India. In some respects women in Andhra Pradesh retain more rights in their natal family than in North India. They sometimes inherit land from their mothers, but the bulk of a family's agricultural property is divided equally among the sons. Women are not included unless there are no sons.

19. Mary Katzenstein, 'Towards Equality? Cause and Consequence of the Political Prominence of Women in India', *Asia Survey*, vol. XVIII, no. 5 (1978).

20. Harijan men in the Andhra Pradesh Assembly and in Parliament also tend to remain in office for long periods (Kistaiah, 'Social Background'; A. Roy, 'Caste and Class: An Interlinked View', *Economic and Political Weekly*, vol. XVIV, no. 7/8 (1979) partly because the constituencies reserved for Scheduled Castes tend to be safe Congress seats. However, we still need to consider why Harijan women benefit as well as Harijan men. In fact a higher proportion of Harijan women MLAs than Harijan men MLAs have long political careers in state-level politics (Wolkowitz, *Gender as a Variable*).

21. This point is made by many observers of caste in the Indian subcontinent, for example, Nur Yalman, 'On the Purity of Women in the Castes of Ceylon and Malabar', *Journal of the Royal Anthropological Institute*, vol. XCIII, 1963; Sharma, 'Segregation and its Consequences'; S. C. Dube, *Indian Village* (London: Routledge & Kegan Paul, 1955); Karen Leonard, 'Women and Social Change in Modern India' *Feminist*

Studies, vol. III, no. 3/4 (1976); Government of India, *Towards Equality: Report of the Committee on the Status of Women in India*, 1974.

22. Kistaiah, 'Social Background'.
23. Yalman, 'On the Purity of Women'; Leonard, 'Women and Social Change'.
24. Sharma, 'Segregation and its Consequences'; Government of India, *Towards Equality*.

12 State, Culture and Gender: Continuity and Change in Women's Position in Rural Vietnam

Christine Pelzer White

An explicit analysis of the role of the State and State policy adds an important dimension to the study of the interaction of culture, education and society. The literature on the sociology of education has been dominated by two polar views: education as social leveller versus education as reproducer of the existing class system. Separating out the State, society and culture allows for a more nuanced analysis and places the discussion on a new plane.

In this chapter I propose to pursue the question of official Vietnamese attempts to promote cultural change in the countryside by focusing on the Vietnamese socialist State's attempts to transform deeply engrained cultural ideas and practices of women's subordination and inferiority. The Government officially supports the principle of equality between men and women. I will examine education as one of a number of instruments of change under State control with gender equality as one (albeit rather secondary) aim. I will focus on three State programmes which seem to have had an important impact on male–female relations in the countryside: rural education and training, rural co-operativisation, and the marriage law. My contention is that they are closely interconnected in their effect, reinforcing each other. Change in the education system alone is not enough to cause fundamental change in gender relations. The case of Vietnam shows that even educational reforms which are accompanied by quite fundamental changes in the systems of production (co-operatives) and reproduction (the family) are not sufficient to cause a complete transformation of such a basic aspect of traditional social and cultural life as gender relations. This can be analysed as stemming in part

226

from the social limits of State-induced change (that is, social resistance to change), and in part from the fact that a State which is a
product of the society which it governs (rather than a colonial or
neo-colonial imposition) is deeply influenced by the very 'traditional'
attitudes which it is attempting to transform. State transformation of
society is therefore a conundrum rather like pulling oneself up by the
boot straps: it is difficult to find the necessary leverage.

For liberal reformers, education has held pride of place as a
promising opening for progressive social change. In the Weberian
sociological tradition, the introduction of a State-sponsored system of
universal education has been seen as an instrument of egalitarian
social change mitigating existing class, age and gender inequalities.
Education plays the key role in the transition from an 'ascriptive' to
an 'achievement' based society. On the other hand, Marxist critiques
which have gained currency over the past decade have rejected the
concept of education as instrument of social transformation in favour
of the argument that the educational system reproduces and reinfor-
ces the existing social system (for example, see Bourdieu and Passeron, 1977).

These debates have counterparts in the literature on women. For
example, during the International Women's Year (1975) a UNESCO
document declared that 'in the long run, education will prove to be
the most effective channel for achieving equality between men and
women and ensuring the full participation of women in development'. The once widely-held belief that State education in industrialised nations has brought equality of educational opportunity for
women has been effectively disproved by feminist critics, but some of
the same authors hope that a reform of the existing unequal system
would make a most significant impact on women's unequal social
position (See Byrne, 1978).

On the other hand, the argument in Marxist feminist literature is
that the roots of women's subordination lie in the organisation of
relations of production and reproduction (for example, Edholm,
Harris and Young, 1977; Young, Wolkowitz and McCullagh, 1981).
The educational system, in conventional Marxist terms a superstructural phenomenon which can only reproduce the material base, does
not receive much attention, even though in Althusserian analysis, a
degree of superstructural autonomy is recognised. In sum, a UN/
developmental stream of feminism puts greatest emphasis on education and training for women as the highroad to equality, while
socialist feminism stresses the priority of tackling women's subordi-

nation in both work and the family, or, as the title of one collection of essays expresses it, the need to transform both 'marriage and the market' (Young, Wolkowitz and McCullagh, 1981).

As socialist Vietnam has undertaken reform of market, marriage and education, it seems a promising area for examining these theories in a specific socio-cultural context. I would like to contribute to the discussion by taking all three areas and examining the interrelationship between them.

Co-operativisation appears to have contributed to raising the status of educated rural youth in Vietnam. As the Polish rural sociologist Galeski has pointed out, the professional training of the sons and daughters of peasants counts for little on their return to the village in Poland since in a peasant farm family system based on private ownership, educational diplomas are devalued; 'the only "title" which counts is the title to the land' (Galeski, 1972). In Vietnam, collectivisation of land made it possible for co-operatives to set up experimental plots staffed by technical teams of educated young peasants (both men and women). These State-trained youth therefore had a base for confronting the conservative views of their elders against State-promoted new agricultural techniques, improved seeds and new crop mixes and planting schedules. It took both education and a State-sponsored co-operativisation programme to establish educated young people as effective agents of Government-sponsored change in the villages: *Vietnam Courier* is full of tales of their accomplishments, including many young women. This was a new and authoritative role for young women with no counterpart in the traditional society and culture.

However, educated young women promoting Government-sponsored initiatives are not typical of all women: they have graduated not only from school but also (thanks to the changed structure of employment opportunities) from the authority of their parents, but have not yet subordinated themselves through marriage to the demands of husband, children and in-laws. It is a period of relative autonomy from 'the family' which in Vietnam as elsewhere often ends or is curtailed with marriage and especially children.

In the socialist normative system, devotion to family is suspect and seen as 'unsocialist' in a man, especially a Party member, but is promoted for women: women are encouraged to give special devotion to family and children, whereas men should 'help'. Although women are encouraged to enter formal employment and assume political posts in socialist Vietnam, which is a significant break from tradition, the State's family policy is that women must continue to have a special responsibility for the care of children, and their husband's parents, which is a continuation of traditional views. (However, it is not the norm that women in the Party sacrifice themselves for their family. See Le Duan, 1969, p. 117.)

In an earlier article I have examined socialist, and particularly, Vietnamese, views of the family, defined as 'the basic cell of society', and the difficulties this institution poses for both women's liberation and for socialist transformation of agriculture (White, 1982). The interrelationship between reforms in relations of production and reproduction is illustrated in Vietnam by the fact that a marriage law challenging both parental control of their children's marriages and male right to more than one wife was introduced at the same time as the co-operativisation campaign. In Vietnam's peasant family farm system (universalised among the peasantry by the socialist Government's land reform of 1953–6), traditional forms of marriage were the major means of recruitment and control of labour. Co-operativisation contributed to the equalisation of male–female relations by transforming wives, unmarried daughters and daughters-in-law from 'unpaid family labour' to co-operative members paid in workpoints. In other words, after co-operativisation, women's work in agriculture was remunerated by the same system as the men in their family, who no longer had a personalised control over the output of 'their' land nor the field labour of 'their' women.

I wish to focus here on one important common denominator or thread which runs through all three areas: authority or power relations. What were the traditional, what are the new (or transitional), and what are the proposed (future, normative) gender authority relations in school, in work and in the family in Vietnam? Discussing the aim of the transformation of gender relations as achieving 'equality between men and women' in effect obscures the fact that in the new (transitional) as well as the proposed (normative, future) socialist society a substantial percentage of social relations are increasingly role-specific rather than diffuse and personalised.

If 'women's liberation' or the achievement of equality between men and women were part of a project to create a totally egalitarian and status free society in which no person was subject to the authority of another, the project of equality between men and women might be achieved with no more difficulty than any other aspect of the transformation. However, this anarchist vision is far from that of the 'proposed society' of Vietnamese socialism, which incorporates a

large range of unequal relations, including obedience to or respect
for political, managerial, educational and familial authorities.
'Equality' in this context implies that in some situations women could
be in positions of authority over men – a cultural change more
complicated to achieve simple 'equality'.

According to the pre-revolutionary Confucian cultural norms,
women could have little or no authority in any sphere, political,
economic, educational, or family. Women were formally barred from
village and political life: there were no women in the 'council of
notables' which governed the village, nor were they part of the village
political community which met in the *dinh* (communal hall). At
ceremonial feasts in the village hall which mapped the social standing
of the village community, the lowest category was seven-years-old
boys; women could not join the feast, although they cooked the food
(Nguyen Hong Phong, 1959). Women did play a major role in
household economic management, both keeping the family budget
and increasing the household income through trading (traditionally a
woman's sphere). However, since according to traditional Confucian
cultural norms a woman was always to be both incorporated within a
family and subject to male authority within the family (as a daughter
to her father, as a wife to her husband, and as a widow to her son), a
woman's economic management and enterprise was, normatively at
least, always subject to male control and therefore not legitimated as
'authority'. Some rare elite women achieved an education and even
taught, but this educational authority was limited to teaching daughters of the elite or the unpaid social service of educating the children
of the masses; women did not teach the sons of members of their own
class (Nguyen trong Hoang, 1971, pp. 128, 141–2).

In Vietnam now there have been some fundamental changes in the
traditional attitudes towards women's work and towards acceptance
of women in positions of authority. In education not only is there
relatively little difference in male and female school enrolment (Tong
Cuc Thong Ke, 1982, p. 103), but the majority of village-level
schoolteachers are women. A new social role for women in the
countryside has opened up: *co giao*, 'Miss Teacher', who teaches her
pupils norms and practices which may conflict with those of the
parents. Vietnamese studies cite with approval cases where rural
students admonish their parents (for example, for not boiling water,
or for quarrelling) on the grounds that 'Miss Teacher would not like it'.
When a little boy in kindergarten tells his father 'Dad, you've been
quarreling with mother, the teacher will not be pleased', the new

national norms of more egalitarian family relations are being introduced into the household through new female authorities in the village school (*Vietnamese Studies*, 30, 1971, p. 122).

However, women's present leading role in primary level education (teaching children) as well as in health (care of the sick) is conceptualised as an extension of women's traditional role in the family. For example, the Party's Secretary General Le Duan has stated that 'a doctor is like a good mother', and therefore an appropriate job for women in Vietnam.

Similarly, women are seen as making good co-operative accountants as an extension of their traditional role as the keeper of the household budget. It is also argued that accountancy 'takes a lot of patience and women are more patient than men'. As in many other countries, the educational system in Vietnam conveys a double message: that although professional training and jobs are open to men and women, some jobs are 'naturally' better suited to women, and girls tend to be channelled into feminised spheres of work. For example, *all* creche and nursery school attendants are women. Young men are not allowed to train as carers of very young children: many older Vietnamese peasants, men and women alike, still find it ridiculous enough that young women should go off to school outside the village to learn how to be. . . babysitters. Even if the Government were to raise the issue of training male creche attendants, as is the policy in Sweden, it would not be likely to get very far with this programme, especially in rural areas, particularly given the shortage of male compared to female labour in the countryside.

In sum, certain spheres of authority are seen as particularly suitable for women, such as authority over young children. This certainly has widened the scope of authoritative roles open to women but falls short of full gender equality. Women's entry into the traditionally male roles, especially in positions of economic or political decision-making, has been much more problematic except while most men were away at the front. During the war, there was a policy (1967 law) to promote women to leading positions in the countryside. The percentage of women acting as co-operative chairmen and other management posts shot up. Furthermore, with young men away in the army, young rural women had even greater access than young men to professional training outside their villages. During the war it was reported that men in the army were very proud of the progress that their wives were making while they were away at the front. After demobilisation, however, it seems that husbands were not happy with a wife of higher status position, whether in co-operative management or in a technical job at the district or provincial level.

The 'agony aunt' or 'lonelyhearts' (Thanh Tam) personal advice column in *Phu Nu Viet nam*, the weekly newspaper published by the Women's Union, has included many letters from women facing hostility from husbands because of their higher status jobs. One vivid example came from a woman working as technician in a district level irrigation service. During the war she had been chosen by her co-operative for further technical education, and at that point, her husband off in the army had been very proud of her achievements. However, after he was demobilised and returned to the village as an ordinary co-operative member, he felt humiliated that she had a higher status job and put great pressure on her to resign and return to the village as a co-operative member like himself. This culminated in an incident when he arrived drunk at her office and shouted abuse at her. 'Dear Thanh Tam, what shall I do?' Her main argument against the pressure from her husband was that the Government had invested money in her education, and that it was her duty to the State to make use of her technical education. I would venture to say that in the years since the end of the war various versions of this family drama have been played out in hundreds if not thousands of peasant households. I wonder what was the reception of the exemplary story published in *Phu Nu Vietnam* in 1976 of a happy couple in which the woman worked as a State cadre and the husband worked as a member of an agricultural co-operative (*Phu Nu Vietnam*, no. 488, 18–24, August 1976). Was this article seen as a utopian or idealised account at variance with social experience?

To conclude, in a developing socialist society such as Vietnam with a rapidly growing professional career structure, the educational and training opportunities for women is an important topic of study. The situation in Vietnam during the war, that is, relatively better access to professional education in agricultural subjects for young peasant women than for young peasant men, was very unusual. In peacetime conditions, since the age period during which most professional education is undertaken corresponds with women's peak child-bearing years (late teens and twenties), many women in Vietnam as well as elsewhere have to 'drop out' of education while their children are small. In cities, women are often able to take up professional job training later through adult education facilities when their children are in school; for rural women this possibility is more restricted. The present policy of encouraging women co-operative peasants, the bulk of the manual agricultural labour force, to work harder through the incentives of the subcontracting system may well be making it even more difficult for women to have time left over for education in addition to their field work and household work.

Bibliography

Ahmed, W., 'The Husband is the Employer', *Ceres* (Rome), 44, (March–April 1975)

Bourdieu, Pierre and Jean-Claude Passeron, *Reproduction in Education, Society and Culture*, (London: Sage, 1977)

Bowles, S. and H. Gintis, *Schooling in Capitalist America: Educational Reform and the Contradictions of Economic Life* (London: Routledge & Kegan Paul, 1976

Byrne, Eileen M., *Women and Education* (London: Tavistock, 1978)

Casella, Alexander, 'The Structure of General Education in the Democratic Republic of Vietnam,' *Studies and Documents* vol. 1, no. 9 (1975) (Geneva: Asian Documentation and Research Centre, Graduate Institute of International Studies)

Edholm, F., O. Harris and K. Young, 'Conceptualizing Women', *Critique of Anthropology*, vol. 3 no. 9/10 (1977)

Elgqvist-Saltzman, Inga and Susan Opper (Dept. of Education, University of Umea, Sweden), Research cooperation between developed and developing countries: women, education and equality', paper for University of Lancaster 5th International Conference on Higher Education, 1–4 September 1981

Galeski, Boguslaw, *Basic Concepts of Rural Sociology*, (Manchester University Press, 1972)

Goode, William J., *World Revolution and Family Patterns* (New York: Free Press, 1970)

Ho Chi Minh, 'The draft law on marriage and the family' (October 1959) in J. Woodis (ed), *Selected Articles and Speeches, 1920–1967* (New York: International Publishers, 1969)

——'Talk to district cadres attending a training class' (18 January 1967) in *Selected Writings* (Hanoi: FLPH, 1977)

Lawton, Denis, *Class, Culture and the Curriculum* (London: Routledge & Kegan Paul, 1975)

Le Duan, 'We must view the Women's Question from a class standpoint' (1969), in *On the Socialist Revolution in Vietnam*, vol. 3 (Hanoi: FLPH, 1967) pp. 111–29

Le thi Nham Tuyet, *Phu nu Viet nam qua cac thoi dai* (Vietnamese women through the ages) (Hanoi: NXB hoc xa hoi, 1975)

Mai thi Tu, 'Vietnamese women in the 80s' *Vietnam Courier*, 10 (1981) pp. 19–23

Mai thi Tu and Le thi Nham Tuyet, *Women in Viet Nam* (Hanoi: Foreign Languages Publishing House, 1978)

Marr, David, *Tradition on Trial, Nineteen Twenty to Nineteen Forty-five* (Berkeley: University of California Press, 1981)

Molander, Cecilia, *Vietnamese Women* (SIDA report)

Nguyen Hong Phong, *Xa thon Viet nam* (Vietnamese Villages) Hanoi: NXB Van su dia, 1959)

Nguyen Khanh Toan, *20 years' development of education in the DRV* (Hanoi: Ministry of Education, 1965)

Nguyen trong Hoang, 'Traditional education in Vietnam', *Vietnamese Studies* (Hanoi) no. 30 (1971) pp. 127–44)

Nguyen Van Huong, 'Women's Rights in the Democratic Republic of Viet Nam', *Vietnam Courier* (Hanoi) 35 (April 1975) pp. 8–12

Ortiner, Sherry B. 'Is female to male as nature is to culture?' in M. Rosaldo and L. Lamphere, *Women, Culture and Society* (Stanford, Ca.: Stanford University Press, 1974) pp. 67–87

Sandy, Peggy R., 'Female status in the public domain', in Rosaldo and Lamphere, *Women, Culture and Society*, pp. 189–206

Tong Cuc Thong Ke (Statistical Service), *So lieu thong ke Cong hoa Xa Hoi Chu Nghia Vietnam*, 1981 (Statistics: Socialist Republic of Vietnam, 1981) (Hanoi, 1982)

UNESCO, *Women, Education, Equality: A Decade of Experiment* (Paris: UNESCO Press, 1975)

Vietnamese Studies (Hanoi), special issue on: 'Education in the DRV', no. 5, 1965

Vietnamese Studies, special issue on 'Vietnamese Women', no. 10, 1966

Vietnamese Studies, special issue on 'General Education in the DRVN', no. 30, 1971

Vu Quy Vy, 'Family Law', in *An Outline of Institutions of the Democratic Republic of Vietnam* (Hanoi: FLPH, 1974) pp. 156–84

Wang, Bee-Lan Chan, 'Chinese Women: the relative influences of ideological revolution, economic growth, and cultural change', in B. Lindsay (ed), *Comparative Perspectives of Third World Women*

Werner, Jayne, 'Women, Socialism and the Economy of Wartime North Vietnam, 1960–1975', *Studies in Comparative Communism*, 14: nos. 2 and 3, (Summer/Autumn 1981) pp. 165–90

White, Christine P., 'Socialist transformation and gender relations: the Vietnamese Case', *Bulletin*, IDS, 13:4 (September, 1982) pp. 44–51

Young, Kate, C. Wolkowitz and R. McCullagh, *Marriage and the Market* (London:CSE, 1981)

Index

The

I responsible
for all bad thing

acceptu

Afshar — "put Nietzsch. & cannot facts - TB"

Roberts — Glen's "moral crisis" - p #249

Dennis — Our against indiscipline - p 17